For Beth and Rob —

with deep appreciation
for your support and
encouragement!

Pat

"*To read Pat Morgan's* The Concrete Killing Fields *is to travel with those our nation has left behind. In bravely revealing her own journey alongside our nation's homeless men, women and children, Pat helps us understand both how we can help them and how we can learn from them. Her own assessment of that journey provides a job description for all those who sincerely want to make a difference in the lives of our country's homeless population. "I'd wept when nobody could see me and laughed when everybody could. I'd mourned more than I ever expected to mourn and I'd danced every chance I got. I' d like to think I hadn't "cast away" stones, but the truth is that I'd cast a lot of stones and gathered up a few more to cast at the barriers to accessing 'the system. Thanks, Pat, for the gift of this book and for your incredible honesty.*"

—FRED KARNAS, Social Investment Officer,
Kresge Foundation, Troy, Michigan; former Executive Director
of the National Coalition for the Homeless,
Interim Director of the U.S. Interagency Council on Homelessness,
and Deputy Assistant Secretary for Special Needs Programs,
U.S. Department of Housing and Urban Development

"*Readers, be warned! Pat's "must tell" testament is compelling and contagious, relentless and raw, inspired and inspiring. Through her persistent voice and action for the silent and silenced ones of our city streets, and her courageous journey from the "comfortable pew" to* The Concrete Killing Fields *of Memphis to the nation's capital to work on national policies and programs to help homeless people... her story will not leave you undisturbed or unchanged. And, it shouldn't! Read and digest* The Concrete Killing Fields. *You will not remain the same.*"

—The REVEREND DR. DOUGLASS M. BAILEY, President and Founder,
Center for Urban Ministry, Inc., Winston-Salem, North Carolina;
former rector of Calvary Episcopal Church (Memphis)
and Assistant Professor of Urban Ministry at Wake Forest University,
School of Divinity

"Pat Morgan is a national treasure. No one understands the problem of homelessness in America better than Pat, and she brings that knowledge to life in the rich descriptions of The Concrete Killing Fields. It is hard to read her book and not reflect deeply on just how easily the people she describes could be ourselves or someone we love. We are all extremely fortunate that Pat has dedicated herself not only to chronicling the plight of the homeless but to doing something about it. Her life is an inspiration to us all."

—MARCUS POHLMANN, PhD, Professor of Political Science,
Rhodes College, Memphis;
American Mock Trial Coaches Hall of Fame;
author of *Black Politics in Conservative America*;
Landmark Congressional Laws on Civil Rights

"Wonderful book. I opened it when I got home from work and didn't put it down until I had finished it at bedtime…made me think about my own life a bit! Pat's writing really shines in the telling of stories of those she met along the way, where her humor, warmth, and humanity shine through."

—GLORIA CABE, Senior Advisor,
Global Partnerships at the U.S. Department of State, Washington, DC;
former chief of staff to then-Governor
Bill Clinton, and Director of the Washington Operations Office
of the '92 Clinton for President and Clinton-Gore campaigns

"Pat Morgan is a model for all who have expressed concerns about the homeless population. She provided care for them and tried to understand the roots of their problems in substance abuse and mental illness. The Concrete Killing Fields *is an account of what she learned. The book is very nicely written and I recommend it to all who have similar concerns."*

—E. FULLER TORREY, MD, Founder,
Treatment Advocacy Center and author of *Nowhere to Go:*
The Tragic Odyssey of the Homeless Mentally Ill, *Criminalizing the*
Seriously Mentally Ill: The Abuse of Jails as Mental Hospitals,
The Insanity Offense: How America's Failure to Treat the Seriously
Mentally Ill Endangers Its Citizens

"The Concrete Killing Fields *is not just a book about struggles or pain or homelessness. It is a beautifully written story about one woman's journey to discover herself, fulfill livelong ambitions, and do her best to provide relief, in whatever form, to those she encounters. You do not need to be a student of the issues or have direct knowledge of the situations Pat describes to appreciate and enjoy this book. Through Pat's elegant, yet direct, prose, she pulls you intimately into the story of a gutsy, strong-willed woman with a goal of making this world a better place. Pat Morgan has spent years doing and living life. Her voice is one that should be heard."*

—BETSY BIRD, Captain, U. S. Navy retired.
Former Military Assistant to the Secretary of Defense,
Public Affairs; Public Affairs Officer for Commander,
Submarine Force, Pacific, Pearl Harbor, HI;
Public Affairs Officer for the Chief of Naval Personnel,
Washington, DC

"A searing glimpse into a lifetime of stories, some yet waiting to be told. A compelling, heartfelt account told with the same passion that Pat Morgan demonstrated while serving individuals previously invisible to many. The stories will remain with you long after reading the last lines of the final chapter."

—DR. JAN YOUNG, Executive Director,
Assisi Foundation of Memphis and
Major General, U.S. Air National Guard (retired)

"In The Concrete Killing Fields, *Pat takes us back to New Hampshire to remind us of why the Arkansas Travelers pulled out all the stops to help elect Bill Clinton President of the United States—and why it mattered to homeless people."*

—SHEILA GALBRAITH BRONFMAN, President,
Southern Strategy Group, Little Rock, Arkansas and
Coordinator, Clinton's Arkansas Travelers, Political Consultant

"Pat Morgan tells a story like no one else and it's a story we all need to know. Her activism, experience, compassion, and intelligence are abundantly clear in making sure the reader understands the people who are homeless. Her tenacity in dealing with this persistent problem and in getting this book published so others can understand is noteworthy. This is an important book."

—PAULA F. CASEY, Editorial Coordinator,
The Perfect 36: Tennessee Delivers Woman Suffrage,
contributing author to *Tennessee Women of Vision and Courage*,
National Federation of Press Women, and
former state president of Tennessee Women's Political Caucus

"Pat Morgan has presented a brilliant commentary on our times in urban America. Her description of the pervasiveness of mental illness, leading to a chain of despair, homelessness and lack of proper diagnosis and medical treatment, cannot fail to touch your soul. And, her painstakingly-accurate detailing of the Clinton/Gore '92 Campaign headquarters located on D.C.'s F Street brought those exciting months back to me like it was yesterday. As she often noted during the long days and nights spent toiling for a 'sea change' in American political policy, President Clinton's philosophies attracted individuals possessing a most amazing array of talents and the most over-educated, dedicated, focused, 'right thinking', and kind-spirited people imaginable. It was an honor and a privilege to be allowed into this elite group of Friends of Bill's, where Pat was our star."

—ALLEN MCREYNOLDS, President and Managing Member,
Mitigation Strategies LLC, Houston, TX
and former Special Assistant to the Secretary
for Lands, U. S. Department of the Interior

"Pat's book is a potent reminder of why so many of us were inspired to pour our hearts and souls into the '92 Clinton for President campaign. It was our compassion for our neighbors, a belief in human good, and a vision for a caring society. Her stories about her experiences in the raw, gritty front lines of homelessness remind us of how much we owe the thousands of men and women who devote their time, their talents, their money—and their lives—to helping those who exist in society's shadows. It was in those shadows that Pat found her calling, while never losing her passion for politics or her belief that each of us can be an agent for change. Her stories about the '92 campaign, especially those about the Washington Operations Office and the Presidential Transition will warm our hearts for years to come."

—BRIAN THOMPSON, Assistant Director for Administration at the Chazen Museum of Art, University of Wisconsin-Madison and former White House Liaison at the National Archives, former Executive Director of the Museum of American Finance in New York

"This book is a real page turner. By interweaving her own struggles and journey with the plight of homeless people, whom she loves so dearly, Pat enables us to experience their humanity and examine our own."

—NANCY HALE LAWHEAD, Founder and former Executive Director, Midtown Mental Health Center, Memphis, Health/Mental Health Advisor to two Shelby County Mayors

"Pat Morgan is extraordinary. The Concrete Killing Fields tells the story of homelessness, addiction, and mental illness in a very personal and compelling way. Pat's personal journey to keep as many as possible from drowning in the river of homelessness is inspiring, and illustrates why the nation continues to need strong will and creative policies at the local, state and national level. Get this book. Read it. Then act!"

—KELLY CARNES, Founder, President, and CEO of TechVision21, Washington, DC; former aide to First Lady Hillary Clinton, former Assistant Secretary of Commerce for Technology Policy, Washington, DC

The Concrete Killing Fields

Pat Morgan

MileHigh Press

The Concrete Killing Fields by Pat Morgan
©Copyright 2014 by Pat Morgan. All rights reserved

Books may be purchased in bulk by contacting the publisher and author at:
MileHighPress@aol.com

MileHigh Press

Cover Design: Nick Zelinger, NZ Graphics
Cover Photo: Chris Desmond, Photographer and Commercial Appeal of Memphis, Nov 2013
Interior Design: Rebecca Finkel, F + P Graphic Design
Publisher: Mile High Press, Ltd.
Editor: John Maling, Editing By John
Publishing Consultant: Judith Briles, The Book Shepherd

About the cover: Photo was taken in Memphis, TN in November of 2007.
The author is doing a street count of homeless people with her team.

Library of Congress Catalog Number: 2013950201
ISBN hard cover: 978-1-885331-55-7
ISBN paperback: 978-1-885331-53-3
eISBN: 978-1-885331-54-0
CIP data pending

1. Political Science   2. Policy   3. Homelessness   4. Mental Illness

Printed in the USA

THE CONCRETE KILLING FIELDS

is dedicated to

the Reverend Dr. Douglass M. Bailey,

whose compassion, respect and

ministry with homeless people inspired

and enabled me to follow him

in answering the call from the

concrete killing fields of homelessness.

Acknowledgements

This book would never have seen the light of day without Judith Briles, The Book Shepherd, her husband and chief editor, John Maling, and the top-notch crew that she called in to publish this book. Just as I have been led in so many ways on the journey described in *The Concrete Killing Fields,* I am sure I was also led to this unbelievably knowledgeable, talented, "snappy, sassy, salty" woman, and her competent, kind, brilliant husband. I am grateful beyond words for their help.

Yet my journey would never have taken place and this book would never have been written without my beloved sons, Milton, Mike and Mitch, who stood by me every step of the way. For their steadfast, unconditional love and understanding, I will be forever grateful. My thanks also to Shannon and Cyndi, my beautiful, brilliant daughters-in-law, who have enriched our lives immeasurably, and to my beloved grandchildren, Vince, Chris, Meredith, and Collin, who keep me young at heart.

Luckily, I never had to seriously contemplate that I would actually become homeless myself because my sisters, Peggy Bringle and Ann Baxter, and my brother, Carlton (Sonny) Phillips were the "safety net" that I knew I could count on for support if needed. Peggy was especially supportive of my writing (and since she was an English teacher, her encouragement was often "the wind beneath my wings"). Although I was determined to pay my own way throughout my wildly improbable adventure in Washington (and did), knowing they were there and would be there for me gave me the freedom to take the risks I needed to take to live out my dreams.

I am also deeply grateful for the friends who have listened to me talk (on and on) about "my book" (ad nauseum) for years without ever rolling their eyes in frustration. To Jo Speak, my BFF (best friend forever) I am especially indebted for standing by me and defending me during some of the most difficult chapters in my personal and political life.

Unbelievably welcome and cherished are the friendships and support of those mental health and health professionals that I cherish: Nancy Hale Lawhead, Marie Williams, Jeanne Daniels Richardson, and Dr. Pam Connor. Also treasured are my friendships with Paula Casey, Mary Silitch, Betsy Bird, and Gloria Cabe, who not only encouraged me but used their professional writing skills and trained eagle eyes to edit the multiple manuscripts that resulted in this book. It would take another book to list all the friends who have encouraged me along the way, but Ginny Webb, my beach buddy, deserves special credit for helping to keep me sane with our annual trips to the surf and sands of Fort Walton, Florida.

My journey in search of a better and more effective way to help break the cycle of homelessness would not have been possible without my mentors: the Reverend Dr. Doug Bailey, the founder and Executive Director of the Center for Urban

Ministries, who, during his superb ministry with homeless people at Calvary Episcopal Church in Memphis, showed me the way to the concrete killing fields; Wilbur (Wib) Smith, the former director of Whitehaven-Southwest Mental Health Center, who opened my eyes and the doors to the mental health system; the Reverend Robert (Bob) Watson (now deceased) who picked me up and dusted me off when I was at one of the lowest points in my life; Dr. Rae Ragland, who had the guts to follow Bob in providing the therapy I needed (whether I wanted to deal with my own issues or not) to survive the rigors of Washington; Dr. Marcus Pohlmann, professor of Political Science at Rhodes College, who opened the doors to the wider world for me; Dr. Mike Kirby, professor of Urban Studies at Rhodes College, who, despite my utter ignorance of computers, guided me through creating the pie charts (critical for getting my degree).

My political mentors include former Arkansas Congressman Bill Alexander, who hired me, a political novice, and got me hooked on politics; Maggie Boals, former long-time Justice of the Peace in Arkansas, whose rock-solid support and sense of humor made politics fun, and Gloria Cabe, former Chief of Staff for then-Governor Clinton, Director of the Washington Operations Office for the Clinton campaign, now Senior Advisor for Global Partnerships at the Department of State, who hired me to work full time on the 1992 campaign, which led to my presidential appointment. I am deeply grateful to each and every one of them. There are not enough words to express my profound thanks to President Bill Clinton, who inspired me to do more than I ever thought a girl from Turrell could do politically, and then gave me the opportunity to do it at the highest level of policy-making in America.

My admiration and appreciation for the national advocates who have, for decades, devoted their lives to ending homelessness is especially strong for Nan Roman, Executive Director of the National Alliance to End Homelessness, Maria Foscarinis, Executive Director of the National Law Center on Poverty and Homelessness, and Fred Karnas, the former Executive Director of the National Coalition for the Homeless, who took his advocacy straight into the heart of the U.S. Interagency Council on Homelessness and HUD.

There are not enough words to express my appreciation for the men and women who search the streets and countryside to reach out to the Alepeachies and desperate families with children of America—and the world. Nor are there enough words to fully express my appreciation for those who provide shelter, health and mental health care, treatment and recovery services for substance abuse—and housing—for homeless individuals and families.

Finally, forever in my heart will be the people of Calvary Episcopal Church who embraced and supported the Street Ministry and made my mission possible.

God bless them all

Contents

CHAPTER 1   The Hearse 1

CHAPTER 2   The City of Good Abode 5

CHAPTER 3   First Day 15

CHAPTER 4   In the Beginning 23

CHAPTER 5   Arthur 29

CHAPTER 6   The Bethlehem Chapel 37

CHAPTER 7   There's a Person Under There 43

CHAPTER 8   Called 47

CHAPTER 9   The Key 53

CHAPTER 10   Alepeachie at TPS 57

CHAPTER 11   A Place to Live 63

CHAPTER 12   I Ain't No Alcoholic 71

CHAPTER 13   Twelve Steps For Do-Gooders 81

CHAPTER 14   Unconditional Love 87

CHAPTER 15   What Do the Voices Say? 99

CHAPTER 16   Breakthrough 111

CHAPTER 17   Going Home 121

CHAPTER 18   Hands Across America 129

CHAPTER 19   The Road to Rhodes 137

CHAPTER 20   Home Again 145

CHAPTER 21   Homelessness Doesn't Mean
Hopelessness—There is a Light 149

CHAPTER 22   My Mother, My Voice 161

CHAPTER 23   Letters From the Grave 167

CHAPTER 24 Body Count 177

CHAPTER 25 We Hardly Knew Ye 185

CHAPTER 26 Housing Now! 191

CHAPTER 27 A Christmas Story 197

CHAPTER 28 Squirrel Park 203

CHAPTER 29 Goodbye, Hello 209

CHAPTER 30 Home in DC 217

CHAPTER 31 The Chinaberry Tree 224

CHAPTER 32 Lessons for a Senate Intern 235

CHAPTER 33 Snow White 243

CHAPTER 34 Boiler Room Girls 249

CHAPTER 35 Peace Park 255

CHAPTER 36 Off and Running 261

CHAPTER 37 Clinton for President 271

CHAPTER 38 Washington Operations Office 283

CHAPTER 39 Clinton-Gore 1992 293

CHAPTER 40 Presidential Transition 305

CHAPTER 41 Lead, Follow, or Get Out of the Way 317

CHAPTER 42 Memoirs of a Turrell Girl 335

CHAPTER 43 In Memoriam 343

CHAPTER 44 The Suicide Club 351

CHAPTER 45 The Last Lesson 359

CHAPTER 46 The Road to Healing 367

CHAPTER 47 Finding Alepeachie 373

CHAPTER 1

The Hearse

During those years we'd listened to

thousands of homeless people tell us

heart-breaking, often maddening stories,

about why they were homeless.

It was early morning when the "hearse" rumbled into the downtown alley and picked up John Marshall where he lay in a dumpster in a pile of debris from the city's streets. It was late afternoon when it dumped him out at the city dump. If a sharp-eyed landfill operator hadn't spotted what was left of a human being tumbling out with the trash, and managed to utter, in an icy whisper, "There's a person under there," the city dump would almost certainly have been John's final resting place—and his only "hearse" would have been a city sanitation truck. It may well have been his execution chamber too, but I choose to believe that he was already dead when the truck lifted the dumpster just high enough to let the refuse from the city streets slide down the steel gullet and into the belly of the beast.

Truth be told, I have no basis for believing that John was already dead. I just don't want to believe he was alive when the truck's compactor began to grind and smash and roar and belch to make room for its next meal. Whenever I think about him, most of the time I tell myself he probably froze to death. It was really cold, and I've heard that freezing is a relatively pain-less way to die—but then the people who told me that hadn't frozen to death, either. If John didn't freeze to death, I prefer to think that maybe he had a heart attack or just passed out in the trash of his tomb and didn't wake up and never knew what ate him. I could have checked with the morgue to see what the autopsy report said about the cause of his death, but I didn't. I really didn't want to know.

The local media apparently found the circumstances of John's tragic demise newsworthy. One of the television reporters even hustled his crew out to broadcast live from the city dump, and the newspaper reported John's death on the front page of the Metro section. The city and county mayors were properly appalled that such a tragedy could happen in their beautiful city, particularly since the alley where John had found refuge in the dumpster was within easy walking distance of city hall, the county office building, the federal building, a half-dozen churches, a couple of emergency shelters, and two drop-in cen-ters for homeless people. John was in plain sight, yet invisible.

Providers of services were distraught, especially those of us who weren't professional social workers, and therefore, either didn't know how to stop—or didn't want to stop—getting enmeshed in the lives of the homeless people we were trying to help. No matter how much we tried to help and no matter how hard we worked, another homeless person had fallen through the full-of-holes safety net of services and shelters and died on the streets.

Brother Jim, a young man whose only credentials for operating an emergency shelter were a good heart and a willingness to try to help, described in tearful detail his many efforts to "save" John ... until somebody pointed out that maybe the reason he couldn't save John was because he didn't know him well enough to even know what color he was—not that it would have made any difference. To Brother Jim's credit, in a city where the racial divide still hadn't narrowed nearly enough to make race irrelevant, he at least, was truly color-blind.

And Brother Jim wasn't the only person who didn't know much, if anything, about John. None of the street people that I talked to knew him, and none of the service providers I asked, and I knew almost all of them, could remember him. I didn't know him either, even though I'd personally worked with hundreds of homeless people during the five years I'd recently spent, first as one of the volunteers and then as the unpaid director/developer of the Street Ministry, a drop-in center in the basement of Calvary Episcopal Church in the heart of downtown Memphis.

The Street Ministry ... Its Services ... and Its Congregation

During those years we'd listened to thousands of homeless people tell us heart-breaking, often maddening, stories about why they were homeless. We'd then done what we could, with and without success, given our limited resources, to help them break the stranglehold of the streets that far too often led to hospitals, jails, prison or the morgue.

Over that time, I was devastated by the rising body count from the concrete killing fields, and frustrated beyond belief with the woefully inadequate, dysfunctional system of social services and treatment resources to help the homeless people who'd come to mean so much to me. I was not giving up, but I'd resigned as director to go back to college full-time to earn a degree. Surely a degree would give me a more credible voice in helping to develop and implement more effective policies and programs—and an effective system—for helping homeless people. I had no idea where going back to college would eventually take me, but wherever it was, I was ready to go.

A few days after John died—now with a full name, John Marshall—he was laid to rest without fanfare but with infinite care by Brother Charles, a caring, committed man of the cloth who operated the other downtown drop-in center ... and the city went back to normal. Politicians went back to regular politicking ... Reporters went back to chasing more traditional ambulances ... And homeless people all over America went right on crawling into dumpsters to collect cans or scrounge for food, or to sleep or stay warm—or die. And I went back to my tiny apartment and began to write about the homeless people who had transformed my life.

However, the more I wrote, the more I realized that their stories and my stories had morphed into our story. They would no longer be invisible.

CHAPTER 2

The City of Good Abode

But it wasn't the four-legged rats

that made my all-time-favorite homeless person

leave the park. It was the two-legged rats

who preyed on him ...

Since nobody but Brother Jim even claimed to have known John Marshall, and since nobody stepped forward to claim his body, John had probably been a newcomer to Memphis, one of the hundreds if not thousands of men who came to or through Memphis during those early years of homelessness, often looking for work or a better life. By the mid-1980s, our Street Ministry records reflected that we'd assessed and helped (or tried to help) homeless people from every state in the Union except Hawaii and Alaska. The vast majority, though, had either been born in Memphis, were long-time residents, or had come to Memphis from neighboring rural counties in Tennessee, Arkansas and Mississippi.

Having lived in one of those counties all my life until my recent move to Memphis, I understood a lot of the history that had made Memphis a magnet for people hoping for a better life.

Memphis, and the Legacy of Shame

Born on a bluff overlooking the Mississippi River, devastated by the Civil War and devastated all over again by the Yellow Fever epidemic in 1872, by the 1980s Memphis ranked as the eighteenth largest city in the United States. For better or worse, it was, and remains, southern to its core. Between gently curving Riverside Drive and the muddy, pulsing river below, is the cobblestone landing where men, women and children were taken from ships and sold like cattle during the most shameful chapter in American history. The names of Auction Street and Exchange Avenue, a few blocks away, reflect Memphis' history as a major center for the slave trade. More than a century later, the simmering rage and silent shame still haunt the Mississippi Delta.

Like a true southern belle from the Bible Belt, the city regularly won accolades for being quiet and clean, but if they'd given an award for the most segregated city, it probably would have won that one too, or at least scored in the top ten.

Overlooking the river and the cobblestones, from the bluff sits Confederate Park, shaded by stately magnolias, crape myrtles and flowering dogwoods. All along the neatly trimmed walkways are shrubs and bushes, lemon-fresh forsythia, and lush, delicate pink and white azaleas. At night, rats as big as cats chase grown men out of those bushes.

But it wasn't the four-legged rats that made my all-time-favorite homeless person leave the park. It was the two-legged rats who preyed on him and other particularly vulnerable homeless men and women inhabiting our streets. Those "rats" had a lot more to do with the reason that for seven long, lonely years, he'd slept under a bush on a narrow patch of grass next to the Methodist church a few blocks away. It didn't matter to him that there were a couple of emergency shelters nearby.

For reasons we didn't understand at first, he preferred to sleep under that bush and scrounge for food rather than stay in a shelter. But for reasons a lot of us did and still do understand, he apparently felt safe and secure in the comfort of the church's enduring presence.

A short block away from the park, but still overlooking the river, sits what is left of Cossitt Library, the city's first public library, established in 1893. As a little girl, I'd dreamed of someday seeing the inside of that Romanesque, red sandstone castle at the top of the hill, especially after my dad told me it was a library. I never dreamed that a few years later, it would be updated and modernized in a way that would render it an unrecognizable architectural nightmare. And it never entered my mind that it would be one of the places where I was always sure to find up to a dozen people rolled up in blankets like human hotdogs scattered all around the outer walls or curled up on cardboard beds under the bushes. At least not until we began counting homeless people on the streets.

Known as "The City of Good Abode" in the forties and fifties, downtown was a mecca for shopping and socializing for upscale and middle-class Memphians, and wealthy planters and their counterparts from neighboring Arkansas and Mississippi. For those of us who obviously didn't fit into any of those categories, rare visits to Memphis to shop for a new dress for Easter Sunday were a big deal, usually offset by the embarrassment of sitting in a line of folding chairs, holding our breath while the clerk called the bank for reassurance that the check was good. It always was.

Like a true southern belle from the Bible Belt, the city regularly won accolades for being quiet and clean, but if they'd given an award for the most segregated city, it probably would have won that one too, or at least scored in the top ten. It was segregated to the core—segregated schools and libraries, segregated waiting rooms, special "colored" days at the zoo, separate water fountains and segregated public transportation. It was "us" and "them."

I didn't live in Memphis during those years. Arkansas was my home in a tiny town so rough and tough they called it "Little Chicago." With three cotton gins in the center that was divided by two railroads encased in knee-high weeds along the embankments, and gravel streets interspersed with our few paved ones, we never had a prayer of getting an award for being clean. But, if they'd had an award for the most segregated small town, Turrell (pronounced "Tirl" as in "girl"), could have won or at least come close.

Never mind that my dad was a Cajun and we had Chinese, Italian, Jewish and African-American people in our little melting pot, along with a couple of fairly well-bred WASP families. And there were a few desperately poor, slothful (probably clinically depressed) families that we were ignorant enough to consider white trash because they lived in such filth.

Only the town's African-American residents, no matter how hard they worked or how clean they were or how well they treated each other—and us—had to go to separate schools, drink out of separate water fountains, sit in separate waiting rooms, climb the steps outside the town's only movie theater and sit in the balcony away from everybody else, and ride in the back of the Greyhound and Trailways buses that came through town—even though they had to pay full fare. There was nothing "fair" about it at all.

But though I lived in that segregated society when I was growing up, and never dared to question it openly until I was an adult, I surely knew it was wrong. That conviction was driven home after I saw a movie about a Mau Mau uprising in Africa and then dreamed that the black people in town were coming after us with machetes and I didn't blame them. Luckily, instead of coming after us with machetes, African-Americans rose up and marched in Memphis, in Arkansas, and across America for equal opportunity and equal treatment and fair wages for their labor. The sanitation workers' strike that brought the Reverend Dr. Martin Luther King to Memphis was rooted in that movement, spurred on by the deaths of the two workers who'd fallen into the compression unit of a barrel-type sanitation truck and were crushed.

When Dr. King "awoke the conscience of a nation," mine was one of them. Unfortunately, I didn't have the courage of my convictions at the time.

Many white people were appalled by the abominable working conditions and the tragic deaths. Many Memphians supported their demands for long overdue recognition, remuneration, and safe and decent working conditions. A few even had the courage to march, standing shoulder to shoulder with the strikers who carried signs declaring "I am a MAN!" a clear and courageous message that no longer would these men tolerate the lack of respect so evident in being called "boy."

Others played peacemaker behind the scenes. Many of them had come of age in the '60s. Others—older—had fought for freedom for millions of people in World War II or Korea only to come home and find that freedom was still denied to people of color in their own country. Some of us were sympathetic to the cause but didn't have the courage to take a stand. Cowardice and ignorance alone, however, weren't enough to explain our passive acceptance of the evil of segregation. We must have been crazy.

The Assassination Changed Our World

The craziness reached its peak in 1968 when James Earl Ray shoved the barrel of his rifle through the window of a run-down rooming house on South Main. The blast that followed killed Dr. King, tearing raw, gaping holes in the hearts and hopes and dreams of his family and friends, hundreds of striking sanitation workers, thousands of Memphians, and millions of Americans, including me.

I wasn't a Memphian then, but I watched and wept as I shared her guilt, shame and pain. And painful it was. The city, already a tinderbox of red-hot, righteous rage, exploded, and

stunned residents found themselves struggling with the shock
and agony that came with the assassination. The sight of tanks
rumbling down the main street of their beloved city was just
too much for the Southern gentility.

Downtown Memphis almost died after that. Some said
it seemed as though somebody had just pulled the plug and
most of the life's blood of the inner city just drained out. Even
the annual Christmas parade fell prey to the fear, and it wasn't
because the tanks got in the way of the parade or the traffic
or the shoppers. Simply put, by 1968, there weren't a lot of
shoppers, so there wasn't much traffic.

The "sit-ins," staged in the sixties at downtown lunch
counters by people who had a lot more courage than I was able
to muster, had frightened some of the shoppers away. Their
refuge was found in the urban sprawl and shopping malls
that had begun years earlier and that would soon characterize
America. That phenomenon had begun with Brown vs. Board
of Education, the 1954 landmark school desegregation case.
Not lost to history is the name of one of those first suburban
developments—Whitehaven—ironically populated today
primarily by middle and upper-class African Americans.

Homelessness had become a part of the urban landscape.

The city's core soon met the
same fate as that encountered
by cities in the Northern industrial rustbelt—a deteriorating
inner city; a declining tax base; a dramatic increase in the
unemployment rate; a soaring crime rate accompanied by
staggering increases in the costs of courts and incarceration;
steep increases in the number of families receiving welfare;

sharp increases in the numbers of people earning or receiving nothing at all; and struggling churches destined to try to deal with it all.

By the time I moved to Memphis in 1982, the city itself was on its way back. Most people were calling it "The Distribution Center of the Mid-South," or the "Bluff City." Hardly anybody called it the "City of Good Abode" anymore, but nobody called it a "rotting backwoods river town" anymore either, as some damn Yankee reporter had done during the riots.

By the mid-1980s, some people were calling it a boom-town, and even downtown was beginning to come back. Out of some of the musty, boarded-up storefronts, hotels and department stores, developers were carving exquisite apartments and condos, some with exposed beams and brickwork from a bygone era, the most prized with roof gardens and views of the river. Many are monuments to the persistence of Henry Turley, a Memphis developer who never lost sight of the magnetic pull of the river and the spectacular sunsets over it which transformed that muddy river into a flowing pink ribbon.

Despite the progress, on any night of the week you still could have fired a cannon down Main Street, by then reborn as the pedestrian-friendly Mid-America Mall, without hitting a soul except maybe a homeless man or woman sleeping in the park or curled up in a doorway. The gentrification that had restored some of the landmark hotels meant that the rooms in what had been the more decrepit hotels were no longer available for the poorest of the poor for a dollar or two a night. Homelessness had become a part of the Memphis landscape. It was alive by day and vacant by night.

The developers transformed the downtown area. Then changes to the landscape occurred. As the 1980s progressed, young professionals, empty nesters, urban pioneers, and people who were hooked on the sun-

But there were other people who sets over the river had begun

helped bring Memphis back. trickling back downtown. Some proclaimed themselves bored with the shallowness of life in the suburbs. Many were encouraged by the promise of the downtown area's renewed interest in the arts and music. Others found living and working within blocks of the legal and financial heart of the city convenient.

Older but young at heart, many enjoyed the weekend carnival atmosphere of music festivals, now taking place regularly in the parks, or the month-long Memphis-in-May activities— activities culminating in the World Championship Bar-B-Que contest in Tom Lee Park and the much more sedate Sunset Symphony concerts.

But there were other people who helped bring Memphis back. In 1968, the year that Dr. King was assassinated, they formed a solid core of conscience in the heart of Memphis. Some of them were among the most highly respected and influential men and women in the city, sitting on boards of charitable institutions, living out their faith in their churches and the community, volunteering their time and talents and giving generously of their money. Luckily for us, some of them still graced the pews of Calvary Episcopal Church in 1978. They, along with other parishioners, had the heart, the conscience and the courage to call to service a new rector of their historic but dwindling church in the heart of downtown Memphis. The Reverend Doug Bailey heard the call and arrived as a passionate priest who would make a difference. He would soon hear—and answer—the call from the concrete killing fields of homelessness. Five years later, I'd answer that call as well, and my life would never be the same.

CHAPTER 3

First Day

I'm worried about you.

We can only give you one shelter voucher a week.

Where do you sleep the rest of the time?

The call from the concrete killing fields came on my first day as a volunteer, one with zero training or experience in social work. Armed with a single sheet of paper listing our meager inventory of resources (three emergency shelters and a couple of faith-based, residential recovery programs for homeless men with alcohol and drug problems), I sailed confidently into Calvary's elegant Great Hall.

The spacious room with French doors leading out into the small courtyard was usually used for social gatherings between and after church services, after weddings or funerals, or other special events. With its polished oak floors, massive antique furniture, rich red velvet drapes and magnificent chandeliers, it also served as the perfect setting for the choir's annual madrigal dinner, complete with medieval costumes and music that, in my experience, only serious musicians want to sing and hardly anybody but Episcopalians really want to hear—and that's after a couple of glasses of wine.

Seated in the armchairs along the outer wall were about ten men, some sitting quietly, others as restless as schoolboys outside the principal's office. One was obviously drunk and at least two were psychotic (although I was too ignorant about mental illness to recognize it at the time). Another one was wearing a hospital bracelet but was lucid, fairly well-dressed and appeared to be in better shape than most of the rest, and one was obviously disabled with major health problems. Most of the rest appeared to be hung over and/or half-asleep except for an older man who sat, slightly apart from the others, in a chair at the end of the row.

The Great Hall was alive; whether it was "well" was a whole other matter. Some of them, as I'd soon learn, were "regulars." They were homeless men that Doug, who had soon seen the need, and then established a Criminal Justice Ministry, and Novella Smith Arnold, the director and life's blood of the ministry, were already seeing frequently, and some of the rest of them would soon be.

The Men in My New "Hood"

Billy was in worse shape than any of them. There was an open cancer eating away at his nose, and his bony hand clutched the world's filthiest raincoat across his chest as he made his way, dragging one leg, to the bathroom. Over the years, I don't think I ever refused any of his requests. I just wrote out vouchers as fast as I could for whatever he asked for. That was usually a voucher to one of the shelters, or for clothes or bus tickets back to Blytheville, Arkansas, after he'd used up or drunk up his monthly disability check.

Doug and Novella were a lot more effective in helping him, delivering him to the emergency room at the MED on more than one occasion. Years later, I ran into Billy at the Exxon station on the corner by the Mission. I don't know what had happened to him, but whatever it was surely qualifies as a miracle. He was clean and sober and his nose had healed a lot; I guess he'd forgotten I was the church lady because he tried to hit on me.

Herbie was there that first day too, ranting and raving about getting the FBI and the CIA to launch a full-scale investigation of the US Post Office because the clerks couldn't find his check. I didn't understand why he thought the FBI and the CIA were going to drop kidnapping cases and international espionage to investigate the post office for losing his check, but then I didn't understand why he was getting a check every month, either. Months later, when the jet planes started landing and taking off from his eyeballs, I understood.

Joe was there too, tall and scary looking, with dirt clods in his hair from sleeping on the ground and pock marks from half a hundred knife fights chipped into his ebony face. When he came back the next week and asked for a voucher, he looked as bad as he had the first week, so I tried to get him to think about how he was living. "I can give you a voucher, Joe," I said, "but I'm worried about you. We can only give you one shelter voucher a week. Where do you sleep the rest of the time?"

"Oh," he said, "ya'll don't need to worry 'bout that. Tuesdays I go down the street to the Methodist Church and get me a voucher; Wednesdays I get one from First Prez, and on Thursdays I come back here and get me some bus tickets to go out to Second Prez for my voucher. I don't get no vouchers for the weekend 'cause I don't want to stay in the mission on Friday and Saturday nights. But y'all need to figger out someplace where I can get me one for Sundays."

I didn't 'figger out" where he could get a voucher for Sundays.

Months later, after I'd gotten to know Joe better, he told me he'd spent 17 years in prison, nine of those years on death row, and before that, he'd been in the army for "four years, eleven months, three weeks, two days, 22 hours, 48 minutes and thutty-two seconds." I think he liked death row better. Even later, he told me a little about how he'd landed in prison on death row. He swore it was self-defense, and it still bothered him a lot that he'd killed a man, even if it was in self-defense. But what just about killed him was the judge telling him that he was sentencing him to die in the electric chair, not because he'd killed a man, but because he'd killed a white man. I never asked him how he managed to get out of prison. I guess I didn't want to know.

... but it didn't take long for me to figure out that there was something wrong with the picture and it wasn't Joe's fault. He hadn't invented the "system"; he'd just learned how to use it.

Joe was falling-down drunk that first day and almost every day thereafter except for one afternoon about four years later.

He came in that day, cold sober and carrying a white poker chip to prove he'd been to the Alcoholics Anonymous meeting I'd been begging him to go to for years. He was so used to seeing me through an alcoholic haze that he almost didn't recognize me. When he heard my voice and realized who I was, he was crushed but started off (with his usual BS) saying, "Iss very true, Pat, you iss very bootiful," but this time he added "but you iss gettin' old!"

Apparently he didn't know I was kidding when I said, "I think I liked you better when you were drunk and just thought I was "bootiful." He looked at me, took the voucher I gave him to buy some work boots and sold them on the corner for a pittance. His next purchase was a bottle of Mad Dog. I never saw him sober again.

Charles looked okay but was actually in really bad shape. He'd just been released from the hospital after his latest treatment for pancreatic cancer, perhaps caused, but surely exacerbated by his alcoholism. As we got to know him, we started calling him "My Charles" because in those early days we were all "enablers." But Novella was world class—even took him home after he had left the hospital and let him live with her while he was recuperating. Months later, after he seemed to have gotten better, she was always looking for him. "Have you seen My Charles?" she'd say, because by then we had several visitors named Charles.

One day while Novella was at the church, My Charles threw a party at her house. Anybody and everybody in the neighborhood was invited. The partygoers proceeded to clean out Novella's liquor cabinet and anything that was edible.

Doug went with her to the house but they still had to call the police to get them all, including My Charles, out of her house. Nobody was surprised about the party but Novella.

By then, a few of us had finally figured out that Charles didn't "belong" to any of us. By mothering and smothering him, we were helping him kill himself. If he couldn't or wouldn't stay sober for his mother or his sister or his significant other or his kids or himself, he wasn't going to stay sober for us. After we stopped enabling and started treating him with the respect he was due as an adult, we heard that he'd gone to Texas and was doing as well as could be expected, given that he had a fatal disease.

Sherman was at the church that first day too, but he didn't look like he'd been sleeping in the streets for a long time the way some of the other men did. His clothes were rumpled, as if he'd slept in them, no

... they simply took the vouchers and slipped silently away, leaving the sickly sweet odor of stale alcohol hovering over the Street Ministry.

doubt because he'd spent the night before in jail, charged with criminal trespass. He was furious and I didn't blame him. I didn't know much at all about criminal trespass, but I thought it was just outrageous that somebody could be arrested and have to spend the night in jail just for trying to stay at a hotel.

Of course, that was before I realized he was trying to stay there without checking in or paying for the room. I even thought he was kidding when he said he'd told the judge that it was going to cost the county money to keep him in jail for the night. If they were going to spend the money, they might as well spend it at the Sheraton, and he'd just stay there because he needed to work on his research and the Sheraton was a lot quieter than the jail.

Sherman was arrested at the Sheraton again the next week, charged with criminal trespass. When he came back to the church looking just like he'd looked the week before, I asked him how many times he'd been arrested at the Sheraton. He just smiled that little funny smile of his and whispered, "A lot."

Years later, he let me read his research. "Investigate all statements made by human beings," he'd written on the first line of the first page of his notebook.

I didn't get the name of the grizzled old man who sat quietly at the end of the row, but decades later I distinctly remember him. By the time I'd worked my way down the line of chairs to where he was sitting, his head had sunk down on his chest.

"Food," he growled when I asked him, in my best cheerful, chirpy voice, what I could do to help him.

"Food?" I chirped.

Again he growled, "Food." Only this time I could clearly hear another growl, but this one was coming from his stomach.

I raced to the church office, snatched a telephone book from the secretary, tore across the Great Hall to the closet where the only available phone was located, ousted the associate priest who apparently thought that just because he was there first he got to use the phone first, and called the Department of Human Services. I found out it would take two weeks to get food stamps but that he could get emergency food from the food pantry at the Methodist Church down the street. The catch was that he'd have to get the voucher first from their downtown office which was going to close in five minutes. His hunger made all else irrelevant. Getting all that information, I flew back across the floor like a speeding bullet to tell him, but he'd disappeared.

I never saw him again, but to this day, I wish I'd just taken him downstairs to the church's kitchen and made a sandwich for him. It would have been so much simpler.

I didn't get the names of the other men who were there that day either. Like hundreds of others who passed our way in the next few years, they simply took the vouchers and slipped silently away, leaving the sickly sweet odor of stale alcohol hovering over the Street Ministry. It never went away—nor did the call from the concrete killing fields—earnest, overwhelming, and relentless.

CHAPTER 4

In the Beginning

... the trickle of street people we'd begun seeing

had soon turned into a steady stream

and then become a flood, threatening

to engulf us and the other downtown and

midtown churches in Memphis. As we would

soon learn, it was also engaging churches and

social services all over America.

If I'd known what I was getting into when I picked up the church bulletin and read Doug's call for volunteers to help him with his ministry with the street people, I might not have called him and signed on. I might not have called, also, if I'd known how long it would take or how much it would hurt to dig into my own life experiences to understand why I felt so connected to some of them.

No, I probably wouldn't have had anything to do with it, but after I started, I couldn't seem to stop. Why was I so driven to write about them and how profoundly they'd changed my life?

It wasn't as though I could write much about John Marshall. I didn't know why he was homeless, how long he'd been homeless, or how long he'd been in Memphis. (Oh, I had a couple of pretty good guesses.) Homeless people were invisible to most, yet their presence vibrated throughout America.

By then, I'd learned a lot about homelessness and homeless people. I learned some from people who'd been providing shelter and services to homeless people for years—even decades—and some from people in recovery from alcohol and/or other drugs and/or their family members. And I was learning plenty myself.

It Started With a Trickle and Became a Flood

The most important teachers came through the front door—one by one—every day of the week. I'd learned more about homelessness from those who knew the most about it—the men and women who regularly or intermittently slept on the streets or in emergency shelters but who soon, or eventually, found their way to Calvary. Word had traveled fast on the "streetvine" with the news that a new program, run by a bunch of volunteers who didn't know enough to ask a lot of questions, was open. As a result, the trickle of street people we first saw had soon turned into a steady stream and then became a flood, threatening to engulf us, the other downtown and midtown churches in Memphis, and, as we soon learned, churches and social services all over America. The flood comprised waves of human misery rivaling that of the Great Depression. Dirty, sick, smelly, sometimes belligerent, sometimes puzzlingly passive, frozen in fear, soaked in alcohol or strung out on drugs, they poured through the doors and into our hearts. They were invisible to most, but they weren't invisible to us.

Just to try to keep up with who was getting—or not getting—what and when from us, I set up a rudimentary filing system, recording their names, the date, what they'd asked for and what we'd given or not given them, on 3 x 5 cards and filed them in alphabetical order in a shoebox.

As the numbers continued to grow, we "battened down the hatches." We welcomed more volunteers and moved our operations from Calvary's Great Hall to a couple of former classrooms and a small office in the basement. We bought cheap file folders to hold the 3 x 5 cards and the very brief form I'd developed to record basic information about our visitors. We then moved the files to a real filing cabinet, and for the next year or so, continued frantically focusing on the symptoms instead of the sickness that was at the core of so much homelessness.

We doled out countless vouchers for emergency shelter, often pleading with the shelter operators or desk clerks to take our new friends back "just one more time" when they'd been barred, and, understandably so, for drinking, drugging, fighting, bringing weapons in, or "acting out" the bizarre behaviors that are the hallmark of severe and persistent mental illness. Vouchers were issued for clothes from the free clothes closet down the street. We even raided our husbands' and sons' closets for more clothes and bummed coats and shoes from our other male relatives and friends. When we'd exhausted those resources, which never took very long, we wrote out vouchers for work boots for homeless men who needed them to get or keep a job (including at least three pairs for Joe, who'd become a "regular" and who promptly sold them every time and used the money to get roaring drunk.)

After we'd raided and depleted the church's First Aid kit, which happened on a regular basis, we used some of our funds to pay for minor emergency supplies as we frantically tried to bind the *It was never enough.* gaping wounds of homelessness with Band Aids.

Moving our operations to the basement had made it possible for us to sit down with our visitors and spend a few minutes getting to know them, listening to their stories, and making them comfortable before we asked how we could help them. In addition, we now had our own phones, making it infinitely easier to try to find resources for the people we were trying to help—and making it possible to do more "screening" of requests to verify stories and verify needs before we doled out our meager resources. It wasn't enough. It was never enough.

Drawn to trying to deal with deprivation that made my personal financial problems look like child's play, I'd quickly begun volunteering most afternoons instead of the one afternoon a week I'd signed up for. As a result, I saw the street people a lot more often and I was pretty sure that I had the problem figured out. The fact that the person (almost always a man) asking for our help didn't have a job or money, a house, apartment, room, furniture, or clothing other than what he was wearing and carrying with him, and not one single family member or friend who could, would, or should take him in for one more night wasn't the problem. Those were symptoms of the problem.

Why he (or, later, she) had none of the above was the problem, and it didn't take an addiction counselor or mental health professional to figure out what the most obvious problems were—alcohol, drugs, and/or mental illness.

But we, at the Street Ministry, still had a lot to learn and far too much of it we'd learn the hard way.

CHAPTER 5

Arthur

"I tol' 'im an' tol' 'im," he mourned,

"I tol' 'im that alcohol wuz gonna kill 'im.

I knowed it would."

The body count from the concrete killing fields had begun for us with Arthur, one of our regulars, in the early morning hours of what would have been a life-changing day for him. In fact, the sun had barely risen when several groups of homeless men streamed out of the Salvation Army's Emergency Shelter and fanned out across the heart of downtown Memphis. Arthur was in the crowd and on most mornings he would have been with the group headed for the nearest temporary labor service. On this particular morning when the rest of that group turned left at the corner, Arthur had turned right as he walked toward his last stop.

He'd been a little nervous when we'd seen him the day before, probably because he was scheduled to check into the hospital the next morning. After a lifetime of struggling to see, a surgical procedure was going to straighten his badly crossed eyes. He was more excited than nervous, though. After he recovered from the surgery, he was going to enroll in adult education classes. No more looking at the pictures on the pages and pretending to read the print for him. No, sirree, he was going to learn to read and write. A whole new life was waiting for him at the Methodist Hospital.

He never kept his appointment.

Memphis has a number of excellent hospitals; most, like the Methodist Hospital, are just east of the immediate downtown area, within walking distance of the shelters where homeless people stay. Arthur didn't want to take a chance on being late for his life-changing medical treatment.

For good measure he had bus vouchers to get to the hospital and back downtown when he was released. Even better, we'd arranged for him to stay at the Salvation Army while he recuperated. Instead of heading for the bus-stop, though, he walked the three blocks to the criminal justice complex and went inside.

It is worth mentioning that Arthur wasn't afraid to walk into the bunker-like building. Frankly, you couldn't pay most of the homeless men in Memphis enough to get them to go near the place. Old fines and old foes were enough to make most of them give the place a wide berth. To our knowledge, Arthur didn't have any old fines or old foes, or young foes either, for that matter. There were no unpaid fines for shoplifting or criminal trespass, no pimps or drug dealers he'd crossed, and no cop whose jaw he'd broken while resisting arrest. According to the street people, "Arthur wasn't no trouble to nobody," and he surely wasn't any trouble to us at the Street Ministry.

Not once in all the months he'd been coming in had he started a fight, swiped all the packets of sugar, or dumped all the peanut butter and jelly sandwiches in the trash can the way some had. Nor had he ever fallen over the furniture, slopped his coffee, slurred his words, thrown up in the wastebasket, wet his pants or passed out in the pew during chapel the way many of the old guys had. We'd never seen him weaving as he walked and nobody ever reported smelling alcohol on his breath. Arthur just wasn't any trouble to anybody.

He wasn't any trouble to the ambulance attendants who answered the call either. They didn't even have to take him to the hospital when they picked him up off the floor in the bathroom of the criminal justice center where he'd collapsed and died. Why bother? Straight to the morgue was the shortest route.

Arthur was from the country, "up around Somerville," he'd told me, and if it hadn't been for the color of his skin, he might have been just a good old country boy—not the rowdy, backslapping kind; more like the quiet, gentle kind that women in the south have been known to stand in line for. If it's said with just the right level of affection, being called a good old country boy is a compliment. The term denotes honor and integrity and a healthy work ethic. It has absolutely nothing to do with intellect or good looks. A good old country boy can be dumb as a post and his eyes can be crossed half out of his head, but you can bet the rent money that the color of his skin will be white.

Nobody ever called Arthur a good old country boy during all the years he lived and worked in the country. What some folks did call him a lot was "Boy," as in "Hey, Boy." The people who knew him and loved him best didn't call him "Boy." At his funeral, his family members stepped forward, one by one, to offer their eulogies. "Arthur was a good man," they said. "He wasn't never no trouble to nobody."

One by one his friends from the streets and shelters stepped forward to offer the same litany. "Arthur was a good man," they said. "He wasn't never no trouble to nobody."

I failed to make the connection.

When my turn came, I gave his daughter his Certificate of Accomplishment from the job-training program he'd enrolled in at our urging and watched her hug the piece of paper to her heart. He'd brought it to us and stood a little taller as we hung it on our "Hero" wall at the Street Ministry. Then I tried to tell his family and friends how much he'd meant to us but the words wouldn't come out right. Part of me wanted to climb up on the roof of the funeral home and shriek, *"I wish Arthur had been some trouble to somebody sometime!"*

I wished he'd been "some trouble" instead of leaving his wife and daughter because he couldn't find work and his wife couldn't make enough to support them but couldn't draw welfare to pay rent and buy food for their child if an able-bodied man lived in the house.

I wished he'd been "some trouble" until he got the kind of health care that would have enabled him to SEE well enough to learn to read and write.

I wished he'd railed at the racism and then gone out and registered voters and maybe even punched out some of the people who called him "Boy" instead of just stuffing all the pain and fear and humiliation and healthy, righteous anger until he just dropped dead on the bathroom floor of the criminal "justice" complex.

Most of all, I wished he hadn't been half blind and illiterate for his whole life and that I hadn't been so damned ignorant and blind for half of mine.

But Arthur had been born black and male in the segregated south when to speak up or out could result in a lynching or a beating or at the very least, the loss of the job a man desperately needed to support his family. And I'd come of age in the '50s when TV sitcom star Donna Reed was the ultimate role model for small-town girls who knew little or nothing about the rest of the world and therefore hoped we could create the perfect family that so many of us longed for if we just kept quiet and did what our role models on TV did.

By the time the '60s rolled around, men and women took to the streets to secure the civil rights I'd taken for granted all my life, or to protest a war I didn't understand and finally hated. My heart was with them, but I was still doing my best imitation of Donna Reed, AKA the "total woman," playing house, busily vacuuming the green and gold shag carpet, making artery-clogging, home-cooked meals, and putting out babies like a popcorn popper.

The week after Arthur's funeral, Freddie, one of his friends, came by the Street Ministry. He must have been a very good friend. Check-in times were set in concrete at Memphis shelters; missing the 6:00 p.m. deadline for check-in meant another night in the streets. Arthur's funeral was at 8:00 p.m., and Freddie had been there. He was still in deep mourning the next week.

According to the unwritten rules that govern writing about homelessness and homeless people, Arthur's story should have ended by now. Stories about homeless people are supposed to tug at people's heartstrings, not to mention purse strings. Any indication that the homeless man or woman in the story is not just a victim of a cruel, heartless society, but may have contributed in some unacceptable way to his or her own homelessness or demise can detract from the tragedy of homelessness. Information that may result in less sympathy for homeless people, or, even worse, be construed as "blaming the victim," if included at all, is usually found at the very end of articles and stories in a sort of "throw-away" line such as, for example: "Arthur is also receiving counseling for substance abuse issues."

"I tol' 'im an' tol' 'im," he mourned, "I tol' 'im that alcohol wuz gonna kill 'im. I knowed it would."

Arthur was a regular at the Street Ministry. We saw him three or four times a week for months. We never suspected that he was abusing alcohol.

"Ever' day," said Freddie.

Alcohol ... the Real Killer

It took Arthur's death to make me understand that while he was illiterate, we were ignorant. Oh, we knew that alcohol could kill and maim and that emergency rooms all over the country were, and still are, overflowing with the victims of alcohol-fueled accidents and alcohol-accelerated assaults. We knew that alcoholics often die from cirrhosis of the liver.

We didn't know that excessive alcohol use is murderous to the central nervous system and the entire cardiovascular system, including the heart, or that some studies reflected (and still reflect) that half the people in America who go to the doctor are there because their lives are falling apart and that people with alcohol-related ailments occupy half of all the hospital beds in use in the United States.

What we didn't know was that alcohol abuse increases the risk for almost every kind of cancer or that chronic, excessive use of alcohol can cause hypertension, stomach ulcers and brain damage; or that it can damage the endocrine and immune systems.

Even then, they are the fortunate ones. One of the first symptoms of heart disease is sudden death.

We learned a lot from Arthur's death. For example, some people can drink as much as a quart of whiskey every day and still not appear to be intoxicated. It's called tolerance, and it means that the body more or less adjusts to the drug in an effort to remain sober. That's the good news. The bad news is that it takes more and more alcohol to just "feel good," even more to feel drunk, and even more not to feel at all.

People all over the world use alcohol. It has the remarkable ability to make us feel powerful, provocative, witty or wise. Some use alcohol to relieve anxiety, deaden pain, camouflage fear, or mask depression. Some find that alcohol dulls the pain of prejudice, crossed eyes, illiteracy and homelessness. For a lot of reasons, a lot of people cross the line from use of the drug ... to abuse of the drug ... to addiction to the drug.

The lucky ones live long enough to regret it.

Arthur wasn't one of the lucky ones, but his death set in concrete the course my life would take, and even though I didn't know where that course would take me, there would be no turning back. Nevertheless, it was the homeless man with his hair all twisted up in top-knots who would so profoundly impact my personal life.

CHAPTER 6

The Bethlehem Chapel

Some couldn't connect immediately—

fingers seemed to bounce off fingers,

tingling with the electricity that seemed to

crackle through the crowd as we connected.

I never forgot it. It was the essence

of the Street Ministry.

The first time I'd seen the homeless man with the top-knots he'd been standing all alone on the corner across from Calvary one afternoon. I'd gotten there only to find that the trouble I'd been afraid would be the order of the day was brewing before we even got inside. The day had started out with a morning temperature of 90, which by noon had climbed to 95, and with the humidity, the heat index had reached a smothering 103. By the time I'd walked the short block from my apartment to Calvary, I was miserable. To make it worse, a couple of volunteers had already called to say they couldn't be there that afternoon, and the other volunteer had called to say she'd be late.

A crowd of at least 50 homeless men had already gathered at the small, ruby-red cathedral-type doors at the side of the church. Some pushing and shoving had already begun as some of them jockeyed to be the first to get inside. Jaywalking across the street, I'd heard the sound of glass breaking and felt the hair rising on the back of my neck as the image of the jagged edges of a broken bottle as a deadly weapon flashed before me. Luckily, this one was still in the brown bag instead of somebody's hand, and the only person who was hurt was the poor old guy on the curb who'd dropped it and was squatting beside it, watching the copper-colored liquid seep through the sack. He was in tears.

Hurrying through the door to the parish house adjoining the church, I bolted downstairs and ran to the Street Ministry office, calling out to Calvin, the church sexton, to unlock the side doors as fast as he could. Leaving the cart with the stacks of sandwiches in the kitchen, he hurried down the hall and I could hear the rattle of the heavy chain coming off the door handles. It clearly helped.

The pushing and shoving subsided as Calvin and I quietly watched the men begin stumbling down the steps, but the overall mood was still surly. I wasn't afraid, but I was apprehensive, and grew even more so as an argument over who was first in line to sign in was threatening to escalate.

Security was rarely a problem. We'd been in business for almost three years by then, and most of our "regulars," the men who formed the core of the crowd that filled our waiting room every day, knew each other and were either friends or knew enough about each other to leave each other alone. The "regulars" weren't there to cause trouble. We knew enough by then to understand that most of the time, the ones we didn't know very well didn't want to cause trouble either. They'd been in enough trouble and had enough problems already—but that didn't mean they'd back down from a fight.

Prayer to the Rescue

Most of the time, just coming inside the church building had a calming effect on them. Everything changed, though, when the weather made homelessness especially unbearable. You could literally feel the friction, and today the tension inside was every bit as high as the temperature and humidity outside. I didn't think we had a prayer of getting through the day without an incident unless we could defuse some of the anger and frustration.

It was seldom quiet and rarely reverent during the Street Ministry's chapel services.

Chapel services always helped but we'd already had our regular, once-a-week, voluntary chapel service and besides, Doug, who could calm the crowd simply by his presence, was out of town, so I couldn't even call him to come down and help if I wanted to. Once before, when he was gone and trouble was in the air, I'd just waded into the smoke-filled waiting room and after I finally got everybody's attention, I asked them to bow their heads and close their eyes. My mouth opened and I prayed like crazy for peace and understanding and tolerance for all of us and our human frailties and inadequacies.

It worked, so for awhile we called on God on an "as-needed" basis until we figured out that something a lot bigger than us was working in that basement—we then started opening the Street Ministry with a prayer every day. Having Him as an opening partner created a cocoon of sorts for each of us.

This time, since I couldn't get anybody's attention, I climbed up on a chair and announced that everybody who needed to be seen quickly should just go to the chapel down the hall and we'd help them there. That got their attention. Almost everybody started moving down the hall to the chapel in an effort to be first and/or get special attention, Then, I scurried back to the office, grabbed a folder, stuck a handful of shelter vouchers and bus vouchers in it and beat it back to the chapel.

Something always happened in Calvary's little "Bethlehem" basement chapel. It was contagious. Even with the altar, pews, stained glass windows, and the kneeling rail that in many churches would command quiet reverence, it was seldom quiet and rarely reverent during the Street Ministry's chapel services. Doug called it his "Holy Zoo" and loved every minute of it simply because he loved the street people unconditionally. And they knew it. But there was more to it than his connection to them and their connection to him.

Something happened to most of us volunteers when we were in there too. It wasn't us and them. It was just us in that holy place.

That day, for some reason, if we'd all been struck mute, it couldn't have been quieter. No doubt they were wondering what was happening and why we had veered so far off our usual routine. Nobody even complained when I asked them to stand while we opened with a prayer, but when I asked them to take the hands of the people next to themselves, something we'd never asked them to do before, nobody budged. To get us started, I stepped over to the aisle between the pews and held my hands out to the men on either side. For a minute, most of us just looked at each other. I just waited. Silently.

Some couldn't connect immediately—fingers seemed to bounce off fingers, tingling with the electricity that seemed to crackle through the crowd as we connected. I never forgot it.

Then slowly, almost furtively, the men began putting their bundles of belongings down and fists that had been clenched a few minutes before turned into fumbling fingers as they, some of whom hadn't reached out to another human being in years, tentatively reached out. Some couldn't connect immediately—fingers seemed to bounce off fingers, tingling with the electricity that seemed to crackle through the crowd as we connected. I never forgot it. It was the essence of the Street Ministry. We were one.

By the time I'd stopped praying and everybody had sat down again, one of the volunteers had arrived, answered the phone and hurried into the chapel to give us the good news. The Memphis Union Mission had declared the day a weather emergency day and all the men could stay there for free that night. Those who wanted, could also spend the rest of the day there. That took care of most of the guys who now relaxed, knowing that they had a place to go where there was more space, better air-conditioning, a TV, better food than the sandwiches Calvin had just put out in the waiting room, and, most importantly, they wouldn't be sleeping outside that night.

After we'd listened to those who were left, and done what we could to help, given the varying levels of intoxication or psychosis, I went back to the waiting room to be sure that nobody else needed help. Sitting quietly in the farthest corner was the man with his hair in top-knots, the one who'd been standing on the corner across the street.

As soon as I walked in, he stood up, heaved a long sigh, picked up the small bundle he had with him, and started slowly toward the door. If he heard me when I asked him if there was anything I could do to help him, he didn't show it. I was sure that he had a mental illness of some kind, simply because of his utter isolation. I didn't want to scare him off by pushing him to talk, so I told him that I hoped he'd come back and we'd be glad to help with whatever he needed. He still didn't respond.

Then I closed up the office and walked the short block home to my lovely, brand-new, air-conditioned, eleventh-floor corner apartment with a spectacular view of the city. As I would soon learn, it was exactly two blocks from where that homeless man with the top-knots would bed down once again underneath one of the oversized bushes between the sidewalk and the wall of the Methodist Church.

CHAPTER 7

There's a Person Under There

... we'd never seen him muttering to himself

or flailing away at somebody nobody else

could see or hear. And he hadn't exhibited

one of the signs of mental illness

that we'd quickly learned to spot.

The summer had long-passed and the rain that had started just after midnight continued throughout the morning. It slacked off just enough around noon for the men to make their way to Calvary from wherever they'd taken refuge. It then settled into a steady deluge. Rainy days meant that fewer men went out on jobs through the day-labor enterprises, and our waiting room was always full. It seemed to me that it was unusually rowdy for a rainy day. No doubt it was because it was early in the month and those of our friends who weren't using their monthly disability checks to buy their way out of homelessness for a few days at a rooming house or cheap motel had apparently used some of their money for booze. As was the norm, they had apparently been sharing their bottles with their drinking buddies. Though definitely not the norm in the waiting room, something akin to a party atmosphere was stirring.

It seemed that everybody was having a pretty good time except the solitary soul in the farthest corner. It was the one who hadn't signed in or spoken to anybody or even indicated that he'd heard us when we asked if we could help him in all the months he'd been coming in. He had utterly ignored our offers of shelter from suffocating heat, bitter cold, or rainstorms—the man with his hair in top-knots.

By the end of the afternoon, we'd talked with all our visitors individually, screened the requests and done what we could to help as many as we could. We'd given out our day's limited resources and the waiting room had virtually emptied out. Diana, one of our gentlest, kindest, most sensitive volunteers, went back to do what one of us always did at the end of the day—make sure everybody who needed help had been offered an opportunity to talk with one of the volunteers. This time, Diana didn't just ask the enigmatic man in the corner if we could help him, she pleaded with him. "It's been so bad outside today, and it's going to get worse. There's a really bad storm coming."

Then she offered our best bribe. "Don't you want to stay at the Salvation Army?" (The Salvation Army was considered the "Hyatt Regency" of the streets by its clientele and vouchers were much prized.) "It won't cost you anything. We'll be glad to give you a voucher. Please take it," she added.

"No, thank you," he said, "I don't like to stay there. It's like a kindergarten class with the teacher out of the room."

Instead of just gathering up the small bundle he usually carried and silently walking out when one of us tried to help him, this time he responded. "No, thank you," he said, "I don't like to stay there. It's like a kindergarten class with the teacher out of the room."

Then he walked out into the downpour that had begun again. For days afterward, Diana would excitedly tell all the other volunteers, her husband, the rest of her family, and anybody else who would listen, "There's a person under there!"

It's not as though we didn't know there was a person under there. It's just that he hadn't let us know who was behind the protective shell of silence he'd been hiding behind and we were all thrilled that he'd opened up for a brief moment. Now we knew that he could hear and speak, and make sense when he spoke. (Not everybody could.) But we still didn't know anything else about him except that he didn't like staying at the Salvation Army.

Our excitement at the breakthrough was short-lived. For weeks after that breakthrough in communication, the man with the top-knots retreated back into his shell, filing silently in with the crowd most days, sitting in the farthest corner, eating the peanut butter sandwiches and drinking the iced tea, water or coffee we served. He'd never signed in and we didn't know his name. We didn't even know if he could read or even whether he could write his name. A few couldn't, painstakingly marking their X on the line. Others took far too long to scrawl nearly illegible letters on the sheet, a clear sign of learning disabilities.

I'd figured from the first time I'd seen him that there was some sort of a serious mental illness. My initial assessment had been underscored by seeing him for months with an utter lack of expression on his handsome, unlined, milk-chocolate face as he sat quietly in the corner while the crowd of half-a-hundred other homeless men (that ever-so-gradually had begun to include a handful of homeless women) milled about and spilled down the hallway. With mental illness, it's common to see muttering—muttering to oneself or flailing away at somebody nobody else could see or hear. That wasn't evident in the man with the top-knots. And he hadn't exhibited one of the signs that we'd quickly learned to spot—the wearing of heavy woolen caps pulled down over ears in 100 degree heat in an effort to keep the "voices" out.

But I had a lot more to learn about voices—his and mine. And a woolen cap wouldn't be able to keep them out.

CHAPTER 8

Called

I knew, on the deepest level,

that back in the basement at Calvary

with 50 to 100 dysfunctional homeless people

and a handful of volunteers, I was where

I was supposed to be.

I'd never expected to lose myself, or find myself for that matter, in the basement of a historic church that had also found itself caught up in the midst of the madness of homelessness. I was a real estate broker and a former banker (occupations not necessarily noted for altruistic motives). I also was a recovering, take-no-prisoners, political activist, still smarting from my second stinging defeat at the hands of voters in Crittenden County, Arkansas, five miles and light years away ... voters who apparently weren't as unhappy with what was happening in the city and the county as I was.

But my political battles weren't the only reason why I found myself at Calvary. I'd agreed to move to Memphis in an effort to salvage what was left of my second marriage, even though it had been pretty much doomed to fail from the moment we both said "I do" and then neither one of us did. It hadn't helped that I'd run for County Judge (an administrative position) three months after we got married, which he thought was a fine idea until I actually did it and he realized he hated putting up yard signs, not to mention pretty much everything else that had to do with yards or houses.

He'd recently walked out on me and our marriage for the first time after only eight months of wedded bliss. In an effort to start over, we'd moved to Memphis, his hometown, only to find, like a couple of idiots, that we'd brought our personal problems with us—and the problems weren't my three sons or his son and daughter who also lived with us. He and I were the problems.

We'd had a total of about ten minutes of pre-marital counseling, not enough to even touch on what we'd soon found were our diametrically opposed perceptions of the meaning and importance of integrity, our polar-opposite approaches to parenting, and our demonstrated inability or unwillingness to live within our means.

Underlying all of those issues was my lack of understanding of the alcoholism and co-dependency that had resulted in the slow, sad demise of my first marriage and soon would result in the scorched-earth end of my second, even though he'd embarked on what would be his snails-pace, but ultimately successful, recovery program a year or so before I'd met him. How was I to know that just "because" an alcoholic no longer drinks alcohol, it doesn't necessarily mean that he or she has recovered from alcoholism. I'd never heard of Al-Anon before my first divorce, and by the time a friend finally dragged me kicking and screaming to an Al-Anon meeting toward the end of my second marriage, it was too late. He'd walked out for the third time by then and I'd finally realized it was a wake-up call, my having hit the snooze-alarm the other two times. For me ... for us ... it was just too late.

But God has a way of helping some of us find healing even when we don't think we need it—or even when we know we need it but don't want it. Within a couple of months after we'd moved to Memphis, I'd found my way to Calvary church where I'd soon begun

Hooked from that first day, I was driven by an overwhelming need to give—just give.

volunteering at the downtown church's food pantry down the street. I was a success at sacking and handing out bags of free food or sack lunches for people who were in a lot worse shape than I was in, some of who were the street people I'd soon be seeing a lot more often at the Street Ministry.

Hooked from that first day, I was driven by an overwhelming need to give—just give. Helping homeless people, I felt, would allow me to do that. I didn't want or expect anything in return, and in the arrogance of ignorance, I thought there was nothing they could do for me anyway. They didn't have a place to sleep, much less a house that I could sell. They were penniless so they couldn't buy a house from me. They couldn't even vote for me. In the event I totally lost my mind and ran for office again, my political battleground was, and would remain for the foreseeable future, in Arkansas.

Politics and Vanity

In retrospect, I think the reason I thought I didn't want anything in return, is that I was tired of people misunderstanding my motives. I'd meant what I said when I was campaigning. I really did want to make life better for people, especially poor people.

I'd won my first political race, represented my district on the county commission (called Quorum Court, in Arkansas), and might have won a second term if I hadn't gotten too big for my britches and run for state representative instead. I lost the race but learned a lot from potential voters during the campaign about how county funds were being used (or, in their opinion, misused) and a lot about the local election process that had historically and effectively disenfranchised many African-Americans. I'd finished up my term on the court, and the finance committee, by going through county records, including invoices in the files, analyzing those expenditures, and then raising holy hell about them.

A couple of years later, I'd run for County Judge (during what should have been our honeymoon period) because I wanted to change those practices. During that campaign, I'd pulled no punches in telling everything I knew about inept, or worse, corrupt government. It outraged a lot of powerful people. I'd topped that off by challenging our local election process, including the illegal appointment of poll workers (judges and clerks) who were municipal or county employees or close relatives of candidates.

But my motives weren't as pure as I liked to think they were at the time. The truth is that when I jumped into the race for State Representative, part of the reason is that I wanted to spend more time politicking and partying in Little Rock with the state's movers and shakers and I thought one of those little license plates with the state capitol on it would look cool on my relatively new, ice-blue, Oldsmobile Supreme Brougham with the sunroof and bucket seats. It is a measure of how much homeless people changed my life that I drove that car for seventeen years while I did everything I could to help them break the cycle of homelessness.

In retrospect, I cannot think of a better way to enrage a lot of people and lose an election—but gain a measure of self-respect.

For many of those years, "Old Blue" sported second-hand, mismatched and threadbare tires, a broken speedometer, a broken air-conditioner, and a cracked sunroof that let the rain ruin the upholstery, carpets, and headliner, and, as often as not, my home-done hairdo. During one particularly difficult financial period, a smog of smoke from the tailpipe obscured everything behind me, and that was after I got it started by lying down on my back on the ground or concrete (depending on where I had parked it or it had quit on me) and hitting something underneath it on the driver's side in the vicinity of the steering wheel with a tire iron as I'd seen Mike, my middle son, do several times when I couldn't get it started by myself.

It didn't matter. I knew, on the deepest level, that back in the basement at Calvary with 50 to 100 dysfunctional homeless people and a handful of volunteers, I was where I was supposed to be, doing what God intended for me to do with my life. I'd been called, and I had no idea that it was only the beginning of my journey in search of the healing that I didn't even know I needed.

CHAPTER 9

The Key

He hesitated for a second,

then his hand reached out and took mine

and more than money exchanged between us.

It was the beginning of trust.

Weeks had passed since our brief breakthrough with the solitary soul with the top-knots. He'd retreated into his zone of silence and sometimes, he didn't come in at all. A week had passed and I hadn't seen him. So I went looking. I walked to Court Square (Squirrel Park, a favorite of the street people) to try to re-connect with some I hadn't seen for awhile and reach out to those who never came in to see us.

Some were too paranoid; some were too proud; some too scared; others too scarred. Since we clearly didn't have nearly enough resources to help the ones who were already coming in, one of the volunteers, clearly frustrated, had asked me why

I was going out looking for more. "Because they're there," I'd replied.

The man with his hair in top-knots was sitting on a park bench by himself, silently watching other people feeding popcorn and peanuts to the squirrels and pigeons. I took a chance and sat down beside him. For awhile, both of us just sat and watched in silence. Since he didn't get up and walk away from me, and because it was killing me that we hadn't been able to help him, I figured I had nothing to lose. I offered him something that I was pretty sure he wouldn't be able to resist—fried chicken—a staple in the south.

"I know you don't like to stay at the shelters," I said, "but it worries me that there aren't many places where you can get something to eat, and you've got to be sick of peanut butter and jelly sandwiches." The slightest flicker of a smile crossed his face—I knew I was on the right track.

One of our few rules at the Street Ministry was that we were never to give anybody cash, even if it was our cash. I was sure we all did it anyway. In fact, just to see if I was right, I'd held a meeting of the volunteers one day and asked if everybody knew the rule about not giving cash. Every head nodded. Then I'd asked, "Is there anybody in this room who's never given cash?" All I got in response were sheepish grins.

"You know where the KFC is?" I asked. He nodded, so I slipped the five-dollar bill out of my pocket where I'd put it just in case he was in the park, softly told him that I was leaving and to pretend that we were shaking hands when I stood up so I could slip him some money. Standing up, I stuck out my hand with the money in my palm knowing that if I'd handed him the cash openly, I'd have been swarmed by every pan-handler in the park.

He hesitated for a second, then his hand reached out and took mine and more than money exchanged between us. It was the beginning of trust. I hadn't asked or expected him to do anything or say anything, and for months afterward, that fragile trust would slowly build. I'd found the key to bridging the gulf between us—something he wanted that I could get for him and that wouldn't, at least in the short term, make him any worse off than he already was.

He still wouldn't sign in and he never accepted our offers of shelter or clothes or anything else.

He never asked us, or me, for anything, not once, but I bought him a lot of KFC and, when he finally tired of fried chicken, food from Jack's grocery on the mall. Eventually, he told me his name. Alepeachie Broadnax. As the months passed, the trust level grew and from time to time, he even responded to a few of my cautious questions.

CHAPTER 10

Alepeachie at TPS

If I'd had any idea that the

Tennessee Preparatory School (TPS)

was a school and home for abused and

neglected children and youth ... I'd have known

a lot more about why he was homeless and

understood why the voices had tortured him so.

"Where'd you go to school," I'd asked Alepeachie, very casually, fully expecting him to say (if he responded at all) "Booker T" or Manassas or one of the other public schools in Memphis. They were all populated primarily by African-American children and youth before (and after) public schools were desegregated.

"Tenn-ess-ee Prep-a-ra-to-ry School," he'd replied, in oh-so-carefully-measured words. Immediately, his words shut me up for the afternoon, scared that I'd ventured too far in asking him about something that he might not want to talk about—like why he'd gone to what I assumed was a reform school for delinquent youth.

It had been one of those rare afternoons when nothing especially nutty had happened at the Street Ministry. For a change, I was feeling rather relaxed when Alepeachie and I left for the day. I'd asked him if he wanted to walk down to the park with me for awhile, explaining that I just wanted to chill out but didn't always feel comfortable sitting or even walking through Court Square by myself—a blatant lie.

There were a lot of people who didn't feel comfortable hanging out in the park where homeless people and panhandlers (some of who were also homeless) tended to congregate, but I was totally at ease with them. I just wanted to learn a little more about him and the little I knew had come mostly from innocuous questions that I'd asked from time to time. Alepeachie was still a puzzle to me.

"What do you do?" and "Where did you go to school?" are questions that I often ask people when I'm trying to get to know them. I certainly wasn't going to ask what he "did" when he wasn't sleeping under his bush or sitting in the waiting room at the Street Ministry. Maybe, I guess, I didn't want to know or was afraid to find out. Where people went to school, though, isn't too personal and whether it's high school, college, or graduate school, at a minimum, it can be the starting point in a conversation.

Who Was Alepeachie and Where Did He Come From?

If I'd had any idea that the Tennessee Preparatory School (TPS) was a school and home for abused and neglected children and youth and how long Alepeachie had been there, I'd have known a lot more. I would have understood why the voices had tortured him so. Why he was homeless. Years later, I would find out.

The comments and "memories" posted on their website by men and women who attended the Tennessee Preparatory School (TPS) during those years are remarkable in that so many have such positive memories of the faculty, the staff, the school where they grew up and the friends they made there.

Perhaps it is no coincidence that the school itself was born of tragedy. A cholera epidemic in 1873 had left many children orphaned but efforts to convince the State Legislature to establish a boarding school for these homeless children had been unsuccessful. The death of Colonel E.W. Cole's 19-year-old son in a train wreck in 1884 proved to be the catalyst.

Already sympathetic and a major supporter for development of the school, he donated what would have been his son's inheritance—a 92 acre estate, including his mansion, which he then equipped to serve as the school, all in honor of his son. By 1887, it had grown so large that Colonel Cole could no longer maintain it and donated it to the State of Tennessee.

I found the first photo of Alepeachie in the TPS' 1974 yearbook, the year I figured he would have graduated, given his age.

The yearbooks posted on the website, especially those produced during the 1970s are, for all practical purposes, indistinguishable from yearbooks that were produced in thousands of other schools during those years. Each one is filled with photos of students of all ages with their classmates, clowning around with friends or involved in extracurricular activities.

The photos reflect that the school fielded championship basketball, football, and track teams. It had cheerleaders and a marching band and sports banquets and homecoming celebrations with homecoming royalty, formals and flowers. It had junior and senior proms, choirs and clubs, including Boy Scouts, Key Club, Jaycees, Junior Achievement, and even Speech and Drama.

The profound difference—and commonality—all of the kids in these photos had been neglected and/or abused, or orphaned. There were no parents waiting to take them home after classes or ball practice or games or other school events.

I found the first photo of Alepeachie in the TPS's 1974 yearbook, the year I figured he would have graduated, given his age. It was there, but not with the seniors. His photo, handsome and smiling slightly, was with 27 other students in the section for "Juniors, Class of 1975." Thinking that perhaps he'd been held back somewhere along the line, I went straight to the 1975 yearbook where I fully expected to see his photo in the section for seniors. It wasn't there; he wasn't listed as "not pictured" and he wasn't in the section for juniors, where I looked, thinking maybe he just hadn't been promoted from the 11th grade.

Working backward, I found him in his class photo as a smiling sophomore in the class of 1974. The yearbook when he'd have been in the ninth grade wasn't available on the website but I kept going. Since he'd been so withdrawn, I was pleasantly surprised to see him as the seemingly happy president of the eighth grade class!

Apparently he wasn't a jock. I couldn't find him or his name in any of the photos of the football, basketball, or track teams. He wasn't in the band either, nor was he in any of the group photos of the various clubs where the names were listed underneath the photos and as far as I could tell, he wasn't in any of the group photos that didn't have names listed underneath.

What is very clear is that he was there.

It got tougher after that, and not because I couldn't find his photo or name. By then, I had already begun hoping that I wouldn't find him there anymore, but there he was in group photos of seventh graders and sixth graders (where he was also listed on the honor roll). The yearbook when he would have been in the fifth grade wasn't on the TPS website, but the yearbook for the year before was. In it, Alepeachie is pictured in a group photo of 4th graders, looking solemn and slightly bewildered, the only African-American boy in the class. He was ten or eleven years old, 200 miles away from Memphis and his family, in a school for abused and neglected children and youth.

I had no way of knowing if he was visited by his family. I had no way of knowing whether his family tried to regain custody, or if or how often he may have returned home. I had no reason to hope that he might have been home with a loving, nurturing family in the two years that photographic records were not available, since he was clearly at TPS the year before and the year afterward. What is very clear is that he was there when he was a ten-year-old child and in every year for which photographic records were available until he turned eighteen.

The school closed in 2002. The website mentions that serious problems in the school's final years were a cause, but there is little doubt that a major reason was a lawsuit filed against the state stating that "Tennessee's foster care system is in a state of chaos and emergency" and that "for too many children, a safe return to their family, adoption or other permanent placement is only a fantasy, not a reality. Instead, far too many Tennessee children are growing up in state custody." It was a quarter of a century too late for Alepeachie.

I knew all too well how it felt as a child to long for a mother's touch, to dream of being reunited with my mother. But by comparison with everything that Alepeachie had endured, what I'd experienced in missing my mother as I was growing up would forever more seem like a Sunday school picnic. I hadn't been abused, neglected or orphaned.

I'd still had a father who loved and supported me, my siblings and my stepmother, and, until he died, I had a place to live.

CHAPTER 11

A Place to Live

Nobody ever told us

they needed a place to live.

It was almost as though the thought of having

a place to live wasn't even in the equation.

It is a sobering thought to realize how quickly we can become accustomed to hearing raised voices and anguished cries. This one was both, and it cut through the din in the waiting room like a bullet, and, for a minute afterward, the silence after the sound was deafening. In one mute movement, every homeless head in the room turned toward the source of the wail as the clean-cut young African American who'd cried out sank deeper into the beat-up leather couch. Oddly enough, it wasn't that his voice was that much louder or that his pain was any more profound than the cries we heard and the pain we saw every day. I think the street people were as surprised as I was at his words.

"I NEED A PLACE TO LIVE!" the man had shrieked.

This was a first. Nobody ever told us they needed a place to live. It was almost as though the thought of having a place to live wasn't even in the equation, having gotten lost in the downward spiral that brought them to the streets and the Street Ministry. "I need a place to stay" is the litany of the lost. Not once in the years I'd been trying to help homeless people had a man or woman asked for help in finding a place to live. We even changed our assessment forms because so many people looked at us in total confusion when we asked them where they'd been living. Now one of our first questions was "Where have you been staying?"

I didn't have a chance to ask the young man where he'd been staying, since a few minutes later, he apparently thought of somebody who might let him "couch surf" for awhile and raced up the stairs and out the door before we'd worked our way down the sign-in sheet to him. If he ever came back, I didn't see him. I just kept on asking homeless people where they'd been staying and hearing responses that would have come straight out of a Homelessness 101 textbook if there'd been one.

"I been stayin' at my mother's but she told me I couldn't come back no more." (Note: one of the first symptoms of substance abuse is trouble at home and trouble at work.)

"My sister was lettin' me stay with her and her kids but she can't let me stay there anymore or they'll throw her out of her apartment." (Note: Feel free to substitute any family member for "sister" and any housing type for "apartment.")

"I been stayin' with a friend." (Note: friend is interchangeable with boyfriend, girlfriend, friendgirl, close friend, or casual acquaintance with a big heart and/or zero understanding of why the man or woman hasn't a family member or other friend to stay with.)

"I got me a cathole where nobody can find me and I'm stayin' there."

By far, the most frequent response was "I been staying at the Mission but I can't stay there tonight 'cause I already used up my three free nights for the month."

That one at least gave us an opportunity to try to wheedle one more night of free emergency shelter out of the Mission, but absent any follow-up questions to figure out why the man or woman had no options other than the streets or shelters, it also meant that in addition to being chronically short-handed, we were often as short-sighted as the street people were.

And that's when it got tougher and tougher to hear and respond to the answers to *Where've you been staying*?:

- I stayed at the bus station last night 'till the guard ran me out.

- I stayed in the waiting room at the hospital but I didn't get no sleep 'cause I sat up all night so they'd think I was waiting for somebody.

- I tore some boards off that ol' boarded-up building across the street and I been stayin' there.

- I been stayin' in my car (truck, old bus, van, whatever).

- I been stayin' in my tent down by the river.

- I was stayin' in the alley behind that apartment building 'round the corner, but some guys beat me up and stole all my stuff and I'm scared to stay there now.

- I got me a cathole where nobody can find me and I'm stayin' there.

Staying vs. Living

It took me awhile, but I was pretty sure I knew why some people "lived" somewhere and other people "stayed." When I was a kid, my dad sometimes let me sit in the squad car with him on Saturday afternoons while it was still relatively quiet. He'd park the black, unmarked car with the bull-whip aerial in a spot where he could see up and down the quarter-mile strip that passed for downtown Turrell, and where it could readily be seen by people going to and from the whisky store, Maud's Cafe, the Chat 'n Chew and the Dew Drop Inn.

While he watched for trouble, I just watched and listened to the static of the police radio and voices saying important stuff like KKC-two-twenty. I've forgotten long ago what my dad told me the code meant but for a little while on those rare Saturday afternoons, it made me feel like I was a part of something exciting.

That was important mainly because during the week, the town was pretty much dead unless Frillis McCord got drunk earlier in the week than he usually did and started causing trouble. Saturdays were different. On Saturdays, the town came alive with people, mostly to buy groceries and supplies and maybe go to the picture show after a week of picking or chopping cotton in the blazing Delta sun on those long rows to nowhere. "A long row to hoe" is a familiar term to those of us who remember what the Mississippi Delta was like in the '40s and '50s. Some, like the sharecroppers and farm laborers and their families who came to town on Saturdays, no doubt remember it better than others.

I loved watching the country folk who'd come to town (not the white ones; they were boring). What I loved were the shrieks of pleasure, the back-slapping, feet-off-the-ground hugging as the black folks literally fell on each other laughing and shouting, reconnecting on the corner with extended family and friends. As the laughter and shouting died down, as often as not the first words out of anybody's mouth were, "Where you stayin'?" I hardly ever heard the whole answer because by the time they got past "I'm stayin'..." and got to "... over to Mr. Wilson's place" or "up the road a piece at Clarkedale Farms," I was already trying to figure out why it was that they asked each other where they were stayin'.

We lived in the white house next door to the Methodist church and before that we'd lived a couple of miles out of town on the Kuhn Plantation in a redwood house with a tin roof, a big yard, and our first indoor bathroom. Before that we'd lived in the apartment at the furniture store that my dad closed when he went into full-time law enforcement. We didn't "stay" anywhere except when we went to visit my stepmother's family in Manila, about sixty miles north of Turrell, for Christmas or for a few days in the summer. Then we "stayed" with Uncle Ed and Aunt Thelma and our cousins or we "stayed" with our step-grandparents. Then we went back home where we lived.

As chemicals replaced cotton choppers and mechanization replaced human cotton pickers and changed the rural south forever, the landowners no longer needed the field hands or the share-croppers. Men and women—hard-working families—who stayed in ramshackle housing and worked the fields on their farms for a small share of the profits at the end of the year. Profits that rarely materialized because they were already owed to the landowner's "company store" for credit advanced during the year. Many of those who fled the farms headed north where there were jobs. Those who couldn't or wouldn't leave the south, headed for the nearest city.

It's doubtful that most of us who had experience with bending double to pick cotton to put in the long, heavy sacks we were dragging, miss that back-breaking work at all. I know I don't, even though my experience was limited to trying to make some money to spend at the traveling carnival that came to town every fall and to a couple of Saturday mornings with my 16-member graduating class to raise money for our senior trip to the nation's capital. (If I'd known that I'd get so hooked on politics; that, as a result, someday I'd find myself sitting in the President's box at the Kennedy Center in Washington, DC, I might not have minded it quite so much.) For most of the men and women who worked in those fields to support their families, the loss of even those God-awful, seasonal jobs meant the loss of any cash income along with the loss of the decrepit housing they were living in on somebody's farm.

A lot of those who'd fled the farms remained in cities like Memphis, but a lot of the better-paying manufacturing jobs in

Memphis and other major cities went ... and hope went with them also. What could be counted on to stay was the stuff that tore a community and its people apart. To make it worse, alcohol stayed; and drugs came and stayed ... and flourished; and domestic violence stayed; and child abuse stayed; and welfare came and marriage went; and families with both their children's parents in the house went; and the children and grand-children of people who never even dared to dream of having a place to live in a home of their own, found themselves still looking for a place to stay.

Alepeachie

When I left the Street Ministry that afternoon, Alepeachie was waiting outside. It took a few minutes, but I finally talked him into letting me buy him some food so he could at least take some with him to his bush. Then, with the brisk wind warning

"I wish I lived in a place like that."

of the winter months to come, he walked with me across the street to my luxury apartment building, peered through the glass door to the lush lobby for the longest time, and then said, without even a hint of envy, "I wish I lived in a place like that."

And then he disappeared; as silently as he had entered the Street Ministry, he vanished. His cardboard bed was still under the bush, but nobody had seen him or knew where he was or if something had happened to him. For all I knew, he was dead. I was devastated but there was nothing I could do but keep going. There were still hundreds of other homeless people who desperately needed help, and apparently, I needed some myself.

CHAPTER 12

I Ain't No Alcoholic

There ain't nuthin' wrong with drinkin'

'cause if there was, God woodna showed

Jesus how to turn the water into wine.

It was my winter of discontent and it was a Friday, a very long one. For starters, I was, as my friends in the recovering community were saying, sick and tired of being sick and tired of alcohol and drugs—what they were doing and had done to people and the people who cared about them, especially me. I was sick and tired of seeing men and women with their guts ripped out, and I was sick and tired of having my guts ripped out. I'd never had time to grieve Arthur's death, and I wasn't even close to acceptance.

Apparently, since there'd been no time for denial or bargaining with God, I'd gone straight to the anger phase of grief and was still stuck there. In retrospect, a lot of my angst was no doubt based in my utter lack of understanding of the role that my co-dependence had played in the demise of both my marriages. Since I hadn't been able to "fix" either of my ex-husbands, I'd set out to "fix" homeless alcoholics and addicts, and they weren't cooperating either. To make it worse, I'd almost given up hope that Alepeachie might be alive somewhere.

I hadn't even wanted to go to the Street Ministry that day, and it wasn't because I was depressed. People who are clinically depressed often find it extremely difficult or even impossible to get out of bed in the morning. It was just the opposite with me. I was going ninety miles an hour, spending almost every afternoon at the Street Ministry and spending weekday mornings and weekends trying to sell real estate. And, even though I'd now been divorced for a year or so, my second ex and I couldn't agree on one primary issue. "I want you in my life," he'd insist, even though he'd

A good friend had taken me aside a few days before to tell me that I needed to slow down; that I was "burning the candle at both ends." She wasn't even close. I was burning it at both ends, in the middle, and looking for another place to light it. Exploding it would have been better.

divorced me, while my response was, "And I want you out of mine." The truth is that I was a lot more mad than sad.

I knew it was at the root of a lot of my problems, but it didn't occur to me that I was basically running from something that I just wasn't ready to deal with—myself and the baggage I'd carried for years.

That afternoon, it seemed that everybody who came in looking for help was either drinking, drunk or high and trying to con us out of something to sell so they could get drunk or drunker or higher. I was totally frustrated because we'd been able to make some inroads into the substance abuse treatment system—a herculean feat. This was accomplished sometimes by talking them into going to the "Nooners AA" meeting where they might get a sponsor who'd help them get into treatment, and sometimes by us getting them into one of the few short-term residential treatment programs and none of the Friday crowd was interested.

Vouchers ... They're an End-All Solution

What most of them wanted wasn't a treatment program. The vouchers were the hot ticket. Since it was late in the month and they'd all used up their monthly allotment of "free" nights at the Mission, some of them wanted shelter vouchers so they'd have a place to sleep off the Thursday night drunk and be rested and ready for the Saturday night drunk. We had vouchers and they knew we had them. The problem was that we'd begun paying the Mission for the vouchers, and we didn't have much money, so we were keeping them for anyone who was at least trying to get his life together.

It didn't do any good to try to explain to them why it would have been a waste of time for us to issue the shelter vouchers when we knew they were drinking. Vouchers for "two hots and a cot" still wouldn't get them past the desk clerks at the shelters. Even when we told the guys to at least try to act sober, the desk clerks knew most of them and just got mad at us for sending them down there when we knew they were drinking and more likely to cause trouble.

Those who'd been thrown out of every shelter in town for fighting or bringing weapons or booze in or for being drunk, didn't even try anymore. They just told people they liked being homeless or that they didn't want to stay in the shelters because the shelters were too dangerous.

Most of the ones who'd come in that afternoon wanted vouchers for personal items. Why? They could and would sell them in a heartbeat on the corner for a fraction of what they'd cost us. We declined. They didn't get bus vouchers to get to "work" at three o'clock on a Friday afternoon either. The vouchers cost us 85 cents apiece and the guys could sell them all day long for a quarter at the bus stop down the street.

We were still battening down the hatches for the Friday afternoon hurricane when the first tidal wave of alcohol hit. Joe was right in the middle of it, slopped to the gills. He'd been there the first day I'd volunteered at the Street Ministry and pretty much every day since, always drunk, drinking, or hung-over. Nobody even bothered to tell him he was walking into the walls. He'd figured it out all by himself. With a happy grin, he was holding onto one of the doorjambs to steady his 6'3" frame while Becky, a diminutive retired teacher, wagged her finger somewhere around his chest level, preaching to him. She was insisting that he absolutely must save 10 percent of whatever money he earned. What was she thinking?

I pulled her aside and reminded her that he hadn't earned a dime since we'd known him, and he surely hadn't earned any money during the years he'd spent in prison. We both just laughed out loud and cried a bit inside. We weren't at all worried that he would hurt any of us. We were right. None of them ever did, even though sometimes our frustration levels were as high as theirs, especially on the Fridays when we volunteers stuck to our script and our visitors stuck to theirs.

Their lines invariably began with a request for vouchers. Ours invariably began with declining their request. With the decline, it gave those of us who couldn't resist trying one more time to get them to go into treatment, another opportunity to waste our breath telling them why. Our friends in the "Nooners" AA group had taught us a lot about alcohol and alcoholism and drug addiction and the role our enabling played in their continuing abuse and addiction. I'd learned the hard way that alcoholics and addicts don't get clean and sober because their families and friends want them to. They get clean and sober when they're sick and tired of being sick and tired.

I was strongly encouraging the other volunteers to do what I was trying to do—get out of the way so that our homeless friends could "bottom out." By that I meant basically getting so sick and tired of concrete pillows and urine-soaked alleys and rat-infested parks that they'd be willing to do something about it.

"I bet ya'll drink, don'tcha, don'tcha?"

Their next line we already knew by heart. "I ain't no alcoholic!" Our visitor would state that categorically, usually in a highly offended voice. Our response to that was usually silence since it is hard to get into an argument with silence. "I can quit anytime I want to" followed immediately. That was best met with silence, too, although after you'd heard the same line a few hundred times, it was permissible to start rolling your eyes right after "quit."

The real pros knew to throw in a little scripture quoting from time to time, with special emphasis on the parts about giving to the needy. If the guilt trip didn't work, as often as not the next line was, "Well, just keep it then. Ya'll ain't nuthin' but a bunch of hypocrites anyways." Then, as if we weren't already ticked off about being called hypocrites and spending our Friday afternoons with a bunch of ingrates while everybody else we knew was on their way to the lake or their other favorite watering hole, one of the "clients" invariably threw in "I bet ya'll drink, don'tcha, don'tcha?"

I never understood why they did that. It never made us more generous. Nervous, usually—defensive, always—generous, never. If we were on our toes, we could try to explain the difference between the use of alcohol and the abuse of alcohol, but it's hard to be on your toes when somebody is "in your face," so everybody always breathed a little easier with the next line: *There ain't nuthin' wrong with drinkin' 'cause if there was, God woodna showed Jesus how to turn the water into wine.*

If that didn't relax anybody enough to loosen a little pocket change, "Jesus drank, y'know" was usually next, and if all else failed, there was always "Don'tchall forget, Jesus was homeless hisself and needed a lil' help." That one had been known to move many a grown man or woman to tears and a couple of bus tickets, but not on Fridays.

Joe launched one last blast as he lurched down the hall. "I CAIN'T BE NO AL-CO-HAW-LIK!" he bellowed. "I AIN'T EVEN GOT NO DUIs!"

"YOU AIN'T GOT NO CAR, JOE!" somebody bellowed back.

"Car, hell," I thought, as I shepherded him down the hall to make sure he made it without falling down or running into somebody; then I made my way back through the crowd muttering, "You ain't got no job. You ain't got no money. You ain't got no food. You ain't got a bed or a place to sleep. You ain't got one single, solitary friend or family member who'll take you in for one more night and help you out just until you can get on your feet again. You ain't got nothing but the clothes on your back and what's left of a half pint of Mad Dog in your hip pocket—and you ain't got no PROBLEM?"

Lazy or Clinically Depressed ... Which Is It?

You wouldn't drink every day if you had a job, you tell us, but the truth is that you lost the last ten jobs you had because you got drunk and didn't show up or got drunk and did show up or you were hung over or drinking on the job and you got hurt. A couple of times, you were just depressed, which is what happens when you drink a depressant, but the boss didn't know why you were just sitting there instead of working, so he fired you because he couldn't tell the difference between clinical depression and laziness any better than the rest of us can.

It wasn't just Joe. We heard it over and over, day in and day out—the mantra of misery, "I ain't no alcoholic." Never mind the symptoms: the daily drinking, the frequent binges, the month-long benders, the blackouts, the shaking hands and the fierce craving for more alcohol. Never mind the truncated transcripts, the string of squandered jobs, the broken bones, broken dreams, and fractured families. Never mind the statistics, the family history of alcohol abuse or the genetic predisposition to the disease. Never mind the rap sheet at the police department with its history of offenses to society in general and human beings in particular. And never mind the profound loss of self-esteem, the depression and the premature deaths.

"I ain't no alcoholic," they said, but what I'd learned to hear was, "I don't want to be an alcoholic. I am afraid to be an alcoholic, and what I fear, I hate. With my whole heart, I don't want to be something I hate."

Joe's father wasn't around much and when he was, he was drunk, and when he was drunk, he was a mean drunk. Joe hated what alcohol did to his father, swore it would never happen to him, swore he would never be an alcoholic. Joe wasn't the first or the last to find that he was the one thing he had always sworn he would never be—an alcoholic.

Even people who were never abused by an alcoholic don't want to be alcoholics. Nobody in their right mind wants to be an alcoholic, a "drunk," a "lush," a "wino." You'd have to be nuts to proclaim, "When I grow up, my goal is to be an alcoholic." Who in their right mind wants to have a crazy-making, chronic, progressive, life-threatening disease that nobody understands, especially when so many people think you are so weak or stupid or morally deficient that you chose to get it and then choose to keep it? Who?

I'd bet the rent money that the millions of Americans who are addicted to alcohol never wanted to be addicted. I'd bet that the millions who abuse the drug just meant to use the drug. I'd bet the grocery money that the millions of other Americans who are addicted to other drugs didn't set out to get hooked. And I'd bet everything I have or ever hope to have, that the millions of family members and friends who are affected by the addicts' addiction never wanted to see the people they love sinking deeper and deeper into the sinkhole of substance abuse.

"I AIN'T NO AL-CO-HAW-LIC!" Joe howled as he staggered up the steps and out of the Street Ministry.

"And I guess I'm Mother Teresa," I muttered.

The Serenity Prayer
When I went back to the waiting room at the end of the day, the poster with the AA Serenity Prayer printed on it practically jumped off the wall and hit me in the face. I knew it by heart.

> *Dear God, Give me the serenity to accept the things I cannot change, courage to change the things I can, and the wisdom to know the difference.*

How was I to know that the courage to change myself would be such a big part of the deal?

CHAPTER 13

Twelve Steps for Do-Gooders

Working the 12-Steps had helped me

immeasurably and made me forever grateful to

my anonymous-to-the-rest-of-the-world sponsor,

but I knew I still had a lot more work to do.

It took awhile but I'd finally realized that what the Street Ministry needed was a good 12-Step recovery program and not just for the street people. I needed one too. I was looking in the mirror. Alcohol or drugs weren't my problem, but most of the people I was trying to help were immersed in them. Being mad at them, not to mention the people and institutions that I thought should be doing a lot more to help them, wasn't doing anybody any good, including me.

Still reeling from the aftermath of the divorce, Alepeachie's disappearance, and the emotional rollercoaster I rode every afternoon in the basement of the church, I wasn't sure serenity was what I was looking for. What I did know was that I was sick and tired of being sick and tired about circumstances and people I clearly couldn't control. I'd been to a few AlAnon meetings and I'd learned the "three Cs." Basically, I didn't cause somebody's addiction, I couldn't control it, and I couldn't cure it, but knowing it and feeling it were two different things. I was pretty sure I needed a 12-step program since my life was becoming unmanageable.

Finding a group that had a 12-step program that wasn't geared toward alcoholics, drug addicts, sex addicts, or gamblers, and finding a sponsor who, in the parlance of the recovering community "had something I wanted" were my next steps.

A few days later, needing to lose a whopping ten pounds to reach my favored maximum weight of 125 pounds on my 5'4" frame, I showed up at an Overeaters Anonymous meeting where I found a wonderful sponsor who literally radiated the "something" I wanted. She even had enough empathy to understand that I needed help even though I wasn't grossly overweight. Still, she'd looked me up and down when I'd asked her to be my sponsor before she asked, "Why me?"

"People I know in recovery programs told me to look for somebody who has something I want ... and you have it," I said, since she'd clearly been "walking the walk" and not just "talking the talk." She was clear-eyed, calm, and yet sympathetic when some of the others at the meeting couldn't control their emotions. I didn't even realize that's what serenity looked like until I met her, and I didn't know what it felt like until I'd been serene enough to lose the ten pounds in six weeks without even going on a diet.

Best of all, when I "worked" my fifth step and "confessed to another human being the exact nature of my faults," including most of the things I'd done that I was most ashamed of, she just rolled her eyes, sighed and smiled at the same time, and chuckled "Is that all?" In retrospect, I didn't tell her the one thing I'd done that I most regretted. I'd buried it far too deeply into my subconscious.

The only downside of "working the steps" was that before she agreed to be my sponsor she looked me (the night owl) in the eye and said, "I'll do it, but we do it my way." It's a measure of how much I needed and wanted her help that I said okay and didn't chicken out even after she told me that she wanted me to call her at 6:00 a.m. every morning.

Early Morning, 12 Step Therapy

"Do you always get up that early?" I'd asked, hoping against hope that she was just trying to accommodate me. "No," she'd replied, "but that's how my sponsor did it and that's the way I do it. And that's the way I did it too, reading, reflecting, writing, and talking to her at 6:00 every morning, including weekends, for six weeks, about a topic she, or later I, wanted to pursue—most of which didn't involve food or weight!

"Working" the 12-Steps had helped me immeasurably and made me forever grateful to my anonymous-to-the-rest-of-the-world sponsor, but I knew I still had a lot more work to do, so I used as a model, the twelve steps that are incorporated to some degree in all of the 12-Step recovery programs. I call my version "Twelve Steps for Do-Gooders."

Step One: Came to realize that my life was becoming unmanageable; that the lives of people I was trying to help had already become unmanageable; that I was powerless to manage their lives for them; and that if I didn't straighten up and do a better job of taking care of myself and my own obligations (including the rent for my apartment), my life was sure to become even more unmanageable.

Step Two: Came to believe that a power greater than all of us, could restore at least some of us, including me, to sanity.

Step Three: Made a decision to turn my will, my life and my futile attempts to control other people's lives over to the care of a wise and loving God.

Step Four: Made a searching and fearless moral inventory of myself and the "help" I was trying to provide to others, often rendered unrecognizable because of my frustration and anger at the very people I wanted so much to help.

Step Five: Admitted to God, my sponsor, and a lot of other people, including myself, the exact nature of my faults, especially my judging, condemning, or mindlessly defending the dysfunctional, counter-productive, sometimes outrageous or downright dangerous behaviors of others.

Step Six: Was entirely ready and willing to "let go and let God" take over as general manager of the world. Actually, I wasn't getting paid for it, anyway.

Step Seven: Humbly asked God to remove my shortcomings, including my fruitless attempts to control others and my carping criticisms of those whose best efforts failed to measure up to my totally unrealistic expectations.

Step Eight: Made a list of all persons I had offended and became willing to make amends and even eat crow if necessary to make a fresh start. This one took a lot of time since, in addition to most of the street people, a couple of priests, and most of our volunteers, I had to dig deep. My list included all my political opponents and a lot of their supporters back in Arkansas. It also included all the service providers in Memphis that I'd smarted off to before I realized they'd been trying to help homeless, mentally ill, addicted, and/or other desperately poor people for years before I ever lifted a finger to help. It was a long list and I smarted as I added each name to it.

Step Nine: Made amends to all those I had offended or hurt except when to do so would have hurt or offended them even more or created an even bigger mess. (This one let me off the hook with both my ex-husbands and all my political opponents and their supporters.)

Step Ten: Continued to take personal inventory—mine, not everybody else's— and when I was mistaken, misguided, manipulative, myopic, manic, moronic, mean, or just a teensie-weensie bit malicious, promptly admitted it.

Step Eleven: Sought through conscious contact with God to improve my conscious contact with reality, remembering at all times that my goal is to put myself and everybody else out of the homelessness business.

Step Twelve: Having had a spiritual, emotional, and intellectual awakening as a result of these steps, sought to carry this message to other wannabee do-gooders in a new spirit of cooperation and dedication to purpose.

Finally, instead of just talking about the Serenity Prayer or saying it, I began to actually pray that wonderful prayer:

God, grant me the serenity to accept the things I cannot change, courage to change the things I can, and the wisdom to know the difference. Amen

Then I found I still needed even more, so I added to that prayer: *and the self-discipline to act—or not act—according to that wisdom.*

CHAPTER 14

Unconditional Love

If one is fortunate enough to give it

or receive it, forgiveness, of others,

of oneself, is the key that opens the door

to unconditional love.

The odds that I'd have such a powerful reminder of why I was where I was supposed to be, doing what God intended for me to do, defied any measure of probability. The trio, a young couple and an older man, had come in as we were about to close for the day. The young couple looked like the kind of folks you see far too often in rural America: dirt poor, shabby but clean and a little embarrassed to be asking for help. The older man who was with them was particularly shabby, with a scruffy beard and a slight shuffle in his walk. He looked as if he could easily have spent some time without a place to live. Unlike most of the homeless men and women we'd seen for the past couple of years, they weren't looking for a place to stay. They just needed money for gasoline. That's what they said.

As we always tried to do when couples or adults traveling together came in, we talked to each one of them separately, giving us a chance to listen to each one, mainly to see if we'd get the same information about what they needed and why they needed it. We wanted to make sure that what we were being asked to do was realistic and would really help.

One of our volunteers took the young man into one of our counseling rooms, another took the young woman into the other counseling room. I sat down with the older man, who appeared to be in his late fifties or sixties, in the waiting room and tried to make him feel comfortable. He was friendly but something just wasn't right. I couldn't put my finger on it, maybe mild mental retardation or brain damage.

"Where're you from?" I asked, for openers.

"Aw, you wooden know," he said.

"I might," I replied.

"Naw," he said, "It's just a lil' hole in the wall up the road a piece."

"Tennessee?" I asked.

"Nope—Arkinsaw," he replied.

"Well, heck, I'm from a little hole in the wall in Arkansas," I said.

"You still wooden know where this 'un is," he said.

"Try me," said I, ready to get on with figuring out why he was with the young couple. We'd had just enough instances to make us cautious where somebody who was getting a disability check would have been a lot better off without whoever was supposed to be "helping" him or her.

A Sudden Reminder of the Past

"Turrell," he said, "half-way 'tween Marion and Frenchman's Bayou."

"Well, I be dog," I said, slipping with alarming alacrity into the vernacular of my youth. "That's my home town! I grew up there."

"Naw," he said, "well, ain't that sumpthin."

"I'll bet you knew my dad," I added.

The thought brought a rush of memories, love, pride and a fresh stab of the old pain. Saturday nights were always wild in "Little Chicago." Think "spring break" but instead of college students running wild, a swarm of men and women whose lives were filled with back-breaking work, deprivation, and discrimination. Saturday nights in Turrell offered an escape for a few hours of hard partying. To eke out a living, the drug store, grocery stores and dry-goods stores that usually closed in the early evening during the week didn't close until midnight.

When I was a teenager, I'd earned my spending money dipping ice cream and making milkshakes for customers at the drug store or selling clothes and household goods to the folks who came to town on Saturdays. Those who came into the store in the evening or close to closing time were just as likely to spend money as those who came in during the day. They just bought different stuff—more like presents for grown-ups than clothes for the kids or other stuff they had to have just to get by on.

The whisky store, Maud's cafe/pool hall (for white people only), and the "tonks" (which would have been called honky tonks if white people were partying there) would have stayed open a lot later but the law required all businesses to close up at midnight. In the south, the "buckle of the Bible Belt," Wednesday evenings and Sundays for church were sacrosanct. One of the tonks was next door to the ice house, which was just across the side yard from where we'd lived for years in the L-shaped apartment that wrapped half-way round our furniture store. This tonk didn't have a fancy name like the Chat n' Chew, the Dew Drop Inn, or the Blue Flame where most of their trouble usually came from. It wasn't even open at night during the week and the man and his wife who owned it and the ice house were really nice. My brother and their little boy played together a lot.

Sometimes on Saturday nights, I'd sit in the dark on the steps of our porch and listen to funky, low-down blues played on worn-out guitars and sung by people who lived the lives they were singing about. I'd watch the ageless, classless mating games, the posturing and preening and partying that today would be called "hooking up." Every once in a while, as I watched the partying ebb, the tonk would erupt in fights and screams, and then I'd watch in half-scared silence as the clock struck midnight and the streets rolled up and Sunday rolled around. In my worst nightmare, I never dreamed that, years after we'd moved to a real house, my father would lose his life on the other side of what had been our furniture store.

Eddie Grice was drunk and looking for his wife and had apparently found her at the tonk next door. Terrified, she'd run from him into the store, by then a grocery store, screaming that Eddie was going to kill her. The storekeeper had called "the law" and either nobody knew or somebody failed to tell my dad or his partner that Eddie had a shotgun. By the time my dad saw the shotgun Eddie was holding across his lap with the barrel pointed at the window on the driver's side, it was too late. Witnesses said my dad yelled, "Throw it out," but instead of throwing it out, Eddie raised the shotgun and pulled the trigger. Somebody said that my dad's gun fired as he staggered and fell, but that he had already been hit by the shotgun blast that tore off part of his head, so it was most likely a reflex action.

Ivan Dickson, his partner, who'd reached the truck by then, shot Eddie and then, helped by some of the townspeople, put my dad in the squad car and sped to the hospital in West Memphis, twenty miles away. The townspeople who gathered were so outraged that my dad had been mortally wounded that not until the town's only doctor arrived on the scene was Eddie transported to the hospital. I don't know if my dad's shot hit Eddie. I never thought to ask. My father died in the early Sunday morning hours and a part of me died with him. His killer had died two or three hours earlier.

All that mattered to me or that ever would matter to me about that night and early morning was that my daddy was dead and nothing would ever be the same again.

In a sure sign of the times, the front page article in the Memphis paper had blared "Berserk Negro Slays Deputy."

The headline for the local, county-wide edition read "Drunk Negro Fires Shotgun Blast Taking Life of Crittenden Deputy," accompanied by a captioned article reporting the number of deputies that had been killed by Negroes (six) and the number killed by white people (one). I guess the reporters didn't know that it didn't matter to me what color the man was who'd killed my father. All that mattered to me or that ever would matter to me about that night and early morning was that my daddy was dead and nothing would ever be the same again.

"Who was your daddy?" the old man asked, bringing me back into focus.

"Carlton Phillips," I said, as the stabbing pain faded into the old familiar ache. For years after my dad was killed, I'd felt that part of me had just been ripped away, a pain so devastating that it had overwhelmed every other loss I'd sustained. As time went by, the raw edges had healed, leaving just the dull ache and the profound sense of loss.

My dad was 49 when he died. I was 18 and loved him with my whole heart. He was my rock, a man of courage and the most unselfish person I had ever known or may ever know. If he had a dollar, everybody in the world had a dollar. On the beat-up old cash register in *"Why, shore, I knew Mr. Phillips," he said. "I 'member when he got killed.* our furniture store he'd hung a small sign. "I cried because I had no shoes until I met a man who had no feet." He extended credit to country folks who would never have had cook stoves or refrigerators or tables or beds if he hadn't gone the extra mile in extending credit. The man who killed him owed him money.

One of my favorite memories is of the day I went "collecting" with him. He only did it when people who'd bought furniture or appliances from him hadn't paid in months and he really needed the money to pay our bills. Clouds of dust had swirled up behind our red pickup truck with "Phillips Furniture Company" proudly emblazoned on both doors as we bounced our way down country roads, winding through the fields, stopping at several weather-beaten farmhouses and shacks before we found anybody home. It was cotton-chopping time, which meant that anybody big enough to hold a hoe was in the fields. I guess we must have been really broke (and I never claimed that my father was a good businessman).

The young woman who opened the screen door was barefoot, wearing a house dress clearly made from the flowery printed cotton sacks that had held flour before being stitched into clothing. I knew because all three of the grocery stores in Turrell sold those huge bags of flour. Three tiny children peeped at us from behind the open doorway, two of them in homemade, droopy diapers. Inviting us inside, the woman insisted that we stay for lunch, which we did, my dad and I each choking down a biscuit made of flour and water, smothered in molasses. He didn't even bother to ask her if her husband had left her any money to pay him after that. Instead, he took his last five dollar bill out of his worn wallet, and despite her reluctance, insisted that she take it and buy something for the children. That memory was the essence of the dad I remembered.

He understood poverty better than most. He'd been orphaned at the age of six, lived with his mother's family until he was fourteen and then, armed with a fourth grade education, left Cajun country for West Memphis where Noah, his oldest brother, lived. Once there, he'd worked at the ice house for a quarter a day and slept on a pool table at the pool hall at night.

I don't know why he didn't live with his brother because they were always close as we were growing up. My best guess is that he probably wasn't welcomed with open arms by his brother's wife, Aunt Lula, who hated it when they spoke Cajun French and she didn't know what they were talking about. He'd had three other brothers but one had not survived childhood, and the other two had died in their early twenties, one of tuberculosis, the other when he fell off an oil rig and broke his back. My dad and Uncle Noah had hitchhiked across Arkansas and Louisiana to bury him and had to dig his grave when they got there.

Carlton Phillips grew up, and sometime during the following years, got a job at the Scott-Kelly Furniture Store, and married the girl who'd become my mother. Their first child, Dorothy Lee, a blue-eyed, blonde-haired cherub, died of pneumonia, in his arms, when she was only 18 months old. Three months later my sister was born; 18 months later I came along; and 16 months later the twins were born. We moved to Turrell and Dad opened his own furniture store (with a poker table in the back) on the south end of the quarter-mile strip of town.

Then my mother got on a bus one day to go shopping in Memphis and never came back home. If my dad ever blamed my mother for leaving him with four little kids he never said so, and if his temper was the reason—or part of the reason— why she left, I never blamed him. After he remarried, he moved his business and us across the railroad tracks to the building where he'd respond to the call that resulted in his death.

The old man's voice pulled me back. "Why, shore, I knew Mr. Phillips," he said. "I 'member when he got killed. I wuz in town that night and soon's I heard about it, I went rite over there. I wuz one of the first ones that got there and I wuz the one that found some of his false teeth layin' there in the gravel where he fell. I picked 'em up and took 'em to Mr. Ivan to give to Miz Phillips."

Mr. Ivan, Dad's partner, who'd been a deputy sheriff long before my dad went to work full time as a deputy, gave them to my stepmother. I don't remember how I came to be in possession of those personal items that are all that remain of the father I knew, except his memory. I think I simply claimed them when my stepmother quickly moved on to her fifth husband. A little cardboard prescription box holds bits of Dad's dentures. A larger box holds the blood-stained package of Lucky Strikes from his shirt pocket, the police badge I refused to turn in to the County Sheriff who was thoughtless enough to ask for it, the blackjack that always protruded from the back pocket of his well-worn trousers, the painfully thin wallet with a single dollar bill (less than a week after payday), and his beat-up, foot-long, aluminum flashlight.

We hardly ever saw him without that flashlight and we never asked why it had those dents in it. We knew. Most of the time he'd just take whoever was drunk and acting out to wherever he was staying, but if he had to arrest him and he put up a fight, he used the flashlight to subdue him instead of the blackjack he was required to carry but never used. He got really upset when any of us even picked up his blackjack even though we were just fooling around. Hitting somebody with it could hurt somebody really badly or even kill them, he said.

When I could talk again, I said, "I still have the pieces of his false teeth that you found. Thank you for caring enough to pick them up and not just leave them lying in the road."

"I couldn't do no less," he said. "Mr. Phillips was a pretty good man e'bn with that temper. Whoo-ee, did he have a temper."

"Yes, he did," I whispered, remembering our abbreviated trip to a nearby town one bitterly cold night to see *Birth of a Nation*. All the grownups in town had been raving about it. As cold as it was, he'd driven 15 miles to see this one with us kids riding, covered up with blankets, in the back of the truck. I'd barely settled in with my nickel bag of popcorn before he came out of his seat, swearing like a sailor, and bundled us right back into the back of the truck. Years later I learned that it was a highly racist film made in the late twenties and re-released in the forties.

"I ain't never been the same since."

The old man coughed, probably to get my badly wandering attention. "You're right," I sighed, "to be as easy-going as he was most of the time, he really had a temper. I know I never wanted to be the one who made him mad."

"Me neither," he said, "not after he come after me swingin' that flashlight. I ain't got no fambly to speak of; them young-uns in there is my sister's kids come to take me to South Caroliney. I cain't get no job, cain't hardly read, quit school, didn't have nowhere to stay. One time this colored fambly was lettin' me stay with them out on Mr. Walker's place and somebody called the law and told them a white boy was sleepin' at some colored folks' house. That's when Mr. Phillips showed up. I wuz asleep but I woke up when he come in and yanked me up."

"You know better'n to be sleepin' here," he said, "and that's when he whopped me upside the head with that big ole flashlight he always carried. And you know what," he said, in a faraway whisper, "I ain't never been the same since."

And you know what? I would never be the same again either. I don't know if my father thought the man (only a youth at the time) was taking advantage of any girls or women in the family or whether he was enforcing the segregation that was part and parcel of living in the south in the 1940s. What I do know is that in being forced to accept the reality of my father's sins, I was forced to face the reality of mine as well—his misguided, angry blows, my years of silent acceptance of the unmitigated evil of segregation and the pain that my indifference to such a terrible injustice must have caused.

By then, both of the volunteers had finished talking with the couple and one had written out the voucher for gasoline and only needed a nod from me, which was a good thing, because I couldn't say a word for hours afterward.

If one is fortunate enough to give it or receive it, forgiveness, of others, of oneself, is the key that opens the door to unconditional love. Like the peace that passes all understanding, it is a gift from God.

CHAPTER 15

What Do the Voices Say?

This time I was the one who was silent,

struck dumb with fear that even though he

seemed totally unconcerned about what the voices

said, anything I said would be wrong or worse.

It was a beautiful spring day and all my agonizing over what had happened to Alepeachie had ended. He'd come in a few days before and had seemed really surprised that I was so glad to see him. I was more than glad. I was ecstatic. I hadn't known if he was dead or alive, or if he was alive, where he was and what was happening to him. He'd been to West Palm, he said, as casually as I'd have said I'd been to West Memphis. This was another lesson for me. Having a mental illness doesn't render one incapable of figuring out how to get to where one wants to go, nor does it necessarily keep one from going there. He looked good, too, and seemed more at ease than I'd ever seen him. Wintering in West Palm must do that for people.

He'd been coming in every day, let me buy him KFC several times, and on this particular day was the only person left in the waiting room when I went in to make sure everybody had left before we locked up. I expected to find it empty since a lot of our more peace-loving friends, including Alepeachie, usually left at the first sign of any kind of distur-bance and several of the people who'd signed in had left instead of waiting their turn to see if we could help them.

The afternoon had been fairly calm until a man that none of us recognized had gotten into a screaming match with somebody that nobody else could hear or see and then stormed out the door. I'd followed, at a discreet distance, and watched helplessly as he flailed away at whoever or whatever was tormenting him. I didn't know what the "voices" were saying to him or trying to get him to do or stop doing. I didn't have a clue who or what he was fighting with, and I didn't know how to help him.

Some of them were so sick they didn't know they were sick and therefore couldn't comprehend the need for medications.

I could only stand, watch, and wonder—again—who was responsible for seeing that he got the help he needed. Until I did, I couldn't shake the feeling that it was me.

We'd been trying to help homeless people for years; many of them were mentally ill, and we had yet to make inroads into the mental health system. It wasn't as though we had problems identifying people who were struggling with mental illness or identifying the mental health centers they were or had been connected to, or even making appointments for them to get help.

The problem was that they never kept the appointments no matter how many times we reminded them, or how many bus or taxi vouchers we gave them to get there, or how many times I offered to take them myself. Some of them were so sick they didn't know they were sick and therefore couldn't comprehend the need for medications. Others knew they needed them but didn't want them because of the side effects, painful to some, numbing (as in feeling like a zombie) to others. Or they were afraid that they'd end up in the hospital.

Being totally out of touch with reality, having no insight into one's condition, eating out of garbage cans and sleeping on the streets or in abandoned buildings, and slugging it out with lampposts weren't enough to get somebody into a treatment facility, jail usually, but not treatment, unless the people who ran the jail transferred them to the hospital.

They needn't have worried. We'd hit a brick wall in trying to get people into the only acute care, mental health facilities that we knew of, especially for people without money or, as far as we knew, insurance.

To be admitted, voluntarily or involuntarily, the person had to be "imminently" suicidal or homicidal. I knew, because I'd finally persuaded (basically bribed with local bus vouchers) Sherman into letting me take him to see a psychiatrist at the mental health center where he was already a consumer of mental health services (aka, a "patient" to those of us who weren't up to date on political correctness). I thought that if I could just get him in to see the psychiatrist, the psychiatrist would help me get him admitted to a hospital.

Sherman wasn't actually homeless, but he came in every day to get a bus voucher to get back home. We wouldn't give him one to get back downtown but we couldn't stop him from walking back. We'd therefore just settled into trying to get him home every night so he wouldn't have to sleep on the street or go to one of the shelters where he said it was always too noisy for him to do his research. He said he had to come back downtown every day because he was waiting for Ho Chi Minh to show up so he (Sherman) could share with him his secret plan to end the Vietnam War, which by then had been over for more than a decade.

I wasn't really worried that he was going to fly to Vietnam on the plane that he'd drawn and then folded into shape (complete with wings) before he showed it to me. But I did think there was an outside chance that he might try to flap his arms and go off a tall building thinking he could fly, or try to hijack a real airplane and get somebody killed in the process. The woman answering the phone and making appointments at the mental health center had been very sympathetic and told me that if I'd bring Sherman out to the center, she'd work him into the psychiatrist's schedule. It had cost me a week's worth of bus vouchers to get Sherman to go with me but he seemed to enjoy the ride in Old Blue.

We'd barely taken our seats in front of the psychiatrist's desk when he practically shouted at Sherman, "You planning to kill yourself?"

"No," my test case responded, rather nonchalantly.

"You planning to kill somebody else?" barked the shrink.

"No," his consumer of mental health services, who wasn't consuming any, responded, with a bemused smile.

"Well what are you doing in my office?" barked the shrink, "Go on, get out of here." It was a good thing he didn't ask me if I felt like killing somebody.

But it was what had happened a few days before that had made me realize that we needed to know if Alepeachie ever heard voices, and, if so, what the voices said. I'd wondered about it but hadn't asked him because sometimes the simplest question could set off a paranoid rant from someone who only an instant before had seemed fairly rational. I didn't want to take a chance on losing the fragile tie we'd established.

By then, I'd listened to enough stories told in whispers or shrieks about poisonous anti-psychotic medications, conspiracies, aliens, the government in general, and the CIA, FBI, and Pentagon in particular, to understand that auditory and/or visual hallucinations were symptoms of serious mental illnesses, especially schizophrenia. None, however, had come close to the bizarre tale the perfectly normal-looking man who'd come in a few days before and quietly waited his turn, had to tell.

The Man and Marilyn

Not much over five feet tall, the man was quiet, calm, clear-eyed, clean and neat, conservatively dressed in khaki pants and a sport shirt, and well-spoken. He seemed perfectly normal to me. I guess he must have been impressed with how easy it had been for me to solve his shelter problem for the night. All I'd done was give him a voucher to the Union Mission. Instead of leaving after he got the voucher, though, he hung around and then caught up with me in the hall after the crowd had thinned out.

> *He didn't know why none of the prospective employers couldn't hear or see her. They just looked at him funny when he tried to make her go away.*

"Can you help me with something that's very powerful?" he asked in a confidential, almost conspiratorial whisper.

"I don't know," I whispered back, "I went toe-to-toe with the good ol' boys and the local political "machine" back home and I'm still standing. If I can help, I will."

That's when he told me about Marilyn. According to him, Marilyn was 80 percent gorilla and 20 percent human and hid behind a big shield all covered over with human skin. But it wasn't Marilyn's appearance that bothered him the most. He was a musician, he said, and he'd been trying to get a job playing piano on Beale Street. Nobody, though, would hire him with Marilyn following him around telling everybody that he'd killed Leslie's son ... when he really hadn't. He didn't know why none of the prospective employers couldn't hear or see her. They just looked at him funny when he tried to make her go away.

That's when I called the priest.

While we were waiting for Doug to come downstairs, I very gently asked the man if he had tried to make Marilyn leave him alone.

"Yes," he said, quite calmly, "I went to the CIA and the FBI and I went to see her daddy where he works down at the police station in Oxford, Mississippi, but he wouldn't even talk to me about how he happened to mate with a gorilla to turn out Marilyn."

Something told me not to laugh.

When I was sure I could do it with a straight face, I asked, "Did you do anything else to make her leave you alone?"

"Uh huh," he said, without a flicker of emotion. "I stabbed her and I threw acid on her, and next time I guess I'll have to assassinate her."

That's when I called the emergency room at the MED. I knew they had a psyche unit because a couple of weeks earlier I'd managed to get one of our regulars who was threatening suicide admitted. I'd then spent a whole afternoon sitting outside the door to the unit, peeking in the small window in the locked door from time to time to assure him that I hadn't abandoned him as he felt that everybody else in his life had done, probably because of his totally uncontrollable addiction to drugs. This case was a lot different but I knew I couldn't help this poor man. If I'd ever seen a clear-cut, hands-down case for getting help from the mental health system, this was it.

By then, Doug had hurried downstairs and was listening to our visitor tell him pretty much the same thing he'd told me.

Never Could Tell What He'd Do ...

After I'd spent another hour on the phone explaining to half-a-dozen people at the MED what was wrong and what we needed them to do, I called the police and explained our problem to the dispatcher. I hated to do it because Doug and I were going to take him to the hospital ourselves. However, the last person I'd talked to as I worked my way up the chain of command at the MED had told me that we had to call the police to transport him in order for them to admit him. "Never could tell what he'd do," the man at the MED had said.

We didn't know the police would have to handcuff our homeless friend for the ride to the hospital. "Standard procedure," they said, "never could tell when he'd go off."

Luckily, he was a lamb about the handcuffs; just leaned forward and put his hands together behind his back like he'd been doing it all his life. I was going to ride

Standing on the curb, watching the police car drive away that day, I'd had a sinking feeling. If someone who appeared as normal as that man could be that sick and, in my opinion, that dangerous, could Alepeachie possibly be that sick too?

with him in the back of the police car to the hospital but the policemen said "No, never could tell, you know." I went home that afternoon thinking that at least he'd be getting the help he needed.

I must have been nuts. He beat me back to the church and was sitting quietly on the front steps when I got there around noon the next day—said the doctor at the hospital talked to him for a few minutes and then told him he could leave whenever he wanted to.

That's when I lost it. This man couldn't work. Who'd have hired him to play the piano, if, in fact, he could actually play it, when he was complaining that a half-human, half-gorilla apparition was following him around and he was planning to assassinate her/it? He didn't have any money or a place to live. How could I have written a voucher for him to stay at one of the shelters when any minute he might decide it was time to assassinate Marilyn? Where was he supposed to sleep? If talking about assassinating an invisible gorilla that was following him around didn't get him a bed in the psyche unit at the hospital and psychiatric care, what would?

The resident physician who'd assessed him at the psyche ER wasn't any help.

"Well," he said soothingly, "he does have a little problem."

"Well, I think he has a BIG problem, about as big as a gorilla," said I, "and if you don't think he's got a big problem, then I think two out of the three of us has a big problem."

No response from the resident.

"What are you going to do," said I, "if he decides to assassinate Marilyn and your mother or your wife or your sister or your girlfriend or your daughter happens to be standing next to her (it)?

"Well, I'm going to feel real bad about that," said the rez.

By the time I'd finished shooting off my big mouth, the man (hopefully without Marilyn) was gone, having said something to one of the volunteers on the way out about going to Oxford, Mississippi.

Standing on the curb, watching the police car drive away that day, I'd had a sinking feeling. If someone who appeared as normal as that man could be that sick and, in my opinion, that dangerous, could Alepeachie possibly be that sick too? We knew next-to-nothing about him. Could he possibly be dangerous to others? To himself? Was he hearing voices? Seeing people or things that nobody else could see?

It was still on my mind, and I'd been waiting for what I thought might be a good time to talk to him.

"I'm glad you're still here, Alepeachie," I said, when I went back to the waiting room at the end of the day. "Are you hungry?" Picking up his bundle, he followed me into the office where I unlocked the desk drawer, got my purse and gave him enough money to eat at the KFC or wherever he wanted to eat. He never said thank you and I never cared that he didn't. I considered it an honor that he let me help him.

For the first time in my life, I understood on the deepest level how deadly words could be.

In what I felt had become a companionable silence, we walked down the hallway and out the side door of the church that the regular parishioners used and jaywalked across the street in the late afternoon sunlight to Court Square and sat down on one of the park benches. We never talked much. In fact, most of our "conversations" were limited to my comments on the weather or whatever I was seeing. Sometimes, not often, he'd respond with a comment of his own. Occasionally, I'd venture to ask him a question and sometimes he'd answer, usually with a nod or shake of his head, sometimes with a yes or no, and occasionally a tiny tidbit of information.

"Did you see the man who was so upset today?" I asked.

"Uh huh," Alepeachie said softly.

"He must have been hearing voices," I ventured. No response from Alepeachie.

"Do you ever hear voices?" I asked, after a long silence.

"Yes," he said, quietly.

"What do the voices say?" I asked, holding my breath and wondering what it was that had sent him over the edge and into the abyss of mental illness.

"You're no good," he said, very calmly, even nonchalantly, "Nobody likes you. Everybody hates you. Nobody wants you. Why don't you just die? Why don't you just kill yourself? Go on. Do it. Kill yourself."

This time I was the one who was silent, struck dumb with fear that even though he seemed totally unconcerned about what the voices said, anything I said would be wrong or worse, resulting in him doing what his voices were needling him to do. All I knew to do was to try to keep him and the others coming to the Street Ministry until I could get somebody in the mental health system to listen and help. But there was even more to it than the voices that haunted Alepeachie. For the first time in my life, I understood on the deepest level how deadly words could be—and the nightmare that had haunted me off and on for years soon returned to wake me night after night leaving me with the taste of guilt in my mouth.

CHAPTER 16

Breakthrough

"You're running a mental health center here.

That's what you're doing." ...

"Nope," she said. "It's definitely a

psyche emergency room."

There was no politically correct way to say it. The Street Ministry had literally become a madhouse. I must have relapsed from my new-found serenity because I wasn't just frustrated, I was mad as hell. In fact, I'd complained so much about our inability to get mental health treatment for the mentally ill people we were seeing that Marjean Kremer visited me. She was one of the co-directors of the newly organized Coalition for the Homeless, and she came to see what we were doing at the Street Ministry. As a result, I was invited to one of the Coalition meetings so that I could explain to them why we needed help.

It was a total waste of time. Though the people there were too polite to say it, it was pretty clear that none of them thought I knew what I was talking about, except Marjean ... and Selma Lewis, the other co-director. Both of them were highly regarded, local community leaders who'd taken on the job (as VISTA volunteers) of trying to coordinate programs that could or should serve homeless people. Most of what I know today about coordinating resources I learned from watching them in action. And the truth is that I couldn't blame the Coalition members for thinking that I didn't know what I was talking about. After all, who was I to try to diagnose mental illness? I wasn't a psychiatrist or a psychologist. I wasn't even a social worker. I was a real estate broker and a volunteer.

Never mind that by then I'd been in the basement of the church five afternoons a week for a couple of years with 50 to 100 street people on any given day, or that we now had files for more than 2,000 people who'd come to the Street Ministry looking for help, and at least a third of them were struggling with serious mental illness, the chaos created by untreated mental illness, and the dual diagnoses of mental illness complicated by substance abuse.

Mental Illness ... Not That Hard to Spot

It wasn't that hard to figure out. If we didn't spot it immediately from the way they looked or acted, we often found out from the brief series of non-threatening questions we now asked, including questions about their health, medications they were taking, whether they'd been in a hospital, and, if so, which hospital, and whether they had problems with their "nerves."

(There was no stigma attached to having problems with one's nerves.) Their responses would often tell us what we needed to know to try to get help for them. If the medications were Prolixin or Haldol or Thorazine, (psychotropic medications) and/or if the hospital was one I knew to be for people with psychiatric illnesses, I knew I needed to try to connect them to the mental health system.

A couple of weeks after I'd met with the Coalition, a delegation that included Marjean and a couple of people who hadn't been at the meeting, came to the church to meet with us. While I apparently had zero credibility, Doug had a lot, and he'd invited them to meet with us on our turf. We'd just gotten settled in one of the meeting rooms that opened off the dining hall in the basement of the church when Blanche, one of our more sporadic visitors, sat down at the piano in the dining hall and cut loose, sounding just like Jerry Lee Lewis playing "Great Balls of Fire," but on all the wrong keys.

Doug didn't miss a beat, just leaned back, pushed the sliding doors together, and kept on talking. Turning to the tall, distinguished-looking gentleman sitting next to me, who had just introduced himself as Wib Smith, the director of the Whitehaven/Southwest Mental Health Center, I whispered, "That's just Mrs. Peter Frampton, the rock star's wife, playing the piano. She's a musician too but she's under a very strict recording contract and that's why she can't play the piano anywhere except in our church basement." That managed to raise a couple of eyebrows.

Frankly, I was disappointed that she'd apparently come by just to play the piano. Sometimes she came in to talk to us for a few minutes, always leaving me yearning for a people-sized butterfly net as she flitted in and out. Other times she came by to use the bathroom, take a bath and wash her hair. That would have been fine if we'd had a bathtub or a shower. We didn't, but that didn't slow Mrs. Frampton down. The bathroom she used had been carved out of an unused space near the boiler room. One had to take a couple of steps up to the little landing and a couple more down, to get into it. This made it easy for her to turn it into a sunken bathtub/sauna just by locking the door and letting the water in the sink overflow for an hour or so.

The reality is that her craziness was driving us crazy. We'd had zero success in trying to help her or even in getting basic information from her. We didn't know who she really was, where she was from, whether or not she had family, where she stayed, how she survived, how to get help for her, or how to get her to accept help if we found it. But that day, if her concert had been a command performance by a renowned pianist at Carnegie Hall, it couldn't have been better as far as I was concerned. She'd made the point of the meeting far better than I, or even Doug could have done.

The next day, I got a call from none other than Wib, the director of the mental health center, asking if he could bring one of his staff members and come by for a few minutes to see if they could help. Of course, I welcomed the visit. When he got there, he stood in the doorway of the packed waiting room for a few minutes, then turned to me and said, "You're running a mental health center here. That's what you're doing." The woman with him disagreed. "Nope," she said, as she left for another appointment, "It's definitely a psyche emergency room."

The Crisis Unit

Before Wib left, he took me aside and said, quietly but firmly, "I want you to see our crisis unit and meet some people you need to know. Come on, it won't take long." No more than a dozen blocks away, he pulled up in front of what looked like just another big old, run-down midtown house. Inside, it didn't look much better; faded wallpaper, chipped paint and second-hand furniture, but it had friendly, cheerful, comforting, caring, laid-back mental health professionals on-site 24 hours a day, seven days a week to help stabilize people who were suicidal or psychotic and "acting out." If our visitors were willing to go there, they could stay in that non-threatening, non-institutional atmosphere for a few days with access to the medications they needed. I thought I'd died and gone to heaven.

When we left the crisis unit, Wib drove a half dozen blocks back toward downtown to a cheerful, well-kept building where we went straight to the office of Nancy Hale (now Lawhead), the director of Midtown Mental Health Center. She'd been out of town when I'd met with the Coalition and had an emergency that had kept her from coming to Calvary with the Coalition's delegation. She was special. Convinced that the university-sponsored mental health center where she'd worked for a couple of years, didn't share her bedrock commitment to ensuring that the poorest of the poor had the mental health care they needed, she'd quit her job, commandeered some grant money, raised some more and battled to transform an abandoned school building into a first-class mental health center. Its sole purpose was to ensure mental health treatment for the people in our inner-city, poverty-stricken, State

Department of Mental Health-designated "catchment" area. She was smart, kind, tough, concerned, and, as her actions would prove over the next couple of years, more than willing to help.

Because Midtown already had the heaviest indigent caseload in town, and because Wib's center had a few paying clients with private insurance to help offset his costs, by the time we got back to the Street Ministry, he'd offered to loan us a crisis specialist for a couple of hours a day, two or three days a week until Midtown could find the money to pay somebody to help us.

I needed my butt kicked. I'd been so busy ranting and raving about what was wrong with the mental health system that I hadn't taken time to find out what was right about it. What I'd found were some extraordinarily caring, competent people who'd been in the trenches of a poorly funded mental health system for years doing their best to care for people with serious mental illnesses before I even knew they existed.

Wib came back again and again to help, loaning us not one but two crisis specialists, Willie Henry and Mike McMillin, whom we quickly dubbed "Saint Willie" and "Saint Mike." Laid-back, knowledgeable, professional and experienced, they were masters at engaging people with mental illness, at defusing a situation before it escalated into a full-blown crisis, and at showing us by their example how to do a better job of it ourselves. Best of all, they were masters at persuading some, though definitely not all of the homeless mentally ill people they were seeing, to accept medications, crisis stabilization and other mental health services and the limited housing options that were available.

Wib didn't stop with loaning us Willie and Mike. One day he stopped by to put in my hands a copy of a landmark study of the homeless population in Chicago by a highly respected researcher and sociologist, Dr. Peter Rossi. He was pilloried by Chicago advocates for homeless people for telling the truth, but I thought he was wonderful. Despite the deeply disturbing results of his ground-breaking study, my perceptions of home-lessness among people who spent the majority of their time on the streets or in emergency shelters had been validated.

And Wib wasn't the only one who came to help. As soon as Nancy could, she sent a case worker for an hour or so two or three times a week to provide us with a direct link to Midtown's mental health services. When the state made funds available to actually pay for in-patient crisis stabilization, in cooperation with the other four mental health centers, she applied for the funding, reno-vated a building on Midtown's property,

The "staggering levels of disabilities" Dr. Rossi described were exactly what I was seeing every day at the Street Ministry.

developed a state-of-the-art crisis stabilization unit (CSU), and then invited me to serve on the board.

As grateful as we were for the breakthrough with the men-tal health system, we had yet, no matter how much I begged, pleaded or threatened, to break through the system to get help for those who desperately needed inpatient treatment but were adamantly opposed to hospitalization. It wasn't enough for someone to be psychotic, slugging it out with lampposts, catatonic, eating out of garbage cans, losing fingers or toes to frostbite, or trying to survive in 100 degree heat wearing layers of winter clothing. And it didn't matter that at the time, the commitment laws actually allowed for involuntary commitment of people who were so ill that they couldn't meet their own basic needs. The CSU wasn't funded, licensed or staffed to admit anyone involuntarily, and in order to be involuntarily committed to the state's primary acute-care mental health MMHI, one had to be "imminently" suicidal or homicidal. Two psychiatrists, the referring psychiatrist, and a psychiatrist at the institution, had to agree that the person met that criteria. That didn't keep me from trying.

The long-time director of the institution finally told me, "Pat, you know they're committable. I know they're committable, but I can't say they're committable because if I say they're committable, then by law, I have to commit them, and I can't commit them because I don't have enough beds for them." He wasn't talking about furniture. He meant that even though state law required him to commit someone who had been deemed committable, the state didn't provide the money needed to pay for the number of staff required by the state to provide treatment for the people who would occupy any additional beds.

Deinstitutionalization had begun as a noble effort. It needed to happen. It would have been unconscionable to keep people in institutions who responded well to the newly developed psychotropic medications, especially when many of those institutions were reported to be poorly staffed and woefully inadequate, and some were described as "snakepits." Discharging people who responded well to the newly developed psychotropic medications had been the first part. Ensuring that they had the services, treatment and housing to live outside the institution was supposed to be the second part, but, as Wib told me on more than one occasion, "Deinstitutionalization worked. We got them out of the hospitals. It's the other half that isn't working."

There were reasons why it wasn't, and still isn't, working well. It was expected that the dollars required to treat them in the institutions would "follow the patient" to the "warm embrace of the community." It didn't happen, primarily because the Bazelon Center, a leading national advocacy group, had argued successfully (and rightly) that it would also have been unconscionable to keep those who didn't respond well to the medications in those same institutions without significantly improving the facilities and providing adequate treatment. That would require additional staff and improvements to the hospitals themselves, which meant that the hospitals kept the money. But when the money didn't "follow the patients," it left far too many desperately poor, desperately ill people to fend for themselves.

"I know they're committable, but I can't say they're committable because if I say they're committable, then by law, I have to commit them, and I can't commit them because I don't have enough beds for them." He wasn't talking about furniture.

Others, like many of the ones who made their way to the Street Ministry, hadn't been in mental institutions at all or if they had, it was only for short-term stabilization.

And my thoughts transitioned back to Alepeachie. Since he had never signed in, I was afraid I'd lose him if I asked him about his psychiatric history. Because the providers were prohibited from talking to me about it, I never learned if he'd ever been in a mental institution.

What I did know was that we were overjoyed to have mental health professionals helping stabilize and house many of the homeless, mentally ill men and women we'd agonized over for months or even years.

CHAPTER 17

Going Home

None of us thought that making his mother

his payee and moving in with her

and the family was a good idea, but

Alepeachie had the right to make the decision.

If we hadn't been disappointed so many times when we thought for sure that one of our homeless friends had finally escaped from the concrete killing fields, we'd have been throwing confetti and toasting Alepeachie's success with iced tea. Instead, we greeted the news that he was going home with cautious optimism, deeply grateful that, thanks to Willie and Mike, he wouldn't be sleeping under that bush, at least for awhile, but concerned that his housing arrangement might not last very long, given that he'd gone to school at a state school for abused and neglected children and youth.

Since it had taken more than a year for me to gain Alepeachie's trust, I was surprised but ecstatic that the trust level had so easily transferred to Willie and Mike. I think part of the reason was that those who don't talk much tend to watch and listen a lot. From his seat in the corner of the waiting room and his chair when he was in the office with me, Alepeachie had apparently liked what he'd seen and heard as they interacted with other homeless people.

Part of it could have been that we'd never demanded, or even asked anything of him and he'd never had to "sing for his supper" or "shuck and jive" to get our attention (nor had anybody else). We cared about him and I think he knew that we had his best interests at heart. I know we did.

After he'd told me what the voices were saying to him, even though he'd given me no indication that he considered them much more than a nuisance, I'd begun mentioning how well the people Mike and Willie had helped were doing and finally screwed up the courage to ask him if he'd let them help him too. Telling him that he might need to go into the CSU for two or three days so they could make sure the medications were working the way they were supposed to do, I asked him if he'd mind.

I held my breath. His simple response was music to my ears. "I'd love it." God only knows how many nights he spent under that bush because I was afraid to ask him if he was willing to go into a short-term mental health facility. The vast majority of the mentally ill people we saw would rather sleep on the streets and forage for food than be hospitalized, and we'd lost more than a few simply by mentioning it.

The next day, I'd brought in Willie and Mike to meet with him privately. They had then gone into overdrive to get him admitted to the CSU, then doubled down to ensure that he got his disability benefits, including Medicaid, to pay for health care and mental health services and medications. That included Supplemental Security Income (SSI), then and still, for most homeless mentally ill people, the critical first step toward securing on-going services and housing.

I'd asked Alepeachie one day if he was getting a check (which everybody understood to mean a disability check), and he'd said he wasn't. It never occurred to me to ask him if he'd ever gotten one before. Willie and Mike, experienced, top-notch mental health professionals, trained to ask the right questions in the right way, did, and obviously Alepeachie had already been approved since they managed to get his check jump-started in a matter of weeks, when it ordinarily always took two or three years to get somebody approved. Now, not only would he start receiving his whopping $325 check every month, he was also due $7,600 in retroactive benefits for the years when, for whatever reason, probably because they couldn't find him, he hadn't received his check. Most bushes don't have an address attached to them.

With money, Alepeachie now had options. He could have gone into a group home, which none of us thought he'd be willing to do given that he'd slept outdoors for years rather than stay in shelters with other homeless people. We might have been able to get an apartment for him in public housing, where his rent, based on his income, would have been really cheap, but public housing in Memphis in the 1980s was forty years old, decrepit and often dangerous. Just paying the rent for his own apartment in a private apartment complex would take most of his check, but with a representative payee to help him manage his money, and with food stamps and Medicaid he could make it.

None of us thought that making his mother his payee and moving in with her and the family was a good idea but Alepeachie had the right to make the decision as to where he wanted to live and he'd made his decision.

The Importance of Having a Home

Part of me went with him, the part that understood better than most of the mainstream people I knew, how much he wanted to be with his mother and how much having a home to go back to meant. After my freshman year in college, I was working for a small law firm in Memphis and staying (as opposed to living) with Peggy, my sister, and her roommate in their two-room apartment.

I slept on the couch in the bedroom just off the kitchen, that is, until her roommate got mad and moved out. She had every right to be angry. She was an early bird and I was a night owl, and I wasn't helping to pay the rent. The bank refused to cash my paychecks because the lawyers I worked for didn't have enough money in their account. Nevertheless, unlike many people who stay with family members or friends and sleep on their couches or the floor, I didn't feel like I was homeless. I still had a home to go back to.

That had changed about six weeks later when my dad was killed. My stepmother clearly expected me, the middle-kid, the pleaser and wannabee fixer, to take my dad's place as the breadwinner. I felt my only option was to quit my non-paying, white-collar job in Memphis and go back to Turrell to try to help support my sister and brother who'd be going into their senior year in high school that fall.

The only job in town was a minimum-wage job as a shipping clerk at the only "factory" in town (half a dozen women sewing brassieres in an old, rundown storefront building behind the whisky store). But it wasn't sweeping up or staggering up and down the street to the post office loaded down with bulky boxes of brassieres or materials to make brassieres that I couldn't deal with. The old farmhouse that my dad and stepmother had bought and moved into town was still there, and I could stay there, but it wasn't a home anymore. The glue that had held the family together had evaporated in the puff of smoke from the shotgun blast that took my father's life.

A month or so after I went back to Turrell, I got a card from Orgill Brothers, an old, well-established warehouse distributor in Memphis saying they had a job opening and telling me to call if I was interested. (I'd filled out an application for a job there when I couldn't cash my first paycheck from the lawyers.) I raced back to the house, called Orgill Brothers, learned that the job would pay me more than I was making at the factory, caught the next bus to Memphis, went back to my sister's apartment, and went to work.

Feeling guilty, I went back to Turrell every weekend and gave my stepmother $20 of my $36 take-home pay. Peggy never said a word about the rent—ever. That fall, she got married and though I offered to sleep on the couch, the newlyweds just smiled at each other, gently declined my offer, and, since I didn't have a car, gave me a ride to West Memphis where I could stay for free in a rooming house/hotel that had our last name in large stone letters on the top.

Carrying my suitcase and my stuff, I climbed the steep stairs to the second floor of the Phillips Hotel, built and operated by Uncle Noah, my dad's brother, and his wife, Aunt Lula, for decades. The downstairs of the building housed a grocery store and a small thrift shop. The "hotel" primarily served construction crews looking for a clean, cheap place to stay while they were in town to work on the railroads, highways and bridges at the gateway from Arkansas to Memphis.

Uncle Noah had died a few years before my dad. Aunt Lula, who hadn't forgotten the Great Depression and was the most frugal person I have ever known, let me have the room rent-free. She never rented it anyway since it had French doors with no locks and looked out on Broadway, West Memphis' main street, just steps away from notorious 8th Street, where drinking, brawling, and gambling went on 'round the clock. I wasn't too afraid. I knew the construction guys wouldn't let anything happen to me.

To hold on to my new job, I paid another employee who lived in West Memphis, $2.50 a week to pick me up each morning and drop me off every afternoon. Given that I had $13.50 left, my meals came from the vending machine at the office and the grocery store downstairs, with a weekly splurge at the cafe down the street for the blue plate special of the day, usually a greasy mess.

Six months later, I married Milton, my freshly-divorced, 19-year-old high-school sweetheart, who'd married another girl one weekend, even though I hadn't known he was even dating her. Heck, I thought I was still "going steady" with him. They'd separated after six weeks and he and I had run into each other a couple of months later. He'd asked me to go out with him so we could talk and since I was still in love with him, I went. I don't know if I would have gotten so involved with him again before his divorce was final if my dad hadn't been shot and killed that night, but he'd been there for me then and almost every night since.

After our overnight honeymoon at the Shell Lake Motel a couple of miles out of town, I'd moved in with him and his parents in their two-bedroom bungalow. It was a very close-knit family and it was clearly a home. They just weren't mine. It hadn't helped that when he'd told his mother, with me sitting there, that we were getting married, she'd said, "Well, that's too bad."

She was right, of course, but standing at the door of the Street Ministry and watching Alepeachie leaving with Mike, who'd be taking him to live with his mother, I remembered how I'd felt the year we stayed with my in-laws, and hoped with all my heart that he'd feel, and be, at home. And every time I got a chance, I'd tell his story, hoping against hope that it would be a success story.

CHAPTER 18

Hands Across America

... local politicians held hands

with the same advocates who made their

lives miserable on a daily basis. Conservative

businessmen and women held hands with

bleeding-heart liberals; preppy-looking students

held hands with kids from the ghetto; ...

On a Sunday afternoon in May of 1986, in a line that stretched for 4,152 miles, millions of men, women, and children held "Hands Across America" to raise consciousness and money to fight hunger and homelessness in one of the richest countries in the world—America. Like many of us in the line that day, I was full of hope. If I'd known then how the money netted from that unparalleled outpouring would be used as "seed money" to help jump-start or provide on-going support for programs for homeless people all over America, or how it would directly affect the lives of some of the homeless people we were trying so hard to help, I'd have been ecstatic.

The brainchild of Ken Kragan, an accomplished veteran of mass philanthropic fundraisers, he and other "Hands" organizers had hoped to form an unbroken human chain from coast to coast. If it had been possible for all five to seven million of us (depending on whose estimate one chooses to accept) to hold hands in a straight line, we could have done it. It wasn't, of course, for obvious reasons.

... in Memphis we had 54 Elvis impersonators.

Beginning on the edge of the Atlantic Ocean at New York City's Battery Park, the line curved through sixteen states, ending at the edge of the Pacific Ocean at Long Beach, California. Along the way, it snaked through Washington, DC where President and Mrs. Reagan and the White House staff joined the line of average citizens that curled in and out of the front entrance to the White House lawn.

Moving south, it came through Memphis where Paula Casey, a local activist with a heart as big as a hotel, had ensured a strong turnout of VIPs, thousands of regular people, and 54 Elvis impersonators. It then went west and passed directly through Little Rock, Arkansas, where it cut straight down Capitol Avenue and past the Clinton for Governor headquarters just down the street. The governor's good friend, Bev Lindsey, had organized Clinton staff and supporters to join the line.

Holding hands along Capitol Avenue, in the middle of the street, were Governor Clinton, and his wife, Hillary Rodham Clinton. Also holding hands with that group was Gloria Cabe, an Arkansas State Representative I'd heard of but hadn't met. Years later, she would help open the door to an opportunity that I couldn't even have envisioned.

As a measure of interest in the event, Massachusetts Senator Ted Kennedy issued a formal protest that none of the New England states were included. He wasn't alone. More than a few political leaders in the South, the upper Midwest, and cities in the Northwest protested against the route that was chosen to span the continental United States.

Understandably, given numerous lakes, vast deserts, mountains and sparsely populated areas of the country, there were lots of gaps in the chain, some of them miles long. I doubted, however, that any of them were any bigger than the gaps in the social service "system," designed and funded to provide services with limited funds to as many people as possible, but woefully inadequate in reaching the homeless people we were seeing.

Though the event didn't live up to its organizers' highest expectations, it was, by all accounts, an unprecedented outpouring—and no wonder. According to *TIME Magazine*, McDonald's promoted the project on 300 million tray liners and Citibank promised $3 million and included information about "Hands" in mailings to its 25 million credit card holders, while Coca Cola pledged a whopping $5 million and put ads on its bottles. "We're out for exposure," was the blunt admission of one Coca-Cola executive.

I couldn't have cared less what their motivation was. Corporate patronage made "Hands" possible. The organizers had hoped to raise $50,000 to $100,000 by charging participants $10 to $35 each to participate, so that most of the revenues derived from the event could be channeled directly into aid for homeless and hungry people. That didn't happen; by Memorial Day only $20 million had been raised and organizers were offering to let people join the transcontinental human chain free of charge. Frankly, we included people in our line in Memphis regardless of whether they'd paid to participate. People in other cities probably did too, and that's no doubt one of the reasons why the organizers didn't reach their monetary goal.

What I loved most about the event was that on the ground, "Hands" was a human connection. Nationwide, egged on by "Hands" staff and 40,000 volunteers across the country, local politicians held hands with the same advocates who made their lives miserable on a daily basis. Conservative businessmen and women held hands with bleeding-heart liberals; preppy-looking students held hands with kids from the ghetto; housewives held hands with middle-age hippies, senior citizens held hands with rock stars, and homeless people held hands with people who cared from coast to coast.

On the twentieth anniversary of "Hands," Buck Wolf, reporting for ABC News on Facebook, wrote that the event "was all to take part in one of the noblest failures in the history of American popular culture." But he also wrote, "Still,

'Hands' managed to raise $20 million for soup kitchens and shelters throughout the country." What he didn't note, probably because he didn't know, is that those funds were also used to help other programs that were doing all they could to help homeless, mentally ill, addicted men and women get the help they needed from an under-funded, struggling, full-of-holes mental health system.

Finally, we had a rudimentary system for helping homeless people access disability benefits, the mental health system and housing.

In Memphis, some of the money allocated to Memphis from "Hands" was used to pay for the Street Ministry's first paid staffer, Jackie Arnold, a kind, intelligent, compassionate and dependable social worker with the patience of Job and the persistence of Saint Paul. She was a Godsend, working part-time to help bring consistency to our efforts and do the follow-up that was critical to getting help for our friends from the social service system. Some of the "Hands" money went to Midtown Mental Health Center in Memphis to pay for half of the salary for Memphis' first full-time professional outreach worker for homeless mentally ill people. The other half had been allocated by the City of Memphis after Barbara Sonnenberg, a sympathetic city councilwoman who hosted her own local television show, asked me during one of her programs to tell her one thing that the city could do to help, after I'd just spent twenty minutes overwhelming her with the magnitude of the needs.

It was a no-brainer. I asked for money for an outreach worker for homeless, mentally ill people and it probably helped to convince her committee to approve the request when I told them that we weren't mental health professionals at the Street Ministry and we didn't want the money for ourselves. Instead, I asked them to allocate the money to Midtown Mental Health Center, which they did. (They should have known there was a method to my madness.)

Kim Moss, a case worker at Northeast Mental Health Center, had just completed his practicum for his masters' degree, interning with us at the Street Ministry. He'd accepted a position with the Alliance for the Blind and had just gone to work there, but as much as I hated to steal from the blind, I called him and persuaded him to interview for the Midtown position. He was a superb case worker and he was a phenomenal outreach worker. Best of all, he already knew many of the homeless people he'd be working with; they knew and trusted him, and Midtown out-stationed him to the Street Ministry. Within a matter of weeks, he had stabilized and housed some of the mentally ill people we had agonized over for years.

The rest of Memphis' share of the "Hands" money went to Family Services, a well-established social service agency, to pay the salary for a representative payee to manage the meager disability benefits for homeless people who were too disabled to manage on their own. On our recommendation, diminutive Lauren Wexner, one of our Street Ministry volunteers, was hired. Her compassion was matched only by her courage.

Finally, we had a rudimentary system for helping homeless people access disability benefits, the mental health system and housing. It wasn't perfect. It would take time to ensure that outreach/case management and representative payee services didn't duplicate efforts, get in each other's way, or unwittingly undermine the work of the other, but it worked. It still wasn't enough to meet the needs, but more help was on the horizon—from the much-maligned federal government.

The Homeless Persons Survival Act

Buried in the basement with an ever-changing group of 50 to 100 homeless people and a handful of volunteers every day, I wasn't aware of it, but that same year, the U.S. Congress passed "a few small parts" of the Homeless Persons Survival Act, and later that same year, other parts of the Act were introduced as the Urgent Relief for the Homeless Act. If approved, Federal funding would now be available to help pay for emergency shelter, food, and mobile health care (vans and staff to go where homeless people were). It would also fund transitional housing, programs where homeless people could stay for a period of time while receiving services to help them break the cycle of streets, shelters, extremely tenuous, temporary housing arrangements, and, for far too many, jails and hospitals. It wouldn't make up for the Federal funding for mental health and housing that had been gutted in 1981, but it was a start.

The year also saw President Reagan signing, with concern and "some reluctance," the State Comprehensive Mental Health Plan Bill, which included a new program of State mental health planning grants. And, in what we know now to be a sad footnote, it also included what the president saw as the enactment of "superfluous new authorities such as that for Alzheimer's disease research, education, and information dissemination activities."

CHAPTER 19

The Road to Rhodes

*I was on my way and even though
I didn't know where I was going, I knew,
on the deepest level,
that I was on the right path.*

It had been the summer of my discontent. Willie, Mike, Kim, and Lauren, ably assisted by Jackie, had been enormously successful in stabilizing and housing some of the homeless mentally ill men and women we'd agonized over for months, even years—including Alepeachie, but it still seemed that for every one they managed to stabilize and house, two more appeared to take their place. It was clear to me that we could only fish a finite number of bodies out of what I called "the river of homelessness," and the sickest ones we couldn't catch at all.

The summer was almost over and what I really wanted was to spend the morning on the balcony of my apartment with the Sunday paper, but something told me to get up, get dressed, and go to church. So I did. One of the readings that morning had come from the third chapter of *Ecclesiastes*. One of my favorites for its content and its poetry, it begins:

"To every thing there is a season, and a time to every purpose under the heaven;

a time to be born, and a time to die; a time to plant, and a time to pluck up that which is planted;

a time to kill, and a time to heal; a time to break down, and a time to build up;

a time to weep, and a time to laugh; a time to mourn, and a time to dance;

a time to cast away stones, and a time to gather stones together;

a time to embrace, and a time to refrain from embracing;

a time to get, and a time to lose; a time to keep, and a time to cast away;

a time to reap, and a time to sow; a time to keep silence, and a time to speak;

a time to love, and a time to hate; a time of war, and a time of peace."

At 48, I'd been through a lot of seasons and something was happening within me. I'd never been more sure of my purpose on earth and I sensed that the time was right for me to move ahead with that purpose. I just didn't know how to do it. I'd been born in what seemed like another world and a part of me had died along with my father, mother, and stepbrother. I'd planted seeds of doubt and seeds of hope and "plucked up" some of both. I hadn't killed anybody even though I'd felt like doing it a few times, and, thank God, I'd done a lot of healing.

With the help of some wonderful professionals, I'd broken down a few barriers to the "system," and I'd spent the past five years trying to build up the Street Ministry and those who came seeking our

What we were doing would never be enough.

help. I'd wept when nobody could see me and laughed when everybody could. I'd mourned more than I ever expected to mourn and I'd danced every chance I got. I'd like to think I hadn't "cast away" stones, but the truth is that I'd cast a lot of stones and gathered up a few more to cast at the barriers to accessing "the system."

I'd embraced more people, homeless and housed, than I'd ever dreamed of embracing and refrained from embracing even more who clearly wouldn't, or couldn't, welcome a hug from me (or maybe anybody else on the planet). I'd gotten far more than I'd ever expected or deserved from helping homeless people and lost more of them to the concrete killing fields than I'd ever expected to lose. I'd kept the people and things that were most important close to me and cast away everything I no longer needed or wanted ... and some that I did.

The National Advocate's Playbook? I Believed a Rewrite Was In Order

In frustration, I'd torn up my copy of the national advocate's playbook that said the only solution to homelessness was housing. Now, I was trying to figure out how to stitch together another one that included treatment for substance abuse and mental illness, one based on the reality that we volunteers saw every day of our lives. I had absolutely not honored the part about keeping silent, and I hadn't waited for my time to speak either (but I'd get a little better at it later). I'd definitely been one of those women who love too much, but I'd hated too much too. I'd gone to war with the "system" and then done my best to make peace with the many wonderful people who were doing their best to make the social service "system" work for homeless people.

I wasn't, and never would be, sick and tired of homeless people, but I was sick and tired of homelessness and our inability to bring it to an end, especially for those who were the most vulnerable. With our limited staff, we'd helped thousands of homeless people secure shelter, food, clothing, medicine and transportation—and we'd helped many of them secure their disability benefits, critical for securing housing. It wasn't enough. What we were doing would never be enough. There had to be a better way, and I intended to find it.

Frustrated beyond belief with the lack of resources and my own limitations when trying to communicate effectively with mental health professionals, I knew I needed a more credible voice if I expected people to listen to me. It was ineffective for me to spend twenty minutes explaining what we were seeing and what I thought we should do about it, only to have a mental health professional respond, "Oh, you mean the Gestalt Theory." Damn, I thought I was the first to think of that!

And when Doug had asked me, very gently, before he posted the position for our first paid, part-time staffer, if I'd be hurt if the requirements included having a degree, I'd told him that I thought it should include the phrase, "or its equivalent experience in the field," even though I knew I wasn't going to apply for it. But his question had made me realize that I needed a degree. Now, more than a year later, I was at a turning point and didn't know where to turn. I needed a sign to point me in the right direction.

I hadn't needed a degree to work my way up from file clerk to Assistant Vice President at the bank, and I certainly hadn't needed a degree to sell houses (36 in one year, all by myself), but a lifelong dream of mine had been to go back to college. During my senior year in high school I'd won a one-year, full scholarship to Arkansas State College in Jonesboro, about sixty miles north of Turrell. I'd made the honor roll that year even though I was also a cheerleader for the "Indians" football and basketball teams and we sometimes got to travel with the team. But I'd understood from the beginning that the scholarship wouldn't be extended, and I didn't know how I'd go back the next year.

There were no Pell Grants or student loans then, and I knew my dad couldn't afford it. He'd often said that if he hadn't hunted and fished (not to mention gambled on everything from every basketball game we ever played in, to high-stakes poker games), he wouldn't have been able to support us, and he was right. He didn't make much money at all as a deputy sheriff and money was always tight.

When the check for three dollars that I'd written to the Wigwam for my spending money for the week bounced, I'd caught a bus downtown and landed a part-time job as a secretary at a law office. The hours conflicted with one of my classes, so I'd gone to the professor and gotten permission to change to the same course he was teaching but on a different day at a different time.

"Of course," he'd said, and filled out the form confirming his approval. When I took it to the Assistant Dean, he glanced at it, looked me dead in the eye, curled his lip like Elvis on one of his bad days, and slowly, deliberately, ripped it in half. A serious student, but woefully unsophisticated, it didn't occur to me that I could have taken the job and just stopped going to that one class. It never dawned on me to talk to anybody about possibilities for a work-study program or scholarship.

But even if I'd figured out how to pay for it myself, I couldn't have gone back to college the next year. My dad was killed that summer and I wouldn't have been able to support myself, go back to college, and still help my brother and sister.

Rhodes College

After church services at Calvary, many of us gravitated to the Great Hall for coffee and conversation. Feeling restless and unsettled, I wandered over to a table at the end of the room where a number of brochures and packets of information had been placed. The cover of one of the brochures had a photo of Rhodes College, the stunningly beautiful, ivy-covered, academically challenging, liberal arts college literally next door to Hein Park where Vic (husband #2) and I had lived in midtown.

Rhodes was establishing an adult degree program; they were searching for non-traditional (read that to mean older, minority, and/or economically disadvantaged) students, and had funds for scholarships. I was older; I certainly didn't have the money to go back to college, especially such an expensive one, and I was intrigued. Unfortunately, the deadline for applying had already passed.

> ... *"What were you planning to do with the rest of your life...?"* —Rev. Bob Watson

The next Sunday morning after church, I found myself again drawn to the table with the brochures. This time I read further and found that the Reverend Bob Watson would be one of the mentors for the students. Knowing that Bob was involved was the spark I needed to get moving. It was Bob who'd basically turned my life around one day during one of my counseling sessions after the divorce. I'd cried through most of the session before he asked, "Pat, what were you planning to do with the rest of your life before you met Vic."

"Oh," I'd responded, sitting up ramrod-straight in the easy chair, "I was going to go back to college and go to Washington and write a book and learn to play the piano (not necessarily in that order). That day had marked a new beginning for me. I'd left his study feeling that I'd reclaimed my dreams and once again taken charge of my life.

When I got home from church, I called Bob and told him that I knew the deadline had passed but that I was very interested and hoped I could apply the next year. To my surprise, he replied that the deadline had been extended and that I was just the type of person they had hoped would respond.

I dug up my 30-year-old transcript, filled out all the paperwork for the scholarship, and enrolled at Rhodes. Since this was a pilot program, we five adult degree students were to carry only three hours the first semester, the legendary "Search for Values in the Light of Western History and Religion" course, an "interdisciplinary study of the ideas, beliefs, and cultural developments that have formed western culture," which would include comparisons of mythology and texts from the Bible. I wasn't sure how that was going to help me help homeless people but the bottom line for me was that I could take the class three mornings a week, continue to sell real estate, and still be at the Street Ministry most afternoons. All three of my sons were supportive and no doubt relieved. Since I was only going back to college part-time, they didn't have to worry about Mom going out for cheerleader. Well, not the traditional form—I had become the cheerleader for all those people in my new life.

I was on my way, and even though I didn't know where I was going, I knew, on the deepest level, that I was on the right path.

CHAPTER 20

Home Again

... an apartment or house one is renting,

is the Holy Grail for homeless people.

Nothing we do to try to help homeless people

works without housing.

Unfortunately, but not surprisingly, Alepeachie's housing arrangement with his family didn't last as long as
we'd hoped it would, but then again, it lasted longer than we'd
thought it would. Within a few months, he was sleeping under
that damned bush again. His bush. I don't know how Mike
found out, but as soon as he did, he went looking for him.
"I'm okay," he told Mike. "I'd rather be by myself, anyway." He
told me later that he'd left because there was too much "stuff"
going on at the house. He didn't elaborate on what the "stuff"
was and I didn't ask. I guess I didn't want to know. Given that
he'd gone straight back to his bush instead of coming back to

us at the Street Ministry, it's highly likely that, like most of the homeless people with severe mental illness that we were trying to help, he'd taken the anti-psychotic medications until he felt better and then stopped taking them, with entirely predictable results.

Mike went to Plan B, a room or a little apartment for Alepeachie and a representative payee from Family Services to manage his monthly disability check and whatever money he had remaining from his retroactive disability benefits. For some reason, Alepeachie didn't mind having someone manage his money for him. What he told us was that he didn't think he needed and didn't want an apartment or even a room. He was perfectly content under his bush. He even had some new cardboard for his bed. I wasn't surprised.

Mike couldn't even get him to look at the tiny apartment he'd found for him. Back the two of them came to the Street Ministry one afternoon. Mike wanted to see if I could persuade him. "I'll do anything Mrs. Morgan wants me to do," said Alepeachie, with a sweet smile. "If she wants me to, I'll look at it but I'll want to just kind of walk around in it to see if it feels right." (I still hadn't been able to talk him into calling me Pat, the way I demanded from everybody else.)

The next week they were back again. Alepeachie had done exactly what he'd said he needed to do, walked slowly round and round (and round and round some more) in the tiny, unfurnished apartment until he finally said it felt okay. Apparently, Alepeachie was way ahead of a lot of us with the Feng Shui approach to understanding the energy in a space, especially a space where one plans to sleep. The problem was that Mike and Willie thought he should also have some furniture and he didn't want any, so they brought him back to the Street Ministry to see if I could talk him into letting them find some furniture for him.

"I could sleep under it for awhile."

I gave it my best shot. "I understand that you don't want a lot of stuff, but let them get a few things for you. At least, let them get a table and chairs and a bed for you. You need a bed." Alepeachie narrowed his eyes and scrunched up his mouth as he thought about that for a minute. "If you want me to, I might get a bed," he said v-e-r-y carefully, "I could sleep under it for awhile." Again, I wasn't surprised.

I have no idea how long he slept under the bed they bought with some of the money that was left from his retroactive benefits, but they also bought groceries and used a minimalist approach in outfitting his apartment with the most inexpensive stuff they could find, including blankets, sheets, and pillows, just in case he decided to sleep on his bed instead of under it. Things got better. In fact, he adjusted so well that he soon got a roommate and they moved to a two-bedroom apartment. Sharing the rent gave each of them a little more money in their pockets.

Home ownership is the epitome of the American Dream, but housing—a home of one's own—even if it is just a room of one's own—an apartment or house one is renting, is the Holy Grail for homeless people. Nothing we do to try to help homeless people works without housing. Alepeachie now had his very own apartment home and he was stable on his medications. Compared to how he'd been living, he was a walking, talking success story. I told it every chance I got to anyone who would listen, which was pretty much everybody I came in contact with. I told it to everybody at Calvary, to my family and friends (multiple times), to total strangers at ball games, to church groups and social workers, to college professors and students. I talked Alepeachie "up a storm."

One of the places I told his story was in *Breakthrough*, the Tennessee Department of Mental Health's quarterly publication. I changed Alepeachie's name but the rest of it was true. I described how he'd lived under the bush and how the outreach by the crisis specialists from the mental health system had been so important in connecting him and other homeless people to the mental health system and housing.

I didn't know it when I wrote it, but the story would change dramatically even before the publication went to print, and over the next two decades I would tell his story, including the rest of his story—and the moral of his story—to hundreds and hundreds of people from coast to coast.

CHAPTER 21

Homelessness Doesn't Mean Hopelessness— There Is a Light!

Everything had changed

after we'd connected

to the mental health system.

A year or so after Alepeachie had settled into his apartment and his new life, I realized it was time for me to move on. We didn't encourage the men and women who'd broken the stranglehold of the streets to come back to the Street Ministry unless they needed us. For most, it would have been too easy to fall back into old, dysfunctional patterns, so I didn't feel that I was abandoning them or him. Still, it was with mixed feelings that I submitted my resignation as director of the Street Ministry, and though I still didn't know where I was going or what I'd do when I got there, I knew for sure that I was on the right path.

I'd done well as a student my first year even though I'd continued to work at real estate and show up at the Street Ministry most afternoons while carrying twelve hours the second semester. I threw myself into sociology, psychology, and urban studies classes, was like a dog with a bone in political science courses (just couldn't let go), and treated myself to a writing course that made the wannabee writer in me come alive. After class, on the first day of that course, I went up to the professor and thanked him. "All my life, I've wanted to write," I told him, "and I feel as though somebody has finally given me a pen."

"Don't try to write like a great writer," he'd said, setting me free to write the truth about homelessness and the homeless people who'd taught me so much about why they were homeless.

We'd come a long way at the Street Ministry and we'd made just enough progress and had just enough verifiable "success" stories to convince me that homelessness didn't have to mean hopelessness and that any success story would have to include housing—not shelter, not just a place to stay—but a place to live—and services. Granted, it's doubtful that we'd have been able to psyche ourselves up enough to continue trying to help if we hadn't learned to deeply appreciate the gradual progress we were privileged to see before we got help from the mental health system.

Before we got "help," it hadn't taken much to keep us going—an appointment kept, the white chip waved triumphantly by one of our alcoholic or otherwise addicted friends to prove to us he'd been to his first AA meeting; a letter saying that someone had finally been approved for disability benefits; a spark of hope in bloodshot eyes. A little hope (or a little help) went a long way in keeping us hooked.

The Key ... The Mental Health System

To tell the truth, we hadn't had many success stories until we finally got help from the mental health system. We'd talked some of our homeless friends into going to the AA meetings at Calvary, gotten a few into treatment facilities, called for paramedics lots of times to take men to the emergency room when they'd collapsed or seemed close to going into DTs, but we never really knew anything about the long-term outcomes. Everything had changed after we'd connected to the mental health system.

Jerry was probably our first verifiable success story—young, slightly built, disheveled, with dirty, stringy blond hair, apparently scared out of his wits at being on the streets and ready to fight at the slightest glance or touch. I didn't realize how sick he was, but I was worried enough to ask Wib to talk to him one day when he'd dropped by to see how things were going.

In retrospect, I think Wib probably represented a father image because they connected immediately, despite Jerry's paranoia. Wib told me later that Jerry was so sick that it was the first time in all his years of working in the mental health field, there was unanimous agreement among his colleagues.

Every professional who'd assessed or even come in contact with Jerry had immediately agreed on his diagnosis and the need for treatment.

Months later, Wib took me to see one of the group homes his mental health center operated. Jerry was there, safe and happy (maybe a little too happy, but it was exponentially better than he'd felt before) as he threw his arms around me and planted a big, sloppy kiss on my cheek.

Then came Brown. He'd been coming to the Street Ministry every day for months. I never knew how he got there, probably just followed the crowd. He never remembered to sign in. He never remembered where he'd spent the night. He couldn't remember if he used the voucher we'd given him the day before to stay at the shelter. When he managed to remember where he was going long enough to get to the shelter or if he just followed the crowd, he couldn't remember the shelter rules long enough to abide by them, just wandered out whenever he felt like it and then couldn't get back in. He didn't have a clue where he was going to sleep or eat, and if he was scared or worried, it never showed. In assessing Brown's motivational level, Saint Mike asked him, "If you were lost in the woods and you were hungry and it was going to start getting dark soon, what would you do?"

Brown heaved a gentle sigh before he answered. "I'd just wait," he whispered, "somebody would find me." He was right. He hadn't been in the woods as far as we knew, but he'd surely been lost and somebody had found him. Within a matter of weeks he was safely housed, no longer lost in the fog of homelessness.

I'm still not sure if the amotivational syndrome, so often present in people who get "wasted" on a regular basis, is due to excessive use of marijuana, or if the people who smoke marijuana on a regular basis just don't have a lot of motivation to start with. I am very sure, though, that the syndrome was no stranger to Brown, (or a lot of other people I knew, homeless or housed), but then again, maybe it's just harder to know where you want to go with your life when you can't remember where you've been.

On the other hand, "Lucifer" knew exactly where he'd been—curled up like a dog in the corner of somebody's garage. Since he believed he was the devil incarnate, he didn't think he deserved better. Little more than a bag of bones in a filthy t-shirt as full of holes as the social service system's "safety net," he didn't think he deserved food, but the hunger pangs periodically drove him out of his own private hell and into our basement offices. We'd done everything we knew to do, including chasing him down the street, pleading with him to take the extra food we'd bagged up to take with him after he'd wolfed down the sandwiches we always kept on hand. By the grace of God, Willie was there one day when he came in, whisked him off to their low-key, home-like crisis stabilization unit, got him stabilized on medications and then into a group home where he'd be cared for. Willie always made it look easy.

Feisty, funny, spunky Frannie Lou, was a special challenge. A woman from the Rape Crisis Center had brought her to us, fresh from the emergency room and wearing a high, stiff medical collar like the ones people wear when they have a neck injury or want the insurance company to think they have one. I could smell the antiseptic seeping out of it from across the room. She'd come to Memphis with her boyfriend from up north; they'd had a fight and he'd put her out on the street. Three men had then snatched her and thrown her in their car; then all three of them had raped and beaten her before they slit her throat from ear to ear and threw her in the Wolf River. If the river hadn't been so polluted, she'd probably have drowned but she managed to float on top of all the crud until she could grab hold of the weeds and crawl up the embankment to the side of the road. A compassionate motorist found her and called for help.

I tried to get her into the domestic violence shelter but they couldn't take her because she wasn't married to or living with any of the three men who had beaten and raped her. The Salvation Army's shelter, which had social workers to help her, was full but could take her the next day, so, even though I hated to do it, I'd put her in a cab, given her an extra cab voucher to get back, and sent her to a shelter every bit as shaky as she was. The shelter operator threw her out, collar and all, for smoking a cigarette on the porch after hours. She and the brand-new boyfriend she'd met at the shelter then walked the 15 blocks back downtown. The shelter operator wouldn't even call a cab, not that one would have shown up at a shelter in that neighborhood at night without a police escort anyway.

The Salvation Army would have admitted her the next day but they wouldn't let her new boyfriend stay with her in the family shelter. The two of them then spent the night in an abandoned building. In fact, they spent a lot of nights in that abandoned building, dubbed "Hotel Siberia" by the street people. When her new boyfriend hit her and "busted her lip," she finally let us arrange for her to stay in a boarding/care home while her claim for disability was being processed. That didn't last long—the men at the home "messed" with her, so she punched out one of "the old buzzards" and walked out.

When she got her victim's reparation money from the Crime Victims Center, she got a room and a brand-new boyfriend, one she'd met in our waiting room, and let him move in with her. Now she was safe from everybody but herself and him. Both of them abused alcohol and he beat her with a baseball bat. Desperate to get her away from him, I tried to get her to go back home, telling her that surely her mother would take her in. We'd have paid for a bus ticket to get her back home but Frannie Lou wouldn't go— said she didn't get along with her mother.

"What's wrong?" I'd asked, "Did she ever abuse you?"

"No," she said, rather nonchalantly.

"Never hit you, hurt you?"

"Nope," then added as an afterthought, "but when she was drinkin' she'd chase me down and try to choke me with the cord to the iron."

One day Frannie Lou had shown up drunk, staggering and hysterical at the Street Ministry, crying that she was being thrown out of her room for not paying the rent, and the landlord was going to keep her little TV and her stuff. She then proceeded to cuss out all the Junior Leaguers who were volunteering that day. Doug would probably have signed a check for her to stay in her room for a week or so, but he wasn't there to sign a check that afternoon and I surely didn't have the money.

I called the MED's ER, got lucky enough to talk to a sympathetic nurse who promised to watch out for her and see that she got medical detox, since she was taking Thorazine, and then called a cab and stuffed her into it. As the cab careened out of the parking lot in the rain, Frannie Lou was hanging out of the window. "WHAT AM I 'SPOSED TO TELL 'EM WHEN I GET TO THE HOS-PI-TUL?" she screeched.

"Tell 'em you're sick! I yelled back."

"I ain't gonna tell 'em I'm sick!" she yelled, her voice fading away in the distance as the cab sped away. "I'm gonna tell 'em I'm drunk!"

I was at my wits end. All the volunteers were mad at me because I refused to bar her from coming in for a couple of weeks as a punishment for cussing all of them out. I couldn't do it. I didn't blame them for being mad—but they hadn't been there the day rape crisis had brought her in with her incredibly violent story. Then Kim came to the rescue, helped her get her disability benefits—her "crazy" check she called it— intervened with her abuser and got her into an alcohol treatment program at Midtown. One day when she'd come by the Street Ministry office, she'd spun around in the chair and started typing away on our old beat-up typewriter. I was amazed! Whereas I'd concentrated entirely on her problems, I hadn't thought to find out if she had any job skills. Kim helped her get into a community college. Years later, she was still housed and doing well.

James, almost blind and struggling with a developmental disability, in trying to see the line to sign, had put his nose within six inches of the printed voucher; then

Some weren't difficult to help at all.

he'd ever-so-slowly printed his name and given me a blazingly beautiful smile. Orphaned at the age of 10, he'd been in and out of institutions and foster homes for most of his life. He'd never had a job except for the one at Goodwill and he'd quit that after two months. They had him hanging up clothes, he said, but he wanted to "learn to read more better," so he'd left. He was looking for a place to stay when he found the Street Ministry, but more than that, he wanted to know if we could help him learn to read and write. That made my day—all I'd had to do was write out a voucher for the Salvation Army for the night and call Kim to tell him where James would be. Meeting him the next morning, Kim arranged for him to share an apartment (with Alepeachie), made sure he got his benefits, and connected him with the Alliance for the Blind for services.

The self-described "Black Greek" required a lot more creativity and no small amount of courage. He'd spent the better part of a year sitting on the steps and sleeping on the floor of the gazebo in Court Square, bristling every time I'd spoken to him, even when I simply said, "Good morning," or asked if he needed any help. His scathing look and sarcastic response to my overtures were enough to quickly send me on my way, but not enough to keep me from coming back to leave an occasional home-cooked meal for him under the Gazebo.

By the end of the summer, it was clear that he was decompensating (a word I'd picked up from my friends in mental health, which means that his mental illness was getting worse). His clothes were in rags and his shoes and socks had disappeared, replaced by a thin-soled pair of bedroom slippers. As fall turned into winter, my concern increased exponentially.

I'd told Kim about him and even though he had a full caseload, he'd been by to see him several times, getting the same scornful response I'd been getting. Then winter hit with a rare Arctic blast. Snow and sleet covered the city and turned Court Square into a snow-white winter wonderland. The Black Greek was nowhere to be seen.

When the snow and sleet melted, he surfaced sporadically, as poorly clothed and shod as he'd been when I'd seen him last. Kim went into overdrive, found him, followed him and figured out how to get him to the emergency room, enlisting the man who owned and operated the peanut shop on Main Street. The owner of the shop had been giving the Black Greek as many peanuts as he wanted whenever he came in and therefore saw him often.

The first time he'd come into the shop after the snow began to melt, the shop owner had seen blood squishing out of his bedroom slippers. It was a stretch by any measure, but the shop owner agreed to ask the police to arrest him for littering his floor (with his blood), with the understanding that the police would take him straight to the emergency room, which they did. When the nurse in the emergency room tried to remove his blood-soaked slippers, some of his toes fell off. Even then, he was lucky that he hadn't lost his feet or his legs, not to mention his life, but as soon as he was able to walk, he checked himself out AMA (against medical advice).

Kim found him the next day in an abandoned car in an alley behind the fabulous Peabody Hotel. It took six policemen to pry him out of the back seat where he'd retreated into a sea of peanut shells. It took an involuntary commitment order signed by the Midtown staff psychiatrist who made the "house call" with Kim, to help get him into Memphis Mental Health Institute, the acute-care mental hospital, and keep him there until he was stable on his medications and well enough to be released. His recovery was so remarkable that he began accompanying Kim to speaking engagements. They were a dynamic duo. Kim had the clinical skills, passion, patience, personality, commitment, credentials and expertise to provide the kind of outreach and case management that is so critical to success.

The Black Greek was a handsome, extremely bright, well-educated, walking, talking example of the miracles that can happen when people with severe and persistent mental illness receive the medications that can help them make rational decisions about their health and safety. Months later, at Midtown for a meeting, I saw him. I had no idea if he'd recognize, remember, or still despise me. He came straight down the hall when he saw me, caught me up in a bear hug and thanked me for caring (and for the fried chicken, pork chops and cornbread I'd left for him at the gazebo). Not long afterward, his family came from California and took him back home.

For five years, I'd spent most of my time trying to help other people deal with their issues. Now it was time for me to deal with my own, including the nightmare that just wouldn't go away.

CHAPTER 22

My Mother, My Voice

There was no escaping the voices

I'd been hearing off and on for years.

The nightmare had returned soon after Alepeachie had told me what the "voices" were saying to him, reminding me of the power of words to make someone's life a living hell. There was no escaping the voices I'd been hearing off and on for years. One of the voices was my mother's voice over the telephone saying the words I'd longed to hear for ten years, ever since she'd told my dad she was going shopping in Memphis, got on a greyhound bus for the 25-mile ride, and never came back. My older sister was seven and the twins were three when she left. I was five, the classic middle kid, ripe for morphing into the "fixer," the pleaser, the peace-maker, little Miss Goody-Two-Shoes. That was me.

The other voice was mine— saying the words to my mother when she called that I would regret all my life.

In one of only two memories I had of her, she'd been all dressed up to go somewhere. I'd wanted to go with her so much that I'd hidden in the back seat of the car. When we got halfway to town, less than a mile from the house, I'd popped up, laughing. She'd laughed and promptly taken me back home. To this day, I have never allowed myself to think that might have been the day she was on her way to catch the bus and leave us.

Once, sometime during the first few years after she left, I thought I'd seen her—a young, blond woman peering intently out the window of a passenger train as it slowly picked up steam on its way out of town. The woman had even turned her head and looked back in my direction as the train moved away. I'd have sworn she was looking at the knobby-kneed kid sitting on the concrete slab porch in front of my dad's furniture store. For awhile after that, in spite of the dust that swirled up every time a car or truck went down the gravel road between the store and the railroad track, I spent a lot of time sitting on that concrete slab—just in case she came back. She didn't.

She wasn't even there when I tied for first place in the school talent show, strolling across the stage singing "Easter Parade," wearing the white organdy dress and carrying the little organdy-covered parasol that my stepmother had the town seamstress make for me, one of the few times that I can recall her doing something just for me. I was in the fifth grade that year, still enough of a dreamer to add to my watching and waiting list the talent scouts from MGM. I thought for sure they'd be coming across the railroad track any minute now to sign me up as I sat, singing away, on the fender of my dad's truck in front of the store.

Pat, This Is Your Mother ...

By the time we moved to the white frame house next door to the Methodist Church and just across the street from the school, I was a teenager, singing with the glee club and playing basketball, surreptitiously searching the faces of all the women in the stands or the audience to see if maybe there was one who looked like me. There never was.

I kept looking though, especially after my stepmother beat my cat to death with a coke bottle in a fit of anger because she thought, probably correctly, that it had killed and eaten her pet parakeet. That didn't excuse her bashing its head into the ground next to the quilt we'd been sitting on in the back yard under a shade tree to escape the oven-like heat inside the house.

On my knees, I'd screamed for her to stop. "Shut up" she'd screamed back, "or I'll give you some of it too!" Still, it wasn't her temper I feared. She'd never been physically abusive to me. I'd been far too much of a pleaser. It was her rejection and jealousy I feared. But in reality, I never blamed anybody but myself for what I did to my mother.

The Fatal Phone Call

"Pat, this is your mother," she'd said when she called a couple of years later.

"I'm sorry," I'd said, looking straight at my stepmother, who sat, watching and listening intently, a few feet away, "my mother is sitting at the dining room table." The next sound I heard was the click as my birth mother hung up the phone. My heart sank. It was the first time since she'd left that she'd called and asked to speak to any of her children, and I had made a terrible, terrible mistake in turning her away. I didn't know where she was and Caller ID hadn't been invented.

I deserved everything I didn't get for doing it—a hug or some show of affection or approval from my stepmother as a reward for having been loyal to her instead of my mother. It didn't happen. It never had happened. But I couldn't use my need for her affection or my fear of her total rejection as an excuse for what I'd said over the phone to my mother. To ... my ... mother. There were many facets to my stepmother's personality, for good or for ill, but she knew a suck-up when she saw one.

That fall, my 21-year-old stepbrother, on his second tour of duty in the bitter cold of a Korean winter, complained of not feeling well, fell asleep on his bunk in an ice-cold Quonset hut in Korea and didn't wake up. Grieving his loss and living with the guilt of not having written to him as often as I should have left little room for wishful thinking about my mother. But I'd made up my mind that I would find her someday.

Two years after she'd called and two months after I graduated from high school, she was dead of a massive head injury. The brief newspaper article that my dad brought to me in the small office at the courthouse in Marion where I was working that summer, reported that her death was one of several deadly accidents reported over the July 4th weekend, and that she had fallen from a moving vehicle near Pensacola, Florida, where she lived and had died two days later.

"I think this is your mother," he'd said softly as he gently handed me the newspaper clipping. Trying not to choke up, but failing, he told me that he was pretty sure the newspaper account was wrong; that when they were married and got into an argument when they were driving somewhere in the car, she would try to jump out. He'd always managed to stop her. This time, the man she was riding with, the man she was planning to marry, hadn't. Her sister, who'd gone to Florida to be with her at the hospital, but found herself making funeral arrangements instead, had apparently sent him the clipping.

The reporter who'd written the brief account no doubt believed she'd fallen to her death. My dad, and the death certificate that my brother managed to acquire decades later, said that witnesses reported that she had jumped, which would have made her death a suicide—to everybody but me. Deep down, I knew better.

After my dad left the office, I'd gone off to the women's restroom where I'd shed some tears for her and for the loss of my dream of finding her someday, but I'd then stuffed my feelings away, gone back to my desk, and buried myself in work.

That fall, I went off to college on a full one-year scholarship, and then, a year to the day after my mother had jumped to her death, my dad had been fatally wounded—and my world had fallen apart. Whatever I'd felt about the loss of my mother or even my stepbrother was totally overwhelmed by the loss of my father.

Now, decades later, my guilt over having turned my mother away would break through the bonds of my subconscious, and I would finally connect the nightmare with my mother's death and the role I'd played in it.

CHAPTER 23

Letters From the Grave

... for me, the sense of loss simply overwhelmed

all other emotions. Through her letters

I'd learn that the sense of loss was sometimes

overwhelming for her as well.

The nightmares had begun again, not long after Alepeachie had told me what his "voices" said to him, but I'd waited for months before I'd made an appointment to see Bob Watson. He'd been a Godsend during my divorce and its painful aftermath and was well aware that I had a lot of deeper issues that I needed to work on. Now my mentor at Rhodes, he was especially kind and helpful, and though I hadn't been ready to open up before, now I was—to a point. Sitting on the edge of the comfortable chair in the study at his home, I'd told him about my mother abandoning us, her suicide, my stepbrother's death, and the murder of my father. I hadn't told him about my recurring nightmare or how I had turned my mother away when she'd finally called, maybe because lumping all those losses into one session had left me feeling especially vulnerable. Both of those unsaid issues were on my mind when I left.

You'd think that it would have eased my conscience to know that until my mother called that long-ago evening, the only direct communication she'd had with any of her children was a card she'd sent to the twins on their birthday almost three years after she'd left. Along with the card, she'd included lockets for each of us girls, plus a dollar for the birthday girl and two dollars for my brother. I'd lost my locket, but a couple of weeks after my dad died, I found the unsigned card, along with the note to my dad that went with it and a few letters she'd written to him.

Letters From the Past

She'd apparently written the first letter a few months after she'd left. Standing in front of the chest of drawers that held my father's few belongings, it was all I could do to carefully untie the string that held the letters together and then hold on to that first yellowed piece of paper, much less read it when I was trembling all over.

Postmarked August 2, 1944, Kansas City, Kansas, it was short, but not sweet. She'd written:

You remember what you said about one of us doing wrong, I made that move. I have chizzled on you since January, why, I don't know. I have lived lies for the past six months. I don't know what has happened to me. Mother has found out and everyone else knows this is the only way out for me. I knew when you found out there would be another fight. I didn't want that to happen again.

I'm sure that's the fight I remember. In my memory, she is lying on the couch, crying hysterically, while a man, surely my father, is banging on the door, demanding that she let him in the house. I am standing in front of her, wanting to help but also terrified when I see her hiding a pistol under a pillow. I don't remember anything else about that night or any other arguments or fights they may have had—no slaps or blows ever being struck, no shoves, not even any arguing. She'd added:

You can take this letter with you and get your divorce easy enough. I knew if I stayed on I couldn't get the kids. I have destroyed my life completely. I am sure mama will stick by you until the kids are much older. Tell them I am dead or whatever you think is best. There is no way of me ever being able to face them or anyone else that I have ever known. Don't be a fool and spend a lot of money trying to find me. I am leaving here, for where I don't know. I hope I can go where no one will ever no me. Take the best of care of the kids. I know you will.

She signed it "Just Plain Mildred."

Over the years, some of my friends wondered why I was never angry at her for leaving. Part of the reason could well have been that she'd left us in good hands. My dad had done his best to take care of us kids. And part of the reason is that after I'd grown up and had children of my own, I learned more about her as a person. People who had known her invariably described her as "fragile." I could certainly see how having her first baby a few months before she turned fourteen, losing that child to pneumonia 18 months later, having her second child three months later, me 18 months later, and the twins 15 months later would have been enough to make even the strongest girl or woman "fragile."

But the truth is that the die was surely cast even earlier. I don't remember anything at all about my grandfather, no doubt because my stepmother told me that my dad had kicked him out of the house and dared him to ever return when he caught him in bed with my aunt, his very own daughter. Chances are he'd abused my mother as well. She must have been frantic to get away from him and from the mother she should have been able to count on to protect her. Decades later, I'd learn that she and a boy/man I'd never heard of had applied for a marriage license, stating that she was 18. She was not-quite thirteen at the time.

But all I'd known before I found her letters or found out how very young and troubled she'd been, was that, for me, the sense of loss simply overwhelmed all other emotions. Through her letters I'd learn that the sense of loss was sometimes overwhelming for her as well.

The second letter, dated almost a year later, and post-marked Flushing, Long Island, New York, began:

Dear Carlton and all: I hardly know where to begin this or what to say. I guess you all are about insane by now. I am sorry I have not written you sooner. I can only excuse myself for four months. I won't go into details tho because you wouldn't believe me anyway. I can't blame you.... You will never no how much I would love to see those kids.

She continued:

Why I have to go on living is beyond me. It sure is a true thing that only the good die young. I will live forever. I was miserable there, just as much as I am here. Except for being with the kids some day when they are grown. I will never be back until the kids are old enough to understand what I have to say. I really think I can make them love me again.

She didn't have a clue that I'd never stopped. But she wasn't just writing to tell my dad how much she wanted to see us or how much she regretted having left us.

I can join the Women's Motor Corp now & go to Europe for a year, that is, if you will divorce me. I hope you have already done so. I am never in one place longer than 3 or 4 weeks at a time. Get your divorce whatever you do. You must not chain your name with mine. I am not looking for a letter from you. But I wish you would drop me a card and let me no about the divorce. I will be here in New York for a couple more weeks. If you need money for the divorce let me no. Waiting for your answer.

Sincerely, Mildred

I haven't a clue whether he responded, or, if he did, what he said. In the last letter, dated almost two years later, and postmarked Hastings, Nebraska, she'd poured out her heart. She had apparently talked to my dad.

Dear Carlton & All,... I hardly know just how to begin this letter. I have so many things to say & yet I can't put them in writing. It was sure swell to talk with you again. I was desperate. So many times I have wanted to write you are call, but kept telling myself it would be bad for you. I don't want to cause trouble between you and your wife. I long to see those kids so bad. Sometimes I wonder if I have not lost my mind. I see them before me but to me they are still babies. When their birthdays come around I want so much to send them something but always afraid you would object. They would ask you a lot of questions that you wouldn't want to answer. Don't ever think just because I have not written that I forgot those kids. I love them so darn much & yet I let them down. I didn't think things would happen as they did. I am paying for it & will continue to do so until I die.

She asked permission to write to us and wanted to send something for the twins' birthday but said she wouldn't without his permission. "There must be a limit to how long a person can go on eating her heart out for the ones she loves & can never do anything for," she'd written, but said she didn't want to make things any worse for him, then added, "I guess I couldn't."

> *If anything ever happens to you are those kids I beg you to let me know. Don't deprive the kids of something they may want some day. I'm still their mother & they really loved me once. Maybe by the Grace of God they will again. That's all I'm living for.*

It was the next line that had brought me to my knees:

> *I can still see Pat's face light up when she saw me coming home.*

When I could see again, I finished reading the letter.

> *Don't think for one minute those things don't haunt me. Well I'll stop before I break again. If you can find time just drop me a card that's all I ask. Give all my love to the kids. As ever. Mildred*

I don't know if he ever risked my stepmother's wrath by dropping my mother the card she wanted so badly or if she ever wrote to him again. What I did realize when I'd re-read her letters the night before I went for my counseling session with Bob, is that buried in the darkest depths of my subconscious mind and in the nightmare that had over the years been my secret, I was partly responsible for her death.

In the nightmare, I was always in a dark, dank, cellar-like room with a dirt floor, dirt walls, and dirt ceiling, sometimes filled with a foul odor. I don't know why it took me so long to realize it was a grave—her grave. Other people were always there too, and though I never saw who they were and none of us ever said anything, I always sensed that a body was buried in that room, that all of us together had killed whoever it was, and if anybody ever found out that I had participated in the murder, I'd be doomed or damned or both.

Raindrops the size of quarters had begun splattering my windshield as I backed out of his driveway and I hadn't driven far when the storm hit full-force, with sheets of rain obliterating the median and on-coming traffic and forcing me to pull over.

I was trapped, with all my defenses down, and I lost it. The flood of tears that I'd bottled up for so long and the words I'd never been able to speak came gurgling out from some seemingly bottomless source, and I heard myself shrieking, "I'm sorry, I'm sorry, I'm so sorry!"

And then the storm passed and I felt my mother's presence as surely as I felt my own. In those few surreal moments I knew that she knew how sorry I was, that she understood and it was okay. Just as I had never blamed her, she didn't blame me.

Jesus said:

Let not your heart be troubled. Ye believe in God. Believe also in me. In my Father's house are many mansions: if it were not so, I would have told you. I go to prepare a place for you. And if I go and prepare a place for you, I will come again, and receive you unto myself; that where I am, there ye may be also.

I never had the nightmare again. I would forever regret what I'd said to my mother and mourn its aftermath, but my words would no longer haunt me as much as they had before; and I would never again doubt the existence of an afterlife. But deep inside, I knew there was something I still needed to do. I just didn't know what it was.

CHAPTER 24

Body Count

... don't know why we as a society

seem to feel that men are more expendable

in the killing fields of war and the

concrete killing fields of homelessness.

I'd finally moved past my own personal nightmare, but now the body count from the concrete killing fields was killing me. Arthur had been the first, falling dead in one of the bathrooms in the criminal justice complex on the morning he was scheduled to have the surgery that would surely have changed his life. Sim, one of our older, more functional visitors, had been next. Someone had found his body in an alley.

Then there was Eugene. I guess you could say he was a regular even though he only came in occasionally for a voucher to spend the night at one of the shelters. Like a lot of the people we were seeing, he was caught in the cycle of homeless-ness. On his "up" cycle, he'd find work and/or a place to stay for awhile. He'd land in the streets and shelters again when the job ended or when the frayed, fragile relationships he had with family and friends simply added burden or stress. What was even worse, was when he couldn't stand being a burden to others. I don't even know whether he'd had a place to stay when he came in the last couple of times we saw him, mainly since he'd shown up with his "lady," Luverna, in tow, saying that he knew she needed help and he didn't know where else to take her.

Eugene was a little guy, younger than Luverna, and she outweighed him by at least 75 pounds. Nevertheless, he'd poured her into a chair in the waiting room with an ease and gentleness that made me think it would be nice to have some-body who wanted to take care of me that way even though I didn't need it. And even if I had, I'd probably have fought it every step of the way.

I didn't think her condition was critical enough to call for an ambulance. Being short on volunteers, I couldn't take her so I asked Eugene to take her to the emergency room to get the Valium pumped out of her stomach. He'd also need to bring her back when she was released. We could then try to get more help for her.

It was a big responsibility for him, but he took the vouchers for the cab when it showed up and helped her out of the chair, through the door and into the cab to the hospital. He brought her back the next day. She was ambulatory, still on rubbery legs and hanging on to Eugene, but at least able to speak more coherently. Luverna said she'd been evicted from her apartment, and had managed to move her stuff to another one. "The city refused to turn the utilities on because the apartment had been condemned," she continued. Then, while she was trying to find a place to stay for herself, her three disabled sons and her baby boy, somebody had stolen all her stuff.

I don't know who or where the father(s) of her four sons were or if a stomach full of Valium and God knows what else had anything to do with at least three out of the four being mentally disabled. (I asked the caseworker at the mental health center but it was against the rules for her to tell me.)

We made an appointment for her at the mental health center, and since she was afraid to call her father to ask him for help, I called him.

He sounded old and tired, no doubt because he already had the boys and the baby. He finally agreed to let Luverna stay with him too, but just until her case manager could help her find another place. I didn't have the heart to ask the poor guy if he had room for Eugene too. We were going to send Luverna to her father's house in a cab, but Eugene told us not to worry about her; if we'd give him some bus vouchers he'd see to it that she got there. As far as we knew, he did. She never came back. Neither did Eugene.

A few days later, he walked down to the expressway and straight into the path of an 18-wheeler. I don't know if he meant to or not; never learned why Eugene was homeless, nor why we didn't spend as much time worrying about Eugene's homelessness as we did worrying about Luverna's. I can't figure out why we, as a society, seem to feel that men are more expendable in the killing fields of war and the concrete killing fields of homelessness. What I do know is that I will always regret not taking the time to ask Eugene where he was going to stay and what we could do to help him.

Nobody had ever explained addiction to me more clearly ...

Applejack, a good old boy from Arkansas and profoundly addicted to alcohol, was next. I'd seen him around just enough to know that he could pour more alcohol down his gullet than anybody I'd ever seen, but he'd never come in to ask for help. One bitterly cold afternoon, I'd found him dumpster diving in the alley in the back of the church. Nothing was visible but his legs and feet with an empty shopping cart sitting nearby. I'd yelled and yanked on his legs until he'd finally raised his head and then talked him into coming into the church where it was warm. It was Applejack. While he snuffled and nursed a cup of coffee, I got on the phone trying to find a treatment center that could or would take him right then.

All the time I was on the phone, he sat in the corner, crying and convulsed with quick, jerky, half-clawing movements. "This alkehol is killin' me," he groaned. By the time he finally stopped crying, his coffee was cold. It was probably just as well. His hands were shaking so hard he couldn't hold the cup still enough to get a good swallow—and even when I held the cup to his mouth, the mucus from his nose dripped right into it.

"Why do you drink so much?" I'd wailed, knowing that lots of people I knew were alcoholics but you could hardly tell it most of the time, and I'd never seen any of them turn up a bottle and gulp it down all at once.

"It's like a itch," he moaned, "the worst itch you ever had in your life, but the itch goes from the bottom of your feet to the top of your head and there ain't nuthin' in the world but you and that itch and there ain't nuthin' you won't do to scratch it."

Nobody had ever explained addiction to me more clearly ... and I might not have fully appreciated what he was saying if I hadn't gotten into some poison ivy at the lake the previous summer and nearly clawed my arm off before I got back to town and coated it with Calamine lotion.

When Applejack clearly couldn't sit still any longer, and I clearly couldn't find a place where he could go for help, he stumbled out of the office. A couple of hours later, I found him slumped in the alley, head back, eyes closed, medicating his "itch" with a half pint of rotgut wine. I didn't know how or where he got it ... and I didn't blame him. It wasn't any crazier than the system.

The man at the treatment center had said they couldn't detox him even though they had a detox bed available. According to the funding regulations, he could only get detoxed there if he was going straight into their treatment program from detox, and though a detox bed was available, they didn't have a treatment bed available. Therefore, they couldn't help him.

Applejack had never been to the Street Ministry before, and he never came back after that day, never asked us for anything, and never panhandled, just picked up those aluminum cans by the hundreds so he could take them to the recycling place for money to buy the only peace he knew. I saw him on the streets with his grocery cart several times after that, but every time I ran into him, it was on a weekend and even I knew better than to try to get somebody into a treatment center in Memphis on a weekend.

Most mornings, he woke up with a hangover. One morning a few months later, he didn't wake up at all. One of the residents of the Riverbluff Condominiums found him lying on the bluff. The next day's paper said it appeared that he'd died of natural causes, but I don't know what's so natural about dying outside on a river bluff with your pants off, surrounded by a pile of aluminum cans, at the ripe old age of 35. One of his buddies must have found him before the early-morning jogger did. Applejack's arms had been crossed across his chest in the traditional death pose and his pants had been neatly folded and laid across his lower midsection.

Even then, we didn't change our official "tough love" approach to helping alcoholics and drug addicts, insisting that first and foremost, they'd have to be willing to at least try to stop drinking and drugging, but more and more, I'd begun to pray, "God forgive us if we're wrong." Was "tough love" the only way—the solution? Even though it didn't always work!

And then there was Robert. A veteran, he'd survived Vietnam only to come home and get in a fight with his wife, who, according to him, ran over him with her car, and, as a result, he had a steel plate in his head. He desperately wanted to go back to college, and the VA would probably have paid for it, at least some of it, but the steel plate in his head made his thinking problematic. He was only in his forties, tall and muscular, but his memory was shot and he wouldn't let us help him get whatever help he could have gotten from the VA.

By then I'd already resigned as director but was serving on the board of directors, and though I still dropped in whenever I could, I wasn't there the day everything blew up. For some reason, he'd gotten really upset with Jackie or one of the volunteers. When somebody told him that he needed to leave, he got even more upset, which led to somebody telling him he was barred for two weeks. Meaning, that he couldn't come back to the one place where he had a connection with people who were at least trying to help him. That's when he really lost it, yelling and cursing and scaring most or all of them half to death. Rusty, the burly kitchen manager, had tried to intervene; there'd been a scuffle, and Robert had been permanently barred.

Robert, who no longer had access to the vouchers for shelter that we'd been providing to him, found himself a "cathole" under the gazebo in Court Square. It was there, where the fire he'd started to stay warm with caught the gazebo on fire and all his hopes and dreams went up in the same smoke and flames that took his life.

My despair was only exceeded by my guilt. If I'd been there, I told myself, I could have calmed Robert down and he wouldn't have been barred and he wouldn't have been living under the gazebo and he wouldn't have died such a lonely, horrible death!

It's been said that guilt is the most unproductive emotion. But guilt is also "that voice within a healthy person that can bring us to a realization that there is a standard that we have fallen short of and a standard we would like to live up to."

I most assuredly hadn't lived up to the standard I'd set for myself, but the guilt I felt was a powerful motivator ... And then came the blow—the final straw—that broke the proverbial camel's back—and heart.

CHAPTER 25

We Hardly Knew Ye

We couldn't give him hope

for a better tomorrow simply because we

actually didn't believe there was hope.

I wasn't expecting the call when it came. In fact, I didn't expect to be around to get that call at all—ever, even though the body count of homeless people had risen every year. I wasn't even supposed to be at the Street Ministry that day. I'd only dropped by the office to meet one of the "regulars" that I'd run into on the street over the weekend. He'd told me that he was finally ready to quit drinking, knew he couldn't do it by himself because he'd tried so many times and failed, and absolutely knew he couldn't do it when he was sleeping on the streets. I'd promised to meet him the next afternoon to help him get admitted to a residential treatment program.

Kim, knowing there wasn't an easy way to tell me, didn't even try to ease into the bad news when he called. "Alepeachie's dead," he said. Worried that Alepeachie hadn't gotten up by noon, James, his roommate, had gone into his room to check on him and found him dead in bed. James, one of the kindest, gentlest men we knew, was inconsolable. So was I. There was no denial, no bargaining with God, no anger, just sorrow and guilt. Alepeachie was only thirty-three; he'd been born the year I graduated from high school. He wasn't supposed to die before I did. But it wasn't just survivor's guilt I was feeling. It was worse than that.

I'd seen Alepeachie only a couple of weeks before. He

The truth is that we'd helped him get everything but a life.

was coming out of the drugstore, eating a packaged ice cream cone, and looking good and perfectly normal, his hair in a neatly cropped Afro. I was in a hurry, on my way to a meeting at Midtown where I was serving on the board of the Crisis Stabilization Unit. I treasured that opportunity to learn more about (and have some input into) the mental health system. Even though I was already running late, but because I was always glad to see him, I'd pulled my car over to a parking place just across the street and waved him over.

"How're you doing?" I'd said cheerfully, fully expecting him to say "fine" or at least "okay."

"I'm not doing so good," he'd responded, even though the expression on his face didn't reflect anything that even slightly resembled pain, worry, anger, or even stress.

I'd then asked, as gently as I could, "What's wrong? You're not hearing the voices, are you?"

"No," he said, "when I take the meds I don't hear the voices, but my life is so empty I still want to kill myself." It was the first and only time he had ever told me that he wanted to kill himself. Because he said it so calmly, almost cheerfully, I didn't think he meant it. Two weeks later, he was dead and I was devastated.

It hadn't occurred to me that it could happen because of something I didn't do or say.

I have a lot of regrets about what I couldn't, or for whatever reason, didn't do for some of the homeless people who played such an important role in my life. None of them compares to my regret for what I didn't do to help Alepeachie that day. I still didn't know enough about suicide to know that we should always take any talk of suicide very seriously. Instead, I offered some inane platitudes that, in my ignorance, I thought would make him feel better. Telling him that I'd see him soon, I went to a meeting that, in retrospect, would have gone on quite well without me. Years later, I still don't understand why I didn't do more for him.

I think I still couldn't deal with the thought that something I said or did would cause another human being to go over the edge. It hadn't occurred to me that it could happen because of something I didn't do or say.

It should have eased my guilt somewhat that at least he hadn't died under that damned bush and that the autopsy found that he hadn't killed himself. It didn't. He had a place to live, and food and medications and a roommate, but those hadn't been enough to give him something to live for. The truth is that we'd helped him get everything but a life. We couldn't give him hope for a better tomorrow simply because we actually didn't believe there was hope. The reality of recovery from severe mental illness, with appropriate treatment and adequate supportive services fully integrated into permanent supportive housing for the Alepeachies of this world had yet to make its way to Memphis, Tennessee.

Three years later, Sam Tsemberis would launch his Pathways to Housing project in New York City to do just that. It remains the gold standard for ending homelessness and vastly improving the lives and health of homeless, mentally ill, addicted, medically fragile men and women—and it costs less than the financial costs of homelessness! The human costs on the other hand, are still incalculable.

A week after Alepeachie died, I stumbled into the funeral home, stood for a few minutes at his open casket, strangely comforted to see his gentle face without a sign of the pain that had marked his life or the massive heart attack that had taken it. I then sat numbly in the back of the funeral home in the kind of isolation that had marked so much of his life. I learned to my surprise that he'd been a veteran. And finally said good-bye in a flood of grief to a man I only thought I knew.

Some of the people who knew me best thought my reaction to Alepeachie's death was out of proportion to the reality of my tenuous, all-too-timid relationship with a homeless man that I knew so little about. They were right. Although they misjudged the depth of my affection for him, and misjudged my despair because I had so hoped he'd be okay once he was housed and on his meds. It wasn't all about Alepeachie.

Decades later, while rummaging in one of my boxes of keepsakes, I found the program from his funeral service. I'd been too upset to pay much attention to it at his funeral, but even though I know he didn't plan his own memorial service, it gave me a measure of comfort. Penned by Helen Steiner Rice, it read:

His death had ripped away my security blanket of feeling that I was actually making a difference in the lives of homeless people.

"When I must leave you for a little while,
please do not grieve and shed wild tears,
and hug your sorrows to you through the years,
but start out bravely with a gallant smile,
and for my sake and in my name,
live on and do all things the same.
Feed not your loneliness on empty days,
but fill each waking hour in useful ways.
Reach out your hand in comfort and in cheer,
and, I, in turn will comfort you and hold you near,
and never, never, never, be afraid to die,
for I am waiting for you in the sky."

Decades later, I hurry through a park or turn a corner or glimpse a human being behind a bush ... and, from under a worn-out overcoat or coarse blanket ... top-knots and empty eyes bring a gasp of remembrance.

Oh, Alepeachie, Alepeachie, we hardly knew ye.

CHAPTER 26

Housing Now!

Estimates of the number of marchers

on that brisk October morning ranged

from 40,000 (the National Park Service)

to 70,000 (Washington Police),

to 150,000 (organizers of the march).

It was one of my first lessons in the culture

of national politics.

Afew weeks before Alepeachie's death, I'd made a
presentation about homelessness at the annual statewide
conference of social workers in Nashville. At the end of the
day, several of us were in a meeting led by Mitch Snyder, one
of the nation's most visible and vocal advocates for homeless

people. He spoke with an eloquence and an anger that both moved me and left me feeling more than a little uneasy. He was trying to persuade us to organize a group of homeless and formerly homeless people in Memphis.

Why? Glad you asked: He wanted them and us to march in the nation's capital with people from all across the country for an event that was advertised as Housing Now!

I'd never marched for or against anything in my life, but since nobody else volunteered to do it, I'd raised my hand (exhibiting an extreme, persistent character defect). I couldn't help it. Housing had been so important to helping Alepeachie and other homeless, mentally ill men and women escape the concrete killing fields.

It was the last thing in the world I needed to do. I didn't have the time or the money. I'd be carrying a full course load at Rhodes in the fall, and I needed to spend the rest of the summer making money to pay my bills—not trying to raise enough money to charter a couple of buses and send homeless people to march in Washington to demand Housing Now!

Back in Memphis, I went to the next Coalition meeting to try to talk them into approving the mess I'd gotten myself into. Most of them thought the idea was nuts—for perfectly valid reasons—but I finally got them to approve it, which wasn't at all the same as taking responsibility for it. I soon found out how hard it was to do something of that magnitude when I didn't have money, a base to work from or support staff to help me.

Years later, one of the national advocates for homeless people told me that after the march, someone had told him that it was the "great homeless exchange of 1989" because so many homeless people swapped places on buses with people on other buses instead of going back home with the folks who'd brought them.

Jeanne Richardson, who'd followed Nancy Lawhead as director of Midtown Mental Health Center, understood the critical need for housing for people with severe and persistent mental illness as well or better than anybody I knew. She bailed me out, assigning Kim to organize a local walk to raise money. Whatever funds were raised would be used to take some of their formerly homeless clients, along with their case managers, and other advocates to Washington. Jeanne, Nancy, and Wib were "sixties" people and all of them had done their share of protesting injustice and misguided policies and marching for causes I'd believed in but didn't have enough guts to support openly.

The morning of the local walk had begun with a light drizzling rain that, by mid-morning, had become just a gray day. It matched my mood. As I drove to the corner where we were to begin the first "Memphis Walks for the Homeless," my heart wasn't in it. Alepeachie had died a few weeks earlier and I was still broken-hearted, and it didn't console me at all for people to tell me that at least he hadn't died on the streets. He'd died in his own bed in his own apartment. I couldn't get past the fact that he was dead at thirty-three and I'd let him down. Nevertheless, since I'd made the commitment to the march, the least I could do was show up.

The Street Ministry and the Vietnam Vet Center had joined Midtown in sponsoring the walk, and my mood brightened somewhat when I saw that a crowd of about 200 people had gathered. We were just about to set out on the walk through downtown Memphis when about 50 students from Rhodes showed up, and, just like in the movies, the sun burst through. It was a relief, but unfortunately, it didn't raise much money, mainly because most of us didn't have much. I needn't have worried. In a matter of days, Jeanne had managed to scrounge up enough money to sponsor the trip for those of us among the approximately 90 people from Memphis who couldn't afford to go. My heart still wasn't in it, but I went anyway and was glad I did.

In Washington, on the morning of the march, a veritable sea

By all accounts, the march was a huge success.

of people milled around the mile-long "mall," the grassy area that stretches from the steps of the Capitol to the Lincoln Memorial. The crowd included rich and poor, students and seniors, veterans, people with disabilities, activists and advocates, social workers, priests, and people who were homeless or formerly homeless, mixed with a sprinkling of dozens of celebrities, mostly actors and musicians, some of who I'd never heard of. By all accounts, the march was a huge success. Estimates of the number of marchers on that brisk October morning ranged from 40,000 (the National Park Service) to 70,000 (Washington Police), to 150,000 (organizers of the march). It was one of my first lessons in the culture of national politics.

The march had been organized by the National Low Income Housing Coalition and was supported by more than 200 organizations, including the U.S. Conference of Mayors, the National Coalition for the Homeless, the National Low

Income Housing Coalition, the League of Women Voters, the Children's Defense Fund, the NAACP and the Enterprise Foundation.

My ignorance was astounding. It was 1989; I was taking classes in urban studies and had written papers on homelessness from my narrow, tunnel-vision, local perspective. Though I'd been in real estate for twelve years, I didn't know anything about the housing legislation we marchers were supporting.

I never dreamed that some of them would be part of my world within the next year or so.

Even if I'd read it, I don't think I would have understood just how much the Affordable Housing Act, enacted in 1992, would mean. I didn't comprehend how helpful it would be in assisting us to house homeless and at-risk individuals and families. The housing it helped create must have been like a real-life refuge for the poorest of the poor, something like the "safe houses" from TV crime entertainment thrillers.

To tell the truth, I felt like a fraud but I marched along, following our leaders, including Tipper Gore, down Constitution Avenue to the Capitol building chanting:

"What do we want?"

"Housing!"

"When do we want it?"

"Now!"

It wasn't that I didn't want housing now, or that I didn't think housing was a major part of the answer to homelessness. Quite the contrary. Nothing works without housing. Plus, housing is tangible. Housing activists and developers can build it, renovate or remodel it, and it stands there, an obvious success story. People can see it; focus on it; measure it; counting the number of houses, duplexes, apartment units or rooms. Politicians can cut the ribbon on one housing unit for one homeless family and every TV station in town shows up. It's impossible to end homelessness without housing.

But we needed much more. We needed, and still need, a mental health system designed and funded to ensure that people receive the mental health treatment and services they need, delivered in the least restrictive setting.

Nobody understood that concept any better than Tipper Gore, who was already one of the nation's leading advocates for mental health. Walking behind that friendly, bubbly, deeply committed woman, I would never have believed that a year later, she'd pluck me from my temporarily assigned desk in Senator Gore's office and announce that she needed to borrow me as her expert on homelessness. The "plucking" took me to the House of Ruth, a shelter for victims of domestic violence. It was there that I'd learn yet one more lesson about homelessness, and a vitally important one at that—from a couple of five-year-olds.

It's impossible to break the cycle of homelessness, much less end it, without housing.

CHAPTER 27

A Christmas Story

I blocked out the faces and tried to get

in the spirit of the season, plastered a fake smile

on my face and tried to pretend that I believed

things would be better soon. What else could I do?

How could I tell them the truth?

Something was different the Christmas after the march in Washington, really different. I was at Calvary to help with the annual Emmanuel Meal, the Christmas dinner that the church served to homeless people, but I wasn't getting my "warm fuzzies." I was supposed to get them. I'd always gotten them. Most of us do-gooders get warm and fuzzy feelings when we do something good for others; keeps us coming back to do more good. Some of us even need those feelings. They keep us going when other people have given up. They make nice, soft cushions, too, when we fall on our butts tilting and jousting with the windmills of the "system."

The street people had already gathered at the side door by the time I got to the church. Most were hunched against the cold, holding on tightly to battered bundles or crumpled paper sacks with all their worldly belongings and more than a few bottles of "anti-freeze" to ward off the frigid temperature. In years past, I'd have been on the inside, enjoying the respite that the deluge of holiday volunteers always brought.

To tell the truth, I knew when I signed up to help serve the turkey and dressing and all the trimmings that there'd be wall-to-wall volunteers and my help really wasn't needed. I knew in my heart I was coming to Calvary to get my warm fuzzies, and that afterward I'd go home and the street people would still be homeless. I don't know how I thought I could feel good. Grateful that I wasn't out there too wasn't a bad feeling, but feeling grateful isn't the same as feeling good.

It wasn't the church's fault that I wasn't getting my warm fuzzies. Everybody else was getting theirs for sure. As always, the atmosphere was awash with Christmas cheer. Volunteers had decorated the hall and prepared the dinner. Top-notch local musicians were lined up waiting to entertain "the homeless." Doug, as usual, held his mainline and not-so-mainline parishioners in the palm of his hand as he told the familiar Christmas story of peace and hope.

I stood with my back against the wall and watched everybody else getting their warm fuzzies, watched the holiday volunteers' faces, glowing with affection and a sense of purpose as they bustled in and out of the kitchen. More importantly, I watched the hard edges of homelessness soften in response to those happy, hopeful faces. But I didn't feel all warm and fuzzy. What was my problem?

Maybe it was because things were so different for me. Unlike most of the street people, I knew I was on the right track; but like most of the street people, I didn't know where I was going. I'd changed my major three times already and all I really knew was that the same magnetic force that had drawn me to the basement of Calvary Church almost every weekday for five years had pulled me away from the regular day-to-day work of the Street Ministry and into the classroom to get the credentials I needed to do whatever it was I was supposed to do.

I missed the Street Ministry. I missed the street people. I missed the warm fuzzies, too. But most of all, I missed knowing, on the deepest level, that during those five years when I was volunteering at the Street Ministry I was exactly where I was supposed to be, doing what I was supposed to be doing.

It had really struck home with me when a young woman who worked at the church had been diagnosed with brain cancer and given six months to live. I mentioned to a friend that I thought the young woman, who was still cheerful and showing up for work every day, was handling it very well. When my friend asked me what I'd do if I knew I had only six months to live, I'd responded, without even thinking, "What I'm doing." I couldn't say that anymore.

I watched the familiar, lined, weather-beaten faces of all the homeless people I'd known for years, saw their watchful eyes begin to soften under the onslaught of Christmas cheer, then caught myself looking for other familiar faces—Alepeachie, Arthur, Robert, Eugene, and Applejack—knowing even as I looked that they weren't there. They were all dead. For them, and for so many others, our help had been far too little and far too late.

I blocked out the faces and tried to get in the spirit of the season, plastered the fake smile back on my face and tried to pretend that I believed things would be better soon. What else could I do? How could I tell them the truth? How could I tell them that the day after Christmas, for most of them, would be just like the day after Christmas last year and the year before. How could I tell them how discouraged and frustrated I'd become at our inability to bring an end to what had become a national nightmare.

Did I dare tell them how painfully clear it was to some of us that the roots of homelessness went even deeper than we feared, and that nothing less than a national commitment to solving a national problem could be successful. And how could I tell them that I was there that day, not to give, but to get, my warm fuzzies at their expense?

I'd stopped my morbid musing and was halfway out the door when Sam, a disabled Vietnam Vet, stopped me. Most of the time, Sam managed fairly well on his small VA disability check; he'd first come to us for help after his check was stolen. He'd come back pretty often after that, and not always because he needed something, but because he needed somebody. I'd come back for the same reasons.

Sam had brought me a Christmas card. On the front was a manger scene and on the back he'd written a note.

"God he love all us
Mrs. Pat Morgan
From Samie Morgan
So i need help from you all.
Mrs. Pat Morgan
This is for you to keep wife you all the time."

Inside the card was printed Saint Luke's hauntingly beautiful account of the first Christmas, "Glory to God in the highest, and on earth, peace, goodwill to men."

Then we hugged and I gave him my last five bucks and went home feeling all warm and fuzzy.

CHAPTER 28

Squirrel Park

My statement was simply,

"If we can bail out our S & L Banks

to the tune of fifty billion dollars,

we can bail our homeless mentally ill

out of jail and our children

out of slum housing."

The morning was sunny and wild. It was late spring and I'd just been interviewed at my apartment by a reporter for WKNO, the local public television station, which was doing a documentary on "Memphis Caregivers." I was one of the three people they planned to feature. I was still a full-time college student, still using the old phone booth in storied Halliburton Hall at Rhodes as my "office" while I tried to sell real estate, but now living a few blocks down the street from Calvary in a tiny, much more affordable apartment. After the interview, the reporter and the camera man followed me as I walked the two or three blocks down the pedestrian mall as I often did, carrying a couple of loaves of bread to feed the pigeons in the park.

Everything was fine for the first block or so. I ran into a couple of the homeless men I knew, spent a few minutes talking with each of them separately and promised both that if they'd meet me at the Street Ministry on Monday after I got out of class, I'd make time to meet them there and give them my undivided attention. Neither of them minded being filmed, especially since we assured them that their faces wouldn't be shown. In fact, like a lot of people, they liked the idea of being on television—sort of validated their existence in a world where they'd been more or less invisible for most of their lives.

... Nevertheless, the documentary would play an important part in the next stage of my journey to wherever I was going.

Moving on to Court Square with the reporter and camera man following several yards behind, I'd walked over to the gazebo to talk to a small group of homeless men when a couple of the Street Ministry "regulars" spotted me. Apparently they'd begun celebrating the weekend the night before or early that morning because they were both drunk, which is why I hadn't gone over to talk to them first. One was so drunk he could barely stand up. The other one staggered over, threw his arms around me, and would have planted a wet, sloppy kiss on me if I hadn't clowned my way out of his grasp.

All the time this was happening, I'd had one eye on a young man lying on a bench on the other side of the park. From where I was standing, he appeared to be sound asleep, but that's how people also look when they've passed out or are otherwise unconscious. When he rolled off the bench and his head hit *You couldn't* with a thud on the sidewalk, I hurried over *have scripted* to check on him. He was still unconscious *what unfolded.* when I called 911 from a nearby pay phone and asked for an ambulance, but he was on his feet and able to talk before the paramedics arrived.

He said his name was Carl and he was still wobbly, but since he had a cut on his head, I was trying to talk him into staying until the paramedics got there and checked him out. I also was trying to get him to tell me if he had someplace to go just in case the paramedics decided he didn't need to go to the hospital. When he said he didn't, I asked if his mother would let him stay with her. At that, he started yelling and cursing his mama, saying she'd put him out of the house and he was never going back. His eviction could have had something to do with the fact that he was drunk enough to pass out on a park bench downtown before noon on a Saturday morning, but I thought it wise not to mention that small fact.

One of the regulars (the drunkest one) saw what was happening, heard him yelling and thought he was cursing me, so he staggered across the park to defend me. I saw him coming and tried to wave him away but he kept coming. By the time he got there he'd already pulled out his pocketknife, flipped the little two-inch blade open and was threatening to cut the guy up if he didn't leave me alone.

To top all that off, while I was trying to get him to put his knife away and, at the same time, trying to get the young man who'd fallen off the bench to just shut up, one of Memphis' 50 gazillion street preachers climbed up on the next park bench and started preaching at the top of his lungs and shouting "repent." Every time he shouted, he swooshed his Bible through the air, which, of course, scared all the pigeons and sent them swooshing through the air. You couldn't have scripted what unfolded.

The ambulance showed up about then in spite of the fact that I'd probably ticked off the dispatcher who had definitely ticked me off when I'd called. I'd told her that a man had fallen and was unconscious and where we were and her first question had been "What color is he?"

"What difference does it make?" I'd snapped.

"We need to know so we can identify him when we get there," she said.

"He's the one lying on the sidewalk with the blood on his forehead," I said, rather testily, I admit. Of course, he wasn't lying on the sidewalk when the paramedics got there so she did have a point, but given the circumstances, we were lucky that he was the only one who was bleeding. The paramedics were always good, but that day they were just great, which could have had something to do with the WKNO crew filming away while they were checking Carl out. In all the hullabaloo, I'd forgotten the crew was still there.

TIME Magazine

When the documentary was aired, the interview at my apartment and the brief interaction with the two homeless men (with their backs to the camera) were featured, but all the footage of the ruckus in Squirrel Park, including the preacher and the pigeons, had hit the cutting room floor. Nevertheless, the documentary would play an important part in the next stage of my journey to wherever I was going. The following spring, *TIME* magazine included me in their feature of "20 Outstanding College Juniors in America," dubbing us "Rising Stars." Marcus Pohlmann, PhD, my political science mentor at Rhodes College, had submitted my name for consideration for the recognition. It was based on maintaining a high GPA at an educationally challenging college and on the strength and quality of the extracurricular activities pursued by the student. TIME particularly welcomed information about the student's activities from the print or electronic media, and WKNO was kind enough to provide us with a video of the clip from the documentary.

When those of us who'd been selected from the approximately 500 nominations met with *TIME* staff in New York, one of the editors who'd reviewed the materials told me that when they viewed the clip, the unanimous consensus was that I'd made the cut (probably because middle-aged women who do street outreach to homeless people make good copy).

In addition to an all-expenses-paid trip to New York, dinner with the publisher of *TIME*, a tour of their offices, a night at Hard Rock NYC for a photo shoot, a *TIME* bookbag filled with mementos, and a $3,000 cash award for each of us, a full-page photo of each student with whatever statement we chose to make was featured in *TIME*. My statement was simply "If we can bail out our S & L Banks to the tune of fifty billion dollars, we can bail our homeless mentally ill out of jail and our children out of slum housing."

George Santayana was a philosopher, essayist, poet and novelist, who famously wrote that "Those who fail to learn the lessons of history are doomed to repeat them." And French novelist, Alphonse Karr, had drawn on an old French proverb when he said, "The more things change, the more they stay the same."

Politically, I couldn't have agreed more, but a year later, everything would change for me. I'd be on my way to where I was supposed to be, to do whatever it was I was meant to do.

Twenty years later, I could have written the same thing but the cost would be even higher than the fifty billion first estimated for cleaning up the S&L Crisis and instead of the Savings and Loan Banks, it would be some of the biggest banks in the country, including some that were "too big to fail."

CHAPTER 29

Goodbye, Hello

... the same magnetic force that had drawn

me into the Street Ministry and then pulled

me back to college, was now pulling me

in a different direction, much further away

and even more challenging.

In retrospect, it's hard for me to believe that I had no reservations about moving to Washington, DC with no plans for what I'd do or how I'd survive when my money would run out in about four months. They would have been dispelled anyway when I turned right onto I-66E toward Fort Royal/ Washington for the last 75 miles of my 880 mile drive from Memphis. There it was, a sign proclaiming the concrete ribbon rolling through the gently sloping hills of Virginia as the John Marshall Highway!

I considered it an omen. I didn't know at the time that the highway had been named for "The Great Chief Justice" of the Supreme Court. John Marshall served from 1801 to 1835 and is still reported to be the single most important figure in the development of constitutional law. What I did know was that it surely hadn't been named in memory of the John Marshall who'd died in the dumpster, or worse, been smashed to death in the sanitation truck in Memphis.

It might not make any sense to anybody but me, but that sign was my sign that I was on the right track. That thought was clear, even though it meant leaving my family, my friends, my church, the Street Ministry, and the street people behind. Yes, my path was becoming clearer with every mile—all 75 of them.

The Trial of Goodbyes

I am not very good at goodbyes. I've said goodbye so seldom in my life, held on to bad relationships when I should have said goodbye and let good ones get away sometimes without even bothering to say goodbye. I hadn't had a chance to say good- bye to the people I'd loved so much—my mother, father and stepbrother before they died—and I wouldn't say goodbye to the people I love most, my sons. I just hugged them harder and longer than ever before and told them how much I loved them, how much I'd miss them, that I didn't plan to stay longer than two to five years at the most, and that I'd be coming home often.

I'd been saying goodbye to Calvary Church for weeks. On Sunday mornings, I'd sat in a pew at the back of the church where I could sneak a peek at the sea of bowed heads I'd grown so attached to over the years, storing up the sights and sounds of the church that had come to mean so much to homeless people in Memphis ... and to me.

I'd said goodbye to my friends in the pews and my buddies in the choir and the volunteers who were the heart and soul of the Street Ministry. I'd said goodbye to Mimsy and thanked her for all she'd done to bring much needed structure and stability to the Street Ministry with her vision and organizational skills. But it was even more than that. My conscience would never have let me leave the street people if she hadn't been there to take my place.

I'd said goodbye to a house full of friends at a big party they'd thrown for me a couple of nights before at Jeanne Richardson's new home. It was the home I'd found and sold to her and her husband after she'd called to remind me that they were looking. She knew I needed the money and, wanting to help those who helped the people she cared about, wanted me to make the commission for the sale. Without it, I wouldn't have had the money to move and then hang on until I could get a job.

I'd promised myself that none of their deaths would be in vain—that I would never forget them, and I would tell their stories every chance I got, in the hope that others might also learn something about homeless people—or themselves— from their deaths.

I knew I'd miss them all, but goodbyes are easier when you feel sure that you'll have the opportunity to say hello again. Saying goodbye to those I feared I might never see again, the street people, was a different matter. I hadn't had a chance to say goodbye to Alepeachie or Arthur, except at the funeral home, and I hadn't had a chance to say goodbye at all to Applejack or Eugene or Robert.

I couldn't bring myself to say goodbye to Doug, my priest, my mentor, my role model, my friend. He'd been there for me more times than I could count as I muddled through the dissolution of my second marriage and its on-going, scorched-earth aftermath. He'd been invaluable in making inroads into the health care, mental health and criminal justice systems. It was Doug who'd recruited volunteers, and every dime we'd spent to help the street people had come from his discretionary account or donations he had encouraged from his mainstream parishioners and friends.

Doug and I'd had our differences, mostly because I was so totally focused on the homeless people I was trying to help that I ignored the problems it sometimes created for him, the volunteers and

But it wasn't the memory of our differences that I would take with me. In his personal ministry with the homeless men and women in his parish, in his unconditional love, and in his forgiving spirit, I had seen Christ.

a few of Calvary's parishioners. Doug didn't have that luxury; the buck stopped with him, which meant that he was the one who took the heat whenever one of the street people who hung around the church hustled the regular parishioners. One even tried to panhandle an elderly woman, a stalwart of the church, who had followed the pallbearers and her husband's casket out the front door after his funeral service.

Yet not once in the five years that I spent working with homeless people in Calvary's basement did I ever hear him raise his voice to one of the street people.

I didn't have guts enough to say goodbye to Mr. Poji. He was 83 and wanted to go to Washington with me. Told me not to worry if I didn't have room for him in my car—he'd just hop a freight and meet me there. I'd found him a few months before at the Circle K on the corner, clutching his stomach to hold the double hernia that filled both his tiny withered hands. The clerk told me he'd been sleeping behind the dumpster. Mr. Poji didn't think he needed any help, but he finally agreed to look at some group homes. I'd driven him around that afternoon to see half a dozen, all of which were so grim that I wouldn't have wanted to live there either.

I'd promised that I'd take him back downtown if he didn't like the last one on my list, a small, midtown nursing home. He'd perked up when we walked into the slightly shabby, but warm, cheery, and homelike atmosphere with a table of little old ladies playing cards. The staff at the nursing home said he slept the clock around after I dropped him off. I was pretty sure he'd stay there instead of following me, now that he had those little old ladies to flirt with. If he ran off, I hoped somebody else would notice him limping around the Circle-K and take him back to the nursing home. It was out of my hands now.

Washington, DC and Senator Albert Gore, Jr.

Driving through the rough-hewn hills of Tennessee and then through the picture-perfect Virginia countryside, part of me was hoping that I wouldn't miss everybody as much as I was afraid I would. Another part was wondering, wistfully, if they'd miss me. Regardless, I was on my way.

I'd been intrigued with social studies in junior high. My class had gone to the nation's capital on our senior trip, and for at least 20 years I'd harbored a not-very-well-hidden longing to live and work in a political junkie's paradise, Washington, DC. I'd put aside my passion for politics when I found myself, literally and figuratively, in the basement of Calvary church, working with homeless people. Here it was again—the same magnetic force that had drawn me into the Street Ministry and then pulled me back to college, was now pulling me in a different direction. A direction much further away and even more challenging.

For the next three months, I'd be enrolled in American University's Washington Semester in American Politics program and serving as an intern in the office of Tennessee Senator Albert Gore Jr.

I'd met the senator when he'd come to Calvary to talk to a large group of us about the topic I was obsessed with—homelessness. I was mesmerized—he was totally on top of the major issues of homelessness, housing and mental health and very much at ease. Not long afterward, he'd announced that he was running for the Democratic nomination for President and I'd told him that if he needed any help in Arkansas to let me know. Within a few weeks, I got a call from the coordinator of his campaign in Arkansas. I readily agreed to coordinate Crittenden County, recruited my old friends, and promptly poured every available minute I had into Senator Gore's campaign. He hadn't won in Crittenden County. Jesse Jackson had carried the county by a slim margin, but Gore had beaten Michael Dukakis three to one. In politics, that's usually worth a really nice letter of thanks for helping, which I'd gotten, but not necessarily an internship, and definitely not a job.

I wouldn't have been on my way to at all if it hadn't been for Marcus Pohlmann, my mentor and favorite professor of political science at Rhodes. He was a brilliant teacher, superb political analyst, and prolific author specializing in racial politics. It was Marc who'd suggested that I might want to do a Washington Semester program at American University to cap off my long-delayed degree.

"TIME is on her side."

Internships were an integral part of the program and I had already secured one on my own. If I hadn't, the university, with its 75 years of "using the nation's capital as a learning tool," would have offered me lots of possibilities, even though I didn't exactly fit in with the goal of their undergraduate programs— "to train young people for public service." And it didn't matter. I might have been over the hill, but my own internal barometer of success was based on my absolute, unshakeable determination to have a credible voice in the national debate on homelessness. It appeared that at least some people were listening to me; and it would seem I was on a roll.

The *TIME* award no doubt had helped ensure the internship as well as American University's prompt approval of my application for admission. An additional factor was the inclusion of my volunteer work with homeless people in a video of *Realtors who Make a Difference* by the National Association of Realtors, for nationwide distribution to Realtors. The local newspaper had also included me in the first ten local people they'd featured in their series on President Bush's Thousand Points of Light initiative.

His speechwriter, Peggy Noonan, was responsible for the brilliant title. She is a fabulous writer who apparently didn't grow up in Turrell, Arkansas, or know very much about mental illness or substance abuse, if she thought we "points of light" could meet the overwhelming needs of homeless people.

Now, thanks to Professor Pohlmann, Rhodes College, WKNO, *TIME*, the national association leaders, Bob Watson and Dr. Rae Ragland (a first-rate therapist who'd picked up where Bob had left off with me), and a whole lot of other people who'd been there for me, I was headed for Capitol Hill in Washington. And if I'd had any reservations about being a fifty-year-old intern (which I didn't), they'd have been dispelled when I saw the Rhodes College newsletter with the article about the *TIME* award. The heading read "TIME is on her side."

CHAPTER 30

Home in DC

I had no idea how much I'd learn

in the twenty-four days I'd spend interning

in Senator Gore's office or how valuable

that experience would prove to be

in the near future.

It was mid-afternoon when I hit the notorious Washington Beltway. Thankful that it wasn't rush hour, I soon crossed into the District of Columbia and easily found the Capitol Park Apartments where I planned to live for at least a couple of years. Just as the photos on the brochure had shown, 103 G Street Southwest was located on a tree-lined street with well-kept apartment buildings and townhouses. To my delight, it was within walking distance of the Capitol and the Russell Senate Office Building where I'd be interning two days a week.

It was also three blocks from the subway station (unless I felt like risking my life by taking the shortcut through the tunnel behind the building to the Metro ... which I did more times than I like to admit).

The apartment was also within easy walking distance of the Potomac River, the seafood market, several restaurants along the waterside (none of which I could afford), and a strip mall, complete with a Safeway, a bank, dry cleaners and a liquor store. And that wasn't all. I could walk to the Smithsonian museums and art galleries, the White House and the nation's most famous monuments, all of which fit into my budget, meaning that admission was free.

On the other hand, whoever had prepared the brochure for Capitol Park Apartments had apparently forgotten to mention Greenleaf Gardens. One of Washington's most notorious public housing projects, it was well known as an open-air drug market, and was only about half a block away. It was literally a stone's throw from the strip mall that I would often walk to, especially when my car wouldn't start.

What the brochure also hadn't reflected, and I hadn't noticed on the city map they'd sent, was the expressway that ran just behind the apartment building. It was the major carrier of the ambulances that shrieked along it every night from the troubled southwest section of Washington to DC General Hospital. What helped to offset the nightly shrieks would be waking up to the welcome roar of "Rolling Thunder" every Veterans Day and Memorial Day and a few other holidays thrown in for good measure. On those days, hundreds of motorcycles poured into downtown DC from that expressway so the riders could honor America's veterans ... and make sure that everybody else did too.

My eighth-floor, junior one-bedroom, rent-controlled apartment wasn't too bad. It was, however, a far cry from my Memphis "digs" through the years. There was the nice four-bedroom, two-story home the mortgage company and I had owned in West Memphis. There was the lovely home in historic Hein Park we'd rented when we first moved to Memphis. And there were the lovely apartments I'd had for most of the rest of the time I'd lived there.

To be sure, it was far better than the housing I'd grown up in and far better than the private room in the coed dorm at American University (my only other viable option) that would have cost me $150 more every month even though it wasn't air-conditioned. My apartment had hardwood floors and a folding door that separated the tiny living room from the bedroom area. The closet space was adequate and, unlike the dorm room, I had my very own bathroom. The miniscule, dingy white kitchen with the small refrigerator and retro stove didn't bother me since I didn't plan to spend much time in there anyway, and I didn't plan to entertain at all.

What the apartment lacked in size and aesthetic quality was more than offset by the sliding glass doors across the width of the apartment that let the natural light in and let me out onto the balcony. From that balcony, I could see the dome of the Capitol, pure as the driven snow in the daytime, aglow at night. The people living in dire poverty and no small amount of terror at Greenleaf Gardens could see that dome from their postage-stamp-size front yards too.

The moving van wouldn't arrive for a couple of days but after unloading Old Blue and making a run to the grocery store, I was prepared for the rest of the weekend. Since

I couldn't afford another night at some fleabag motel, in addition to a couple of suitcases, I'd brought a folding lawn chair, a portable radio, a couple of towels and washcloths, a pillow, and a couple of sheets for my temporary bed, a 99-cent plastic float that I huffed and puffed to blow up as a mattress to sleep on.

I wanted to call home to let everybody know that Old Blue and I had made it even though the heat index had been over 100 degrees. The air-conditioning hadn't worked for years and I'd spent a good part of the two-day drive dipping paper towels in cups of melting ice and patting my face to cool off. Unfortunately, the people from the telephone company wouldn't be hooking up my phone until the next week, and though cell phones had been invented, I didn't have one. It was okay. I was where I wanted to be.

Exploring DC

Eager to be on time for my first day of classes and for my first day in Senator Gore's office, the next morning I set out to learn my way around the area via the Metro, Washington's (mostly underground) transit system. To get to the nearest stop that would take me to the Hill, I walked three blocks, noting with gratitude the police substation in the middle of the second block. Gliding down the escalator into the subterranean world of Washington's subway system was a surprisingly pleasant experience.

We didn't have subways in Arkansas or Tennessee and still don't, but I'd ridden the New York subway— old, invariably crowded, and especially scary when somebody is trying to pick your pocket. The Washington Metro, by comparison, was clean and well lighted, with modern trains that ran frequently, relatively quietly, smoothly, and on time. They crisscrossed the city and extended to the Maryland and Virginia suburbs.

After buying an all-day pass, I hopped on the train to my next stop, Capitol Hill South, a scant few blocks away and literally at the door of the Cannon House Office Building where Congressman Bill Alexander, who'd represented our Northeast Arkansas district for years, had his office. I'd cut my political teeth on one of his campaigns for reelection by coordinating his hard-fought campaign in my home county. He'd carried the county and won district-wide, and I'd been hooked on politics ever since.

Remembering that exhilarating experience, I walked with a lot more confidence past the back entrances to the Capitol on my left and the Library of Congress and the Supreme Court on my right, to the Russell Senate Office Building. Standing on the steps at the entrance to that historic building, I had no idea how much I'd learn in the twenty-four days I'd spend interning in Senator Gore's office or how valuable that experience would prove to be in the near future. I just knew I would learn and most likely, my learning wouldn't be coming from a prescribed agenda.

Where Are the Homeless People?

From there, I walked a couple of blocks to Union Station, Washington's beautifully renovated, active train station that also houses the busiest Metro stop in DC, then made my way, stop by stop across town to American University. At each stop, I got off the subway and went up the escalator to see what the area looked like. At the Farragut North stop on Washington's famous "K" street, where the offices of many of Washington's most famous, wealthy and powerful consultants are located, I counted fourteen homeless people who were clearly mentally ill (and that didn't include the preacher with the bullhorn in the middle of the street), all within twenty yards of the entrance to the subway. Until then, I hadn't seen even one homeless person.

At the Tenleytown stop where American University is located, an elderly homeless man with a gentle face had made his home in a 12 inch-wide window ledge outside an empty storefront building and was busily doing his housecleaning with a spray bottle filled with a clear liquid, spraying the surface of the window and the window sill and scrubbing them dry again. Every time I went out to the university for classes or lectures or special events or to use the computer lab, he was there, still trying to clean his corner of the world.

Lafayette Park was full of homeless, ragged men and women—the White House faced it.

On the way back to my apartment, I took a different route. I got off the Metro at Farragut West, close by the White House, where there was a crowd of homeless people, most of whom were sitting or sprawled close to the walls of the entrance, then walked across the street to Lafayette Park, directly in front of the White House. The park was full of homeless, ragged, haggard men and women. Many of them were clearly mentally ill and many of the rest bore the telltale signs of long-term substance abuse. The sidewalk and grassy strip separating the park from Pennsylvania Avenue and the White House looked like a refugee camp with makeshift tents and homemade signs protesting policies that long ago had lost the attention of the general public.

I had no doubt that many of the people in that park were there in the hope that the person who held the highest office in the land would see them and use his power to make the "voices" or the invisible people or apparitions that tormented them go away.

In the weeks that followed, I learned to navigate my way around the city. I'd find lots of other places where homeless people congregated, mostly in the dozens of parks, other metro stops, under bridges and viaducts, and at the sheltered bus stops. My past five years had trained me to look for places where homeless people congregated, but nothing had prepared me for the number of homeless people sleeping on the heating grates when winter came.

My mission was clear. I was there to see if the president would use his power to make the scourge of homelessness go away.

In a city approximately the same geographical size and population of Memphis, the U.S. Census Bureau, in its first-ever national count of homeless people in the summer of 1990, had counted 4,682 homeless people—almost ten times as many as the 480 they'd counted in Memphis!

I'd come to Washington seeking solutions to homelessness and I had clearly jumped from the frying pan into the fire. As I would soon learn, one of the main reasons there were so many homeless people was that the mental health system in the nation's capital was a disaster—a complete disaster. It was so dysfunctional that it had been placed in receivership, along with public housing and the foster care system.

Nevertheless, since I'd arrived on Labor Day weekend, I walked over to the capitol later that afternoon and found a spot on the west lawn to sit and gaze in awe as the sun slipped out of sight behind the Washington monument, then rose to stand as the National Symphony Orchestra began the evening's performance by playing the national anthem. Then, as the evening ended with the 1812 Overture and the booming of cannons, I watched the fireworks light up the western sky.

I was sure I was where I was supposed to be, but that night I also knew I was where I wanted to be.

CHAPTER 31

The Chinaberry Tree

... to feel the cool marble-sized chinaberries

in my hand as I felt the old excitement

of a new adventure. I'd felt it

hundreds of times before; every time I opened

a new book or turned a page in my life.

A few days later I took the Metro all the way out to the Medical Center stop in Bethesda, Maryland, just outside the city limits of the nation's capital, and then took the shuttle to the National Institutes of Health library. There, along the side of the library, were a dozen or more chinaberry trees. I thought the Metro had taken me home.

Turrell Was My Window to the World

To this day, I don't remember when we moved from the tiny, white clapboard house on the street lined with similar houses, to the apartment that wrapped half-way around the furniture store. By the time I was old enough to look back and try to remember anything, it seemed like we'd always lived in the store on the corner with the chinaberry tree. Technically, I guess we lived in the apartment, but all we really did was sleep in the rooms that opened out onto the big screened porch and eat in the dining room or the kitchen. We rarely used the living room even when it had furniture in it. Life was outside or in the store—around the big pot-bellied coal-burning stove, the only heat we had in the wintertime, or in the breeze and cool hum of the floor fan in the dog days of summer.

Straight across the gravel road that ran in front of the store loomed the steep slope of the railroad track. The daily rumbling of the freight trains that wailed and rattled the windows, and the sleek, shrieking passenger trains that occasionally ran over people who were too dumb, too deaf, or too drunk to stay off the tracks, were as normal as the sweat that poured from our bodies in July. Wild blackberries grew in tangled patches all along the slopes and all the way to the schoolhouse; they kept my mouth purple-black for six weeks out of every summer.

All along the roadbed of the railroad track were agate-sized rocks that I prized. For years, I collected them and stacked them against the wall of my secret hiding place under our four-foot-high side porch. Not like the gravely pebbles scattered over most of the streets in town, they were sandstone, rose quartz and bits of marble, sparkling "fools gold" and stinky yellow sulphur—exotic rocks from exotic places like Rome, Italy, and Bakersfield, California—places that I knew must be a lot different from the only place I knew—Turrell—deep in the heart of the thick, black, gumbo mud clay of the Mississippi Delta.

Just across the gravel road that ran beside the store, squatted one of the town's trio of tin-topped, corrugated steel cotton gins. Two more sat just across the railroad track; one on each side of the gravel road just as it turned into asphalt, stretching its black tongue toward the whisky store. It seemed like all the roads in Turrell led to the whisky store.

The cotton gins were deserted for three-quarters of the year, with quiet, silky webs stretching over gaping windows without glass. Bursting alive in the fall, like hungry bears coming out of hibernation, they roared into a feeding frenzy and gobbled up wagons full of snowy puffs of cotton in beat-up bolls. The air everywhere was filled with excitement and cotton lint. The gins ran round the clock and if one of the gins stopped, the townspeople stopped—all of us—too. Most of the time all that was wrong was that something was just broken or had gotten stuck in the gin. Sometimes, that something was somebody, or a part of somebody who'd gotten too close to the gin's teeth or gotten sucked up and baled with the cotton.

Maybe the gins didn't really sit in sated silence for the rest of the year. Maybe, to my young girl's eyes and ears, it just seemed that way.

Across the weed-grown yard, the yard that we cut with a sling blade when the weeds got so high we got scared of snakes, was the ice house. Thick, glistening blocks of ice lined the cool, dark interior of the tiny building and huge ice tongs hung on a big hook outside the door. It was the coveted place to be in the summer.

Our kitchen was in back of the store. Just past the back porch that ran off of it was what may have been the filthiest gas station known to modern man. This was a real live service station with sweat and grease-caked tools and spilled gasoline and lots of crashing and clunking and cussing. Just behind it was Charlie Wah's grocery store with cases full of penny candy and spiced ham and rag baloney and sodas so big we called them belly washers. I don't know how Charlie ended up in Turrell speaking English and Chinese but he did and sometimes he went back to China. I could tell he'd really been there because he brought us packages of tea in little gilt and gold packages with dragons and Chinese characters in blood-red ink.

One time when he returned, he brought himself a wife. She was pretty and sweet but she couldn't speak English—she just smiled and laughed a lot. The next time he went, he brought her father and mother with him. They couldn't speak English either; his father-in-law just smiled a lot too, but his mother-in-law hardly ever smiled. Instead, she shrieked a lot in Chinese as she staggered around the store. We never knew if she was shrieking at us or just shrieking because her feet hurt. They were just stumps because they'd been bound since she was a little girl. They probably hurt a lot, but just to be sure, we stayed out of her way. I think Charlie's father-in-law must have been scared of her too because he got out of her way about as fast as we did and he was real old then, maybe forty.

The Magic Carpet of the Chinaberry Tree

There was a chinaberry tree too, only it wasn't in front of Charlie's store. It was at the front corner of our furniture store and right in front of the window of our sometimes living room. I always thought the chinaberry tree was kind of magic, having grown all the way from China to finally jut out of the mound of dried mud with bits and pieces of bottle green glass and chunks of concrete left over from when they'd poured the front porch of the store. My stepmother told me if I dug a hole down deep enough, I'd come out in China so I figured somebody in China had planted it and it just got turned around and grew the wrong way and wound up in Turrell, Arkansas, instead of Hong Kong.

Aesop's fables came to life through the leaves.

Sometimes the tree was covered with cotton lint and sometimes it was dusted with black soot from the trains. Always it seemed like it was covered with chinaberries, little green marble-hard, marble-sized, inedible berries that I'd never seen before because nobody else in Turrell had a real chinaberry tree from China.

The tree wasn't nearly as big as the big old, half-rotted oak tree with the tire swing or the tall cottonwood that grew so close to the side porch that we could climb the tree and step over to the roof of the store to play when grown-ups weren't around. The chinaberry tree's low branches were just right for climbing, and after Daddy bought the entire twelve-volume set of encyclopedic "Books of Knowledge" from the one-legged traveling salesman, the branches were just right for holding a little girl with a big book. All I had to do was stick whichever book I was reading into the gnarled branches and hop on my carpet into another world.

Aesop's fables came to life through the leaves. Romeo stood at the foot of the tree and called up to his Juliet with the knobby knees and bare feet, and Rapunzel threw down her stringy, dish-water hair from the tallest branch. The fake gemstones that the town's dressmaker threw away and I found and hid in a knothole in the oak tree, could have come from King Tut's tomb right there on the pages. Daddy's fishing poles looked just like the bamboo that grew in Calcutta. The White House and Mount Vernon and the nation's capitol and every single solitary state had its own story. The insects that covered the porch screens on midsummer nights had names, and poets had dreams and every page sent my grubby fingers flying to the next. Not only did I go to China—I went to places no one had ever heard of in Turrell.

That one-legged traveling salesman left another legacy. He was the one who'd left the card that Daddy had taped to the cash register—the card that said "I cried because I had no shoes till I met a man who had no feet." It had helped to remember that line when I was a cheerleader and lined the holes in the soles of my saddle oxfords with cardboard. The card was still there when Daddy sold the last few pieces of furniture out of the store, packed up the books full of unpaid accounts (ours and theirs) and went into full-time police work.

Sometimes, in the twisted little branches of the chinaberry tree, I hid and pondered important questions—like, why was it that the Italian families in town always seemed to have so much fun?—and why was it that the Jewish families never seemed to have much fun at all, even though they were really nice and the only people in town who seemed to have any money? One family that I baby-sat for, even had an all-purple living room, furniture and all—And why had somebody bound up that poor old Chinese lady's feet like that?—And why did colored kids have to go to the old run-down school they went to when there was plenty of room at our school? A lot of "Whys."

Sometimes I hid behind the leaves and pondered secret questions—questions I was always afraid to ask, like where was my real mother and why did she leave and was the pretty lady with the hat who'd stared at me that time from the passenger train my real mother, come to sneak a peek after all those years ... and maybe even take me with her—and were Topeka and Santa Fe real places—and was that maybe where she was going on the train and would she still be there when I got big enough to go find her.

I never saw the chinaberry tree again after my dad was killed that Saturday night right there on the parking area next to the store. I don't even know if it was still there when I left Turrell. We'd moved to a real house a few years before, and after my dad was killed I could never bear to go past the place where he'd run down the graveled driveway to the truck where his killer was sitting with his shotgun and what was left of a bottle of booze. The Chinaberry Tree, my companion and friend for many years, had become invisible.

Past, Forward to the Present

It'd been 32 years since I'd seen a chinaberry tree when my journey in search of a way to break the cycle of homelessness had led me to the stately, shushed silence of the library of the National Institutes of Health. Walking across the quiet, shaded walkways, I'd seen the trees—at least a dozen, lined up near the entrance of the library, low branched and loaded with chinaberries just like my chinaberry tree in Turrell.

I was 50 years old but I still wanted to climb one of those chinaberry trees, wanted to feel the cool marble-sized chinaberries in my hand as I felt the old excitement of a new adventure. I'd felt it hundreds of times before; every time I opened a new book or turned a page in my life I'd felt the thrill of a truth discovered, a mind set free.

From my limited information, it had seemed that national advocates were claiming that housing was the only solution to homelessness. I'd come to Washington because I was convinced that there was much more to it than housing and we'd never end homelessness until we told the truth about its causes—all of them. A lot of the truth about homelessness was in that library, in books and articles explaining the biochemistry of the brain and body and the devastating effects of alcohol and other drug abuse not just on the body, but on the brain.

A few weeks later, my search for a mental health policy would take me to the National Institute of Mental Health and I would learn even more during what was already being called "the decade of the brain" as researchers plumbed even deeper into the workings of the human brain, including the most critical years in brain development—from zero to three.

But for me on that day, it was enough to feel that my childhood belief in the magic of that chinaberry tree had been right after all. It had surely been planted by God to sprout in the gravel-strewn, gumbo clay of Turrell, Arkansas, to give one of His children a special place from which to grow.

I'd come to Washington because I was convinced that there was much more to it than housing and we'd never break the cycle of homelessness, much less end it, until we told the truth about its causes—all of them.

CHAPTER 32

Lessons For a Senate Intern

"It's not on the agenda," she said pleasantly.

"There's been no directive; it's not there."

The internship exceeded by a country mile every expectation I'd had of what I'd be doing as a Senate intern. Unlike most interns on the "Hill," I never had to do the regular intern work such as answering phones or sorting mail or photocopying or running errands. I even had my own desk, right behind the desk of Jacquie Lawing, the Senator's 26-year-old, Memphis-born and raised, super-bright, hard-working legislative assistant for housing, homelessness and poverty. Jacquie had made it clear the first day that they wanted my internship to be a positive experience and did everything she could to ensure that it was.

I'd started off by reading reams of reports and by the second day was drafting a committee report about legislation introduced by Senator Gore for a White House Conference on Homelessness. The legislation would also have provided funding for staff to organize local and statewide conferences in every state but the White House was opposing the Bill on the grounds that the U.S. Interagency Council on the Homeless was already addressing the issue. (If they were, nobody I knew in Tennessee had heard anything about it.) Frankly, if the internship had ended that day, I would still have considered it an unqualified success. It didn't end. It got better. Senator Gore had dropped by a couple of times by the end of the day, greeted me warmly and given me a "hello" hug and a kiss on the cheek.

During the next few days of the internship, I stayed busy with a variety of duties, which included calling constituents, making a list of providers of services to homeless people in Tennessee, and learning how to draft letters to constituents without getting anybody in trouble. (Jacquie was a master at it). In the weeks that followed, among other duties, I worked on "talking points" (a new concept for me) for a speech the senator was to give about hunger and housing. I'd bombed on that one because I was still seeing everything through the prism of mental health and substance abuse. I'd done better with the next few—including a speech to the National Association of Social Workers and a "floor statement" for the senator to make about the Affordable Housing Act.

The Affordable Housing Act

My background in real estate came in handy in helping to explain the ramifications of the Affordable Housing Act to the senator's constituents. Because it was such a sensitive issue, it took half a dozen re-writes for Jacquie and me to explain in a carefully worded letter to the senator's constituents why he'd voted for the Affordable Housing Act. It would, over the next two decades, help create almost half a million units of affordable housing for lower-income people, but, unfortunately, it would also immediately tighten requirements for qualifying for home mortgages. The more restrictive requirements had been a necessary inclusion, given the widespread abuse of more lenient regulations that had played a major role in wrecking the housing market and the economy, a lesson we'd clearly fail to learn in the near future.

As part of the massive "Housing Now!" march in Washington a year earlier, I'd been among tens of thousands of people encouraging passage of the legislation. But I hadn't read the legislation and even now couldn't tell how it was going to do much, if anything, for the "street people" I knew and had tried to help for years. (It would take a couple of years for me to realize that I was dead wrong about that.)

I felt pretty dumb for not knowing that funding from the McKinney Act was already funding programs for homeless people all over the country.

There was a reason why I hadn't ventured to mention the Affordable Housing Act hadn't been nearly as far-reaching as I'd hoped. With Jacquie's encouragement, I was busy reading everything she had in her files about homelessness, including the four-year-old, landmark, Stewart B. McKinney Act. That Act absolutely, positively would help homeless families and individuals, especially those with mental illness and/or alcohol and drug problems—just like the ones I'd left behind in Memphis but still longed to help. These programs would not only provide funding for shelter, transitional housing, permanent supportive housing, and operations, but also the services and treatment that were so sorely lacking. Not surprisingly, Senator Gore had been one of the sponsors of the legislation.

On the other hand, I felt pretty dumb for not knowing that funding from the McKinney Act was already funding programs for homeless people all over the country, including a transitional housing program in Memphis. That was the one I'd tried to get an unbelievably dysfunctional homeless couple admitted to in one of my more misguided moments. I never knew where the money for the program had come from simply because I hadn't asked.

No, I had a lot to learn and the McKinney Act would be my first, and one of my most important textbooks. Nevertheless, I still managed to forget the section about the U.S. Interagency Council on the Homeless that had been established by the legislation. The Council's role was to coordinate the efforts of the various federal departments and agencies that had programs to help homeless people—programs that would have helped in Memphis. I learned more about the Council a couple of years later when I was picking out where I wanted to work in Washington, but at the time I didn't remember ever having heard or read anything at all about it.

There was an even richer source of information than Jacquie's files. At the end of many of the days I spent in the senator's office, I rode the little open, uncovered, underground shuttle from the Russell Senate Office Building to the basement of the Capitol. On each trip I carried home all of the reports on homelessness, housing, mental health and substance abuse that were available, produced specifically for the Congress by the Congressional Research Services' small army of policy analysts, information professionals and attorneys.

I read all of them, gleaning from the reports about mental illness a lot of the information I needed for my "Search for a National Mental Health Policy," the 80-page research paper I produced that semester after surveying congressional committees, national advocacy groups, national professional organizations and high-ranking governmental officials. It became my personal manifesto.

With each interviewee, along with other questions designed to determine the level of their knowledge about mental health in general, I asked the same question:

Who (or what) entity is responsible for making national mental health policy?

Many didn't presume to know; those that thought they did know, uniformly responded "NIMH" (the National Institute on Mental Health.) Then I went to NIMH and met separately with the two people I'd been told would be my best source, both of whom were caring, mental health professionals. Each of them said, "No, not us. We're a research facility." However, one of them went to her filing cabinet and pulled out a two-page outline for a national mental health policy that had been prepared for Rosalyn Carter, only to be rendered obsolete when President Carter was defeated in his bid for re-election, primarily due to the disastrous economy and the Iran hostage crisis. In one of the first acts of the new President and Con-

The timing was horrendous.

gress, the 1980 Mental Health Systems Act, which would have significantly increased funding and coordinated mental health programs across the federal government, had been repealed.

The low point for me was when, after calling lots of times, talking to lots of his people, and leaving lots of messages on his phone, I got through. The man identified as the sole individual in the White House who could respond to my requests for information about national mental health policy picked up his phone and growled "HELL-O." Definitely not a warm, fuzzy and welcoming hello.

The Associate Director for Health and Social Services in the Domestic Policy Office of the President had answered. He said straight away that his background was in health services administration; and he had no professional background in mental health. He did, though, have a family member with a mental illness. He was, in his own words "anti-credentialist." He was clearly not happy to hear my voice.

The timing was horrendous. The budget summit of 1990 had failed; the White House and Congress were at war, Iraq had invaded Kuwait, and nerves were frayed. "I know why you're calling," he said irritably, after I'd told him who I was and why I was calling. "I've gotten your messages."

He then proceeded to outline the real crux of the issue: "It's not the White House's problem," he said. "The states have all the powers." Likening the federal role versus the states' role in mental health to trying to lead a horse to water, he went on to add, "You can't make them drink." He capped it off by saying,

No one gets everything they want. I don't get all the money I want and you don't get all the grades you want. We are not an entitlement society. There's no silver bullet, and if you're looking for some piece of paper that says "national mental health policy," forget it.

One last effort led me to a senior policy analyst in the executive office of the president. "It's not on the agenda," she said pleasantly. "There's been no directive; it's not there." After that, I was even more determined than ever to do whatever I could to get mental health services for homeless people on somebody's agenda.

CHAPTER 33

Snow White

"Yes," she said, and I watched

her beautiful little ebony face settle

into rock-solid determination. "Yes," she said

again, "Anthony's gonna marry me because

I'm pretty—and I'm white."

Not all of the lessons I learned about homelessness were political. One day Tipper Gore stopped by the office, told the staff she wanted to borrow her "expert" on homelessness, and took me with her to the House of Ruth, a nationally recognized shelter for abused women and children in Washington. She introduced me to the director of the program as an expert, but as usual, I learned something from the real experts on homelessness —a couple of homeless people at the shelter.

Neither one of them fit the old stereotype of homeless people—aging alcoholics with weather-beaten faces and bloodshot eyes and trembling hands. They didn't fit the new stereotype either. Neither of them was high or stoned or mentally ill and they weren't anywhere near the average age of homeless people at the time (35). In fact, neither one of them was a day over five years old!

It wasn't surprising to me that all of the children I saw that day in the shelter's day care center were African-American, and it was even less surprising that almost all of the grown-ups I saw there were snow white. At the Street Ministry in Memphis, 80 to 90 percent of the homeless people we tried to help were people of color and all of us who were trying to help were white. We hadn't planned it that way. I'd tried to recruit African-American men and women to help us and had a couple of first-rate volunteers for a little while, but most of the African-Americans I tried to recruit were already doing so much good they just didn't have time to take on any more.

Some folks at the churches where I went looking for volunteers were afraid that we were "coddling" the street people. Some of them made it a point to let me know that they'd "made it" in spite of racism and poverty and expected others to do the same. Others were so busy supporting themselves and/or their families that they just didn't have the time or energy to come downtown to the Street Ministry. It didn't help much that our program was only open during weekdays; that meant people with regular nine-to-five jobs couldn't volunteer. The truth is that I didn't try nearly as hard as I could have, mainly because I figured that since we volunteers didn't care what color the people we were trying to help were, then the people we were trying to help probably didn't care what color we were either.

Through the Eyes of Babes

The two children playing in the corner didn't know any of this stuff. Akaretha and Anthony were just putting a puzzle together on a tot-size table when I went over to talk to them for a minute. I'd already talked briefly with a saintly young woman who'd smiled and looked lovingly at the children when she told me they were all doing just fine and that homelessness didn't seem to have much of an effect on them.

"They are so damaged emotionally and developmentally."

That assessment didn't exactly square with the studies and reports that I'd been reading. Dr. Ellen Bassuk was, and still is, the leading researcher into the causes and effects of homelessness among women and children. According to Dr. Bassuk, "Homeless children suffer from psychological and developmental problems that can plague them the rest of their lives." Chillingly, one of her studies had found that half the children in a Boston shelter had thought about killing themselves.

With Dr. Bassuk's research in mind, I'd also talked briefly with the shelter's child psychologist. "They are so damaged emotionally and developmentally," she'd said, her face reflecting the sorrow she clearly felt.

"All of them?" I'd moaned.

"All of them," she'd sighed.

With that reality in mind, it stands to reason that I was probably trying a little too hard to be cheerful when I crouched down beside the table to talk to Akaretha and Anthony a few minutes later. Kids know when you're being honest with them and when you're not. Akaretha gave me the coolest stare I'd ever gotten from a four or five-year-old and went right back to working on the puzzle. Anthony ignored me altogether. I had sense enough to stop talking and wait for them to wait for me to get real.

Anthony spoke first. "Me and Akaretha gonna get married," he said.

"You are!" I said, in mock surprise.

"Yeah," he said. "Me and Akaretha's gonna get married and get us a house."

Since I couldn't deal with a couple of homeless five-year-olds talking about getting a house to live in, I tried to move the conversation away from getting a house to live in to talking about something safer, like a couple of five-year olds getting married.

"I don't blame you, Anthony. I'd marry Akaretha too if I were you because she's so pretty." I said. That got Akaretha's attention.

"Yes," she said, and I watched her beautiful little ebony face settle into rock-solid determination. "Yes," she said again, "Anthony's gonna marry me because I'm pretty—and I'm white." And, as the last few words slipped through her clenched teeth, her pudgy, precious, beautiful little black fingers ground Snow White's face into the space where Grumpy's head should have gone.

Seeing the things I saw when I was growing up during the forties and fifties, I couldn't imagine wanting to be black or even brown, but that day, for that hour, I'd have given anything I owned to be any color but white.

I never forgot those children or their story and, along with Alepeachie's story, I'd tell it every chance I got. And my laser-like focus on helping those homeless people who were most vulnerable would forever more include infants and children.

CHAPTER 34

Boiler Room Girls

"Every job has its drawbacks,"

her voice dripping with disgust.

"We have to put up with all those "loonies"

in Lafayette Park."

My political instincts on full alert, I'd figured the woman who strode down the hall of the Old Executive Office Building next door to the White House was one of us as soon as I saw her. Women like us come out of the woodwork in election years, drawn by the power and the promise of a political campaign, and it doesn't matter who we are: businesswomen, college professors, college students, political activists, teachers, lawyers, housewives, secretaries, civic leaders or advocates. We are "us."

Somebody wrote somewhere that the Kennedys called women like us "boiler room girls." Some people call us political junkies or political hacks. Wives of politicians sometimes call us "groupies" (or worse). No matter what we're called, every major political campaign has us, a loyal core group of women who open the mail, stuff the envelopes, work the phone banks, and, depending on how much or how little money the campaign has, sweep the floors and clean the bathrooms of store-front campaign offices all over the country.

Today's women have moved into positions of power within campaigns, advising on issues and policy, researching, marketing, strategizing, run-ning for office themselves—and winning. But out of the media glare, toiling away in

Some of us are lucky enough to believe in the cause and the candidate.

the boiler rooms of many of those same campaigns are the "boiler room girls," the heart and soul of grassroots, front-line politics. Some of us are attached to the candidate by birth or marriage, others by ideology. Some of us are attracted to other political junkies and make lifelong friends, and some of us are simply attracted to "causes." Depending on who is running and the level of charisma of the candidate, some are attracted to the candidate. Some of us are lucky enough to believe in the cause and the candidate. Others couldn't care less about the issues or the "cause" but attach themselves early on to a candi-date, and, by dint of hard work or smart work or their money or their ability to raise money or because of their unquestioned loyalty, make the transition from the campaign's "boiler room" to jobs in political offices—sometimes the highest political offices in the land.

The woman who led my class from American University on a tour of the Eisenhower Executive Office Building, which most of the old-timers and insiders in Washington call the OEOB (the Old Executive Office Building), was attractive, well groomed and middle-aged, a rather well-dressed boiler room girl I thought. Her name escapes me but I'm very sure that she said she was the director of children's mail in the White House's Office of Presidential Correspondence. That's the office where staff and volunteers read and prepare responses to the thousands of letters to the president that are received every year from people all over the country.

I don't remember much about what she told us about the elaborate, French Provincial building that dwarfs the White House next door and sticks out like a sore thumb amid the classic Greek Revival and Roman architectural gems of the nation's capital. I was too busy thinking about and imagining the presence of the people who'd probably walked the same black and white tile floors and climbed the same massive, curving staircases and stood under the skylight domes of the stunning, stained glass of the rotundas.

Our Guide, the Tour and Her "Spiel"

Other than what she told us about the building, most of what our guide talked about was general stuff, like who got to sit where in the Presidental limousine, in the presidential entourage when the president traveled, and where she got to sit in the presidential limousine when she traveled with the President, in particular. Saddam Hussein's troops had invaded Kuwait a few weeks earlier and America was probably going to war to keep our hands on Kuwait's oil. You'd think she could have thought of something else to talk about, especially since she was in charge of handling kids' mail to the president and the president's responses to their letters. For starters, she might have mentioned kids' reactions to the threat of war or practically anything of substance.

Our professor in the Washington Semester in American Politics class had cautioned us against criticizing or otherwise offending our hosts on the site visits even if we disagreed vehemently with what they were doing or saying because it might result in the univesity's pro-

> *"Guns don't kill people.*
>
> *People with guns kill people."*

gram losing its access to the hosts. By then, we'd already met with a lot of people and groups, including a senator, a staff person from a congressional committee, the Coalition to End Handgun Violence, and the National Rifle Association.

Because I didn't want to screw up the university's program, under which students were, and still are, able to meet with senators or representatives or their staff members, other governmental staff, and an impressive mix of not-for-profit advocacy and public interest groups, I'd held my tongue. Even when the man who showed us the NRA office said, "Guns don't kill people. People kill people." Since I'd managed to refrain from telling him that "people with guns kill people," I managed to overlook the airhead commentary.

After our hostess' remarks, she was supposed to give us a brief tour of the West Wing, but the warriors were gathering there. Therefore, after we finished the tour of the OEOB, she led us out to the sidewalk in front of the White House. Somebody in the class mentioned the lush green lawn.

"Ohhhh, yes," she gushed, "isn't it just lovely? The Park Service is just wonderful. No effort or expense is spared in taking care of the White House lawn." She went on to explain that every fall the Park Service comes out to count the squirrels. If there are too many, they take some of them away and set them free in other parks. If there aren't enough squirrels at the White House, they bring in more squirrels from other parks. She said it was to keep the lawn ecologically balanced. That was a new one for me. I have a hunch it's some wag's way of making sure we always have enough squirrels running around the White House. By then, even without counting, I was beginning to think we had at least one squirrel too many running around the White House, but I was just a fifty-year-old college student and a lowly Senate intern, so what was I supposed to know.

Anyway, the lady was really getting into her social director routine and she turned her attention to Blair House, right across the street from the White House. It used to be the home of the Vice President before the government started using it for visiting dignitaries. Physically and functionally it is quite impressive. According to our hostess, no expense was spared in the way foreign guests were treated. If the visitors were from Germany, the government brought in the German-speaking staff, shipped in German newspapers and magazines, had German food prepared and served, and just generally "blew it out." If the next visitors were French, they got the whole routine in their native language and culture. Ditto the Japanese, Chinese, Russians, and any other VIP visitors from abroad. Kind of like the Squirrel Model—spare no expense to keep it in balance.

Our speaker/tour guide got so carried away describing the opulence and the grandeur that finally one of the other students asked if there was anything she didn't like about her job. Waving her hand toward the horde of homeless, mentally ill people across the street in Lafayette Park, she said, "Oh, of course. Every job has its drawbacks," her voice dripping with disgust. "We have to put up with all those "loonies" in Lafayette Park. One of them was even being interviewed on the news the other night. I couldn't believe it. They'd put a sport coat on him and everything, and they were acting like he was somebody. I couldn't believe it—one of the loonies!"

As though someone had just flipped a page, the heads of every one of the other students in our group snapped toward me, wondering, no doubt, if I'd be able to keep quiet given that they'd all heard me tell Alepeachie's story and knew that I'd come to Washington because of homeless, mentally ill people like Alepeachie and the ones living in Lafayette Park. It took all the self control I had, but I didn't say a word in response.

A year later, I would walk past the White House on many nights and invariably think about that lady and what she'd said about those homeless, mentally ill people. Then I'd find renewed energy and pour everything I had into helping elect a president and vice president that I knew for sure not only had compassion for the Alepeachies and future Alepeachies of this world, but were committed to doing everything they could to help them.

CHAPTER 35

Peace Park

... I whispered goodbye

to the young man sleeping under the bush,

slipped all the money I had with me ...

Partially hidden under a bush in Lafayette Park, directly across from the White House, a young man lay in a stupor in the late October sun, his torso and long, spindly legs curled into a fetal position. His head lay in the dirt where the feet of thousands of visitors to the nation's capital had scuffed away the dying grass. A shoe with the entire sole ripped away lay near his hand. He wore what was left of the other shoe, along with a bizarre conglomeration of incredibly filthy rags. Bits of dried grass were woven through his thickly matted hair; a pair of flies buzzed around the tiny drop of saliva oozing past his dry, cracked lips.

He may have been drunk. He may have been high. But whether he was drunk or high or clean and sober, he was clearly mentally ill and obviously homeless. He could have been a younger, sicker version of Alepeachie.

How he could sleep through the din as the protests got louder and louder in "Peace Park" was beyond me. Apparently, I wasn't the only person in America who wasn't exactly thrilled about President George Herbert Walker Bush's plan to dispatch American troops to the Mideast to restore the little oil-rich kingdom of Kuwait to its "rightful rulers."

To be honest, the "rightful rulers" spin had spun out pretty quickly. The next spin was that the real reason American troops were on their way to Saudi Arabia was because of "jobs." Jobs? What this meant was that we had to "protect our interests" in somebody else's oil to keep our economy humming. When that one didn't defuse some of us any better than the "rightful rulers" spin, the latest spin was that U.S. troops were pouring onto the sands of the kingdom of Saudi Arabia, next door to the kingdom of Kuwait, to "protect our way of life."

Protest

It is doubtful that the young man lying at my feet in Peace Park knew or cared that half a million of his fellow Americans were on their way to a place halfway around the world to "protect his way of life." All around him the verbal confrontation between the supporters of the war and the anti-war activists, fueled by the battle of the poster boards, was raging.

"Support our troops!" shouted one poster.

"Support our troops—bring 'em home!" challenged another.

"Lefties go home!" screeched another.

"Send Neil Bush!" implored another.

"Commies, go home to mommy!" whined a preppie's.

"I want my son home alive!" moaned a mother's.

"Win one for the Gipper!" boomed the businessman's.

"A wimp at peace is better than a fool at war!" warned the peacenik's.

"Blessed are the peacemakers," prayed the priest's.

"Looks like druggies out there!" charged the short-hair's.

"My blood for oil? Piss off, Fascist Swine!" stormed the long-hairs.

"Whose blood? For whose oil? For whose way of life?" read mine, scrawled on the back side of an abandoned poster and now held in front of me as I hovered over the boy under the bush.

I understood all too well the pain of loss and the survivor's guilt that follows when somebody you love comes home in a body bag.

I'd made a detour on the way to Peace Park, going to the Wall first to pay my respects and draw courage from the names inscribed on the memorial to the 58,000 Americans who'd died in Vietnam. It's true; the war wouldn't have ended one second sooner if I'd had the courage to step out of my comfortable job and my primary role as wife and mother to at least give lip service to the peace movement during those agonizing years. Adding one more voice in protest would not have helped to save one life, but maybe I wouldn't have carried such a burden of guilt for so much of mine.

I'd finally gotten angry enough to write a letter to the editor of the local paper blasting our city council for passing a resolution supporting Lieutenant Calley, who'd been convicted of the My Lai massacre of Vietnamese peasants, including women, children, and babies in the arms of their mothers. (I'm sure my letter had the city council shaking in their shoes.)

I was serious about protesting Desert Storm, and it wasn't just about the vestiges of Vietnam. I understood all too well the pain of loss and the survivor's guilt that follows when somebody you love comes home in a body bag.

When my arms wouldn't hold my sign up any longer, I whispered goodbye to the young man sleeping under the bush, slipped all the money I had with me, about $15, into one of his pockets, walked all the way back home and gratefully unlocked the door to my apartment. As tiny as it was, and as dangerous as the neighborhood was, I wasn't sleeping under a bush or in one of the makeshift tents that littered Lafayette Park at night and I wasn't on my way to fight in a war over somebody else's oil.

Another Street Ministry?

The following Sunday I visited historic St. John's Episcopal Church, "The Church of the Presidents," that borders Lafayette Park on the north side. I was intrigued that "since the church's first service in 1816, every person who has held the office of the President of the United States has attended a regular or occasional service." The church itself was (and still is) exquisite; the people were as friendly as people could be expected to be in a city where power and access to people who have power are everything.

The music sung by the choir, all paid professionals, was beautiful and the sermon was uplifting. My research revealed the church had come a long way under the current rector's leadership. Progress had been slow during the first two decades of his tenure. Yet he had played a major role in the church's ultimate major shift to a strong social presence. The shift was from what had been thought of as a "society" church that rented the pews to the socially prominent as a main source of funding, to a church more focused on social programs for homeless and other disadvantaged people. I thought I'd found where I was supposed to be, in a church that had a history of helping homeless people, literally a stone's throw from a park full of homeless people, with a pew reserved for the President of the United States. Hot damn!

Stepping out into the sunlight after church, I stopped, shook hands with the rector, introduced myself and told him I was new in town, an Episcopalian, and looking for a church home. He smiled and nodded and held onto my hand until I mentioned that I'd run a drop-in center for homeless people out of the basement of my church in Memphis. He didn't say anything but his deep blue eyes glazed over, his firm grasp morphed into a limp fish and his body language told me everything I didn't want to know. The Church of the Presidents was not where I was going to replicate the Street Ministry. I'd have to keep searching, trusting that when I found where I was supposed to be, I'd know it and whatever I was supposed to do would fall in place.

CHAPTER 36

Off and Running

"I can't believe you're here," the governor said

as soon as I walked in the door and

then straight over to him where I stuck out

my hand and got a quick hug instead

(obligatory in Arkansas politics when the

person is known to be a strong supporter).

The "roll" I'd been on when I arrived in Washington had begun rolling downhill as soon as the semester ended and reality set in. I'd gotten only two interviews from the dozens of resumes I'd sent out, and that was after I'd deleted an entire banking career so prospective employers couldn't figure out how old I was. One of the interviews was way out in Maryland at a group home for people with developmental disabilities. I'd thought the DD in the ad meant dually diagnosed, which probably would have included some homeless people. When the nice lady who was interviewing me apparently noted my lack of interest and asked me if I really wanted the job, I confessed that I didn't.

I drove back to DC, disappointed but still "stepping out on faith" that if I was where I was supposed to be, something would work out. It was a very long drive back.

On the other hand, I'd really wanted the job when I went for the other interview. I didn't get it. I think the director of the program probably thought I was the wrong age, the wrong gender and the wrong color to do outreach to homeless people on the mean streets of Washington—especially since I wasn't familiar with the city, much less the shelters and services for homeless people in the District. After my purse was taken at knifepoint as I was walking home from the subway one night, I didn't mind so much not getting that job.

With my limited funds quickly running out, I'd been resourceful enough to sign up at several temporary employment offices. In a city full of high-stakes, high-pressure deadlines and people who perceive (rightly or wrongly) that their jobs or political futures depend on meeting deadlines, "temps" were in demand. Lots of government agencies, public interest groups, private interest groups, and businesses used temps to answer phones, copy or fax materials, type letters and reports, do data entry, and sort and collate enough materials to overload even the most committed policy wonk.

I'd never taken a computer course but some of the students in the "Mac lab" had shown me a few of the basics, and Professor Mike Kirby had gone far beyond the extra mile to write out for me, step-by-step, how to make pie charts for one of my research projects. On the other hand, I typed 85 words a minute with hardly any errors, I dressed appropriately for office jobs and the young woman at the temporary agency where most of my work would come from said I was the only person who'd ever made 100 on their spelling test. I was clearly employable, at eight to eleven dollars an hour, just enough, if I worked regularly, to get by.

"Then how big is your head?" she sighed.

"I don't know," I laughed, "it's gone down a lot in the last few months."

From February to August, I'd managed to do just that; by "temping" in private or governmental offices all over Washington, taking time out in late May to go back home to graduate with my class. When I went out to the campus to get my cap and gown, the student who was helping me asked me what size cap I needed.

"I don't know," I said, I don't wear caps."

"What's your hat size?" she asked.

"I don't know. I don't wear hats either," I replied.

"Then how big is your head?" she sighed.

"I don't know," I laughed, "it's gone down a lot in the last few months."

It wasn't all bad. In fact, the best part about temping was that I never carried work home with me, physically, mentally or emotionally. When I walked out the door at the end of the workday, my time was mine and I went home most nights to write about the homeless people I'd cared so much about. Instead of a pen and pad of paper, I now used the brand-new word processor I'd bought to type my research paper on and which actually let me save and edit what I'd written! It was an amazing gadget to have.

Bill Clinton Again

It was October, 1991, about three weeks after Governor Bill Clinton of Arkansas announced his candidacy for the Democratic nomination for President of the United States. He was delivering a speech at his alma mater, Georgetown University, and I was in the audience, made up primarily of about 400 Georgetown students. I'd taken half a day off from my new job at the Peace Corps and, with a flickering of anticipation at what was yet to come, caught a cab to Georgetown.

I didn't agree with President George Bush on much of anything, but I did agree with him when he, apparently quoting that

Validation. Everything he had just said echoed my heart and experience.

well-known philosopher Woody Allen, explained his long, varied, and successful political career by telling whoever the interviewer was that "half of success in life is just showing up."

Given that the speech the Governor made that day was the first in a series of issues lectures, the issues he talked about were vintage Clinton, but his delivery was much more restrained than his campaign speeches that invariably brought crowds to their feet. In fact, he even called it his "dismal" speech because he outlined some miserable statistics about the economy and the recession we were stuck in, criticized

Republican presidents and both parties in Congress for having gotten us into the mess, and, in words eerily familiar two decades later, blamed Republicans for stacking the odds "in favor of the rich" during the preceding decade.

On the positive side, he outlined some of his proposals for improving the life of the hard-working middle class, proposals to help the poor "climb out of poverty," and guaranteed health care. The *Washington Post* reported his main points in a couple of long columns; not bad press for a young governor of "an obscure southern state."

Validation. Everything he had just said echoed my heart and experience.

I took a pencil and stenographer's notebook out of my oversized purse, stuck the pencil over my ear, flipped the notebook open and headed for the hallway just off the stage. I needn't have bothered trying to look like a member of the press with the intention of getting through what I assumed would be a crowd clamoring for his attention. Nobody was in the hallway he'd disappeared into and he and a young man he introduced as Jay Rouse were the only two people in the room with the first open door I found. It would be the last time I would ever see Bill Clinton without a crowd jostling for his attention.

"I can't believe you're here," the governor said as soon as I walked in the door and then straight over to him where I stuck out my hand. Instead, I got a quick hug (obligatory in Arkansas politics when the person is known to be a strong supporter).

"Yes, and I'm ready to roll," I replied. I needn't have reminded him who I was though it had been years since I'd seen him. His remarkable recall of names and faces and facts and places was legendary, and I'd been a fixture on the podium or in the crowd at just about every campaign function in Crittenden County when he was running for governor and I was running for local offices. The year he'd won his first race for governor, I'd won my first race for political office as had Gloria Cabe, one of his strongest, most politically savvy supporters. She'd served as a state representative until she became the governor's chief of staff. She would soon leave the governor's office to work on the campaign and would play a significant role in the campaign—and my life.

Clinton was a phenomenal speaker with an awesome intellect and total grasp of the issues. I just walked every street on every block and rang every doorbell in my district asking everybody who came to the door to vote for me; and when I left my campaign materials, I left his as well. I didn't realize it at the time but that may well have helped me defeat the incumbent, a highly respected and successful businessman who was president of the country club, the Chamber of Commerce and the Rotary club, and an upstanding member of the biggest Baptist church in town. I'd been pretty busy in the community myself, serving on boards and doing volunteer work, but I wasn't and never had been a power player. On the other hand, I had sense enough to know one when I saw one.

It would be the last time I would ever see Bill Clinton without a crowd jostling for his attention.

I was on board again when Bill (that's what everybody in Arkansas called him then) ran for re-election in 1980, but in a major upset he'd lost the race, partly caused by his overly ambitious agenda (including having raised the state's fee for car tags by $3), and partly caused by the influx of 120,000 Cuban refugees dispatched by President Jimmy Carter to Arkansas' Fort Chafee for housing (without adequate money to pay for supplies and security).

That event resulted in riots and costs to the state. His opponent's battle cry had been "Car tags and Cubans"— and it had worked, aided by Ronald Reagan's overwhelming victory over President Carter and a mostly unreported but widely circulated whisper campaign that would come roaring back a decade later.

There were supposed to be photos of Bill Clinton burning his draft card, then he was supposed to have been leaning out of a tree burning his draft card, then he was supposed to be sitting in a tree "buck-nekkid" burning his draft card. He was also reported to have a baby by a black woman, except the people who were spreading the rumor used the "n" word. (The rumors about other women had yet to make it to Crittenden County, 120 miles from Little Rock.) He was supposed to have smoked "pot" even though nobody I knew had ever even seen him with a cigarette. One thing "they" never accused him of, though, was using his position for his personal financial gain. Even his worst enemies knew that wouldn't fly since everybody knew he didn't give a damn about making money. He not only couldn't be bought. He couldn't even be rented!

By all accounts, Clinton was devastated by losing the election and I could vouch for that. I'd seen him soon after the election at a state democratic committee meeting in Little Rock. He was coming down the hall, shoulders slumped, his head down, and I'd stopped him. "Don't let them get away with it. Start running now and come right back at them!"

I have no illusion that my advice caused him to promptly begin planning to run for governor in the next election but apparently a lot of people who had a lot more money, power and political expertise than I did told him the same thing. He did exactly that and won.

Ten years later, I still had my original "Clinton for Governor" bumper sticker on my car, now parked at the Capitol Park Apartments in Washington. When people asked me when I was going to take it off, I'd invariably respond "As soon as we elect him president."

My confidence was based on his warmth and compassion and respect for ordinary people that made millions of people, in poll after poll, year after year, report that Clinton "cares about people like me." I'd watched him share those convictions for years with some of the most impoverished people in Arkansas.

That image is so strong that I still remember being at a tiny African American church in Crawfordsville, Arkansas, one evening. The political rally/meeting had been scheduled for 6:00 p.m. or so and only a handful of people had shown up. I was running for state representative but I needed to get home to check on my sons

"Let me see your hands," I'd said. Looking puzzled, he'd held out both his hands. "Nope," I'd said, turning his hands, which dwarfed mine, over so I could see his palms. "Just what I thought," I told him, "nail holes. They crucified you in Crittenden County ... but don't back down. Start running today and come right back at them."

so I was impatient. He wasn't impatient at all; he just spent the time talking with the few who were there, drawing them out and listening to them talk about their hopes and fears as others trickled in.

They were late because they had gone home first for supper and to clean up after a hard day's work on somebody else's farm or after cleaning up somebody else's house or caring for somebody else's kids. There was nothing paternalistic in what he was doing; it reflected a caring and genuine respect for people on the lowest end of the economic totem pole. I never forgot that evening. That's when I became a "true believer" in Bill Clinton, his purpose, and his policies. But he wasn't the only one in the family with a heart.

Hillary's passion was children—all children—everybody's children. She'd joined the Children's Defense Fund as a young lawyer, fresh out of law school, then served on the board and gone on to chair the board for years. Electing Bill Clinton meant that we'd get Hillary too and Akaretha and Anthony would have yet another champion in the White House.

I'd had no idea that within six months I'd be off and running on the campaign trail in New Hampshire for the next President of the United States.

In the few minutes he had before he had to leave Georgetown, the governor told me that the national campaign office would be in Little Rock but they'd be opening a campaign office in Washington and to be sure to give Jay my phone number and address so Jay could contact me when the office opened. I did just that and caught a cab back to my three-month-old, full-time job as secretary to the director of administrative services at the Peace Corps. I'd temped there for three or four weeks and they'd liked my work so much they'd urged me to apply for the job as a permanent employee. They persisted even though I told them from the beginning why I'd come to Washington and that I wasn't at all interested in a permanent job. After the sheriff's deputy knocked on my door at 3:00 a.m. to serve me with an eviction notice when I was only five days late with my rent, I'd decided to accept the Peace Corps' offer.

CHAPTER 37

Clinton for President

I came here to do what I could to

help make a difference in the lives of

homeless people and right now, the best way

I know to do that is to help elect a president

that I know for sure cares about the same people

I care about and will do whatever he can

to help them.

In early January, Jay called to tell me the campaign office was opening and, true to form, I was one of the first volunteers, going there straight from work every afternoon, staying late, and volunteering 12 to 15, or sometimes 18 hours a day on the weekends. Within a couple of weeks, I got a call from Henry Woods, a relatively young but senior-level legislative assistant in Arkansas Senator David Pryor's office. I'd known him for years, ever since we'd worked together on campaigns in Arkansas. Henry had called to let me know that a busload of people would be going to New Hampshire to campaign for Clinton, and invited me to go. Most or all of them were involved in the Arkansas State Society, the social organization for Arkansans working and/or living in Washington. I didn't hesitate for a second, just told him to count me in.

New Hampshire, Here I Come

Despite wearing my warmest winter coat, knee-high boots, and layers of sweaters, scarves, socks, and gloves, New Hampshire was the coldest place I'd ever been but far more hospitable than I'd expected from people about as far above the Mason-Dixon Line as one can go and still be in the United States. In fact, if it hadn't been so cold, I'd have thought I was back in Arkansas where people are usually friendly and generally of the "what you see is what you get" type.

The trip had been a blur. I'd slept on the way up as much as I could, given that I was on a bus hurtling up the New Jersey turnpike in the middle of the night and the driver and I were the only people on the bus who were over thirty and there was a party going on. Arriving in New Hampshire the next morning, we'd spent the next two days making phone calls to potential

voters, stuffing envelopes, and blitzing the streets of downtown areas with campaign materials, subsisting on the coffee,
donuts and pizza provided by the campaign at the various
headquarters. I don't remember where I slept the night we
were there, but I know it wasn't in a bed.

Though I didn't know it at the time, a few of Clinton's best
friends and strongest supporters had been there for weeks,
working closely with his New Hampshire supporters and
paving the way for those of us who would soon swarm over
the state to vouch for his character, his accomplishments as
governor, and our belief in his ability to serve as president.

Among those earliest and strongest supporters was Sheila
Galbraith Bronfman, a long-time friend, neighbor, and
political supporter who'd been
instrumental in getting the
national headquarters in Little

*All of us traveled on our own
time and our own dime.*

Rock up and running. Looking for a way to fully utilize the
Arkansans who wanted to help on the campaign, she'd also
organized the "Arkansas Travelers," a broad cross-section of
scores of long-time personal and/or political "Friends of Bill"
into cohesive groups that traveled in vans, in pairs, or solo,
to campaign door-to-door for Clinton in key states all across
America—starting in New Hampshire. All of us traveled on
our own time and our own dime.

Two decades later, at a reunion of the Travelers held at the
Clinton Presidential Library in conjunction with the twentieth
anniversary of Clinton's first inauguration and publication of
Political Magic, a book about the Travelers and their history-

making role in the 1992 election, President Clinton would once again give Sheila and the Travelers a huge share of the credit for helping him win the presidency.

A week or so after returning from New Hampshire, I was typing out yet another boring letter when Dan, the director of administrative services, called me into his office. Someone had brought him a fax, intended for me, telling me where and when to meet a couple of fellow "Arkansas Travelers" on Friday afternoon to go back to New Hampshire. Dan was a really nice guy and he was very kind in explaining to me that I could get in trouble for my campaign activities.

"You're not going to hand out fliers and things like that or ask people to vote for him, are you?" he asked.

"Of course I am, Dan," I said, "that's what we do when we're campaigning. That's what we did the last time, and that's what I'll be doing this weekend too."

"It's live free or die," I said.

"But you could get in serious trouble for that, Pat," he said, clearly nervous.

"You're 'Hatched,'" briefly explaining that the Hatch Act forbade government employees to do what I was doing. "You could even be (pausing to consider the seriousness of my possible punishment) reprimanded!"

"Well, I guess I'd better quit then," I said, walking into my office and sitting down at my desk where I fired off my resignation. "Please consider this letter my resignation as secretary to the director of administrative services at the Peace Corps, effective Friday, January (whatever the day it was) at 5:00 p.m." Walking back into his office, I said. "Here you go, Dan," and handed my resignation to him. His jaw dropped and his mouth just hung open for a minute or so before he looked up at me with a puzzled look on his face and said, "You weren't kidding, were you?"

"No, Dan, I wasn't kidding," I replied. "Don't you remember? I told you and everybody else in the department before I took the job that I didn't intend to be here for very long, and everybody I've ever talked to here knows why I came to Washington. I came here to do what I could to help make a difference in the lives of homeless people and right now, the best way I know to do that is to help elect a president that I know for sure cares about the same people I care about and will do whatever he can to help them. I'm sorry about the short notice and I'll be glad to come back as a temp, but I'm going to New Hampshire this weekend to campaign for Bill Clinton. And besides, do you know what the state motto in New Hampshire is?"

"No," he said, still looking puzzled.

"It's live free or die," I said.

That week I did everything I could do to get things in order, including producing a desk guide with instructions, policies and procedures for whoever would to take my place, and that Friday afternoon I was off to New Hampshire again.

This trip was more urgent. In typical Clinton style, Bill had barnstormed all over New Hampshire, including many of the smaller hamlets that he would end up carrying, and earning a healthy second place spot in a very crowded field of candidates, with former Senator Paul Tsongas of Massachusetts, an adjoining state, in the lead. The campaign was seriously off-track from the heat generated by the claims of a former TV reporter and lounge singer that she'd had a twelve-year love affair with the governor.

I didn't believe it. When my second marriage had blown up, I'd been a textbook perfect example of the timeless truth embedded in that old saying that "Hell hath no fury like that of a woman scorned," and since it takes one to know one, I didn't doubt that somewhere, sometime, she'd been scorned by one or more men, and one of them could well have been Clinton.

But I also knew that Clinton had bucked some of the most powerful, unscrupulous people in Arkansas ever since he'd first been elected governor, and they'd had plenty of time and plenty of money to pay people to follow him and take photos or collect any other evidence of a long-term affair, or a short-term one for that matter, and they wouldn't have had any qualms about selling whatever evidence they had to the tabloids or giving it to the mainstream press.

After the "bimbo eruption" had hit, Bill and Hillary had done an interview together on national television (20/20 no less, not noted for pitching "softball" questions) in which he'd denied Ms. Flowers' charges but acknowledged having "caused pain" in his marriage. He and Hillary had defended their marriage, acknowledged that there'd been problems but made it clear that they'd worked through them, and stressed that they were committed to each other and, like the rest of us, believed they had a right to some degree of privacy. (Detractors called it politics, but watching them in that interview, I couldn't help thinking that I'd just seen what unconditional love in a marriage can look like.) Polls conducted after the interview reflected that millions of people understood, but it hadn't been enough to stop the steady stream of negative publicity.

Given that context, the campaign's response was a full-court press as the Arkansas Travelers poured into New

Hampshire with many of us assigned to go door-to-door, hand-delivering in the frigid weather across the state 100,000 video cassettes describing the Bill Clinton we knew, who he was, where he'd come from, what he'd done for Arkansas, and what he wanted to do for America.

On that trip, I rode with Henry and Damon Thompson, another young legislative assistant from Senator David Pryor's office. We talked politics all the way there and back until I fell asleep, exhausted, while they took turns driving and sleeping. I was in hog heaven. I didn't know if New Hampshire was where I was supposed to be at the time, and that weekend I didn't much care because I was dead-dog sure it was where I wanted to be.

I was jolted back into the reality of why I was there when a half-frozen homeless man outside a diner in Manchester told me that the week before he'd asked another candidate (from the opposite party) what he'd do for homeless people. The man had barked, "Nothing."

The Worst Recession in Recent Decades

But homeless people weren't the only people in New Hampshire who were hurting. It was an extremely difficult time for many ordinary residents who'd been financially devastated and demoralized by the recession that a reporter for the Union Leader in Manchester would describe in an article the day after the primary.

He'd written that the economy in New Hampshire had "plunged from exponential growth in the late 1980s to the worst recession in recent decades. Banks overextended on bad real estate loans had failed, unemployment shot up, welfare and food stamp cases sky-rocketed and bankruptcies multiplied. With tens of thousands of jobs lost, the recession (had) entered its fourth year."

(Note: Newspapers anywhere in the country could take that quote in 2009, inserting "America" in place of New Hampshire and inserting "millions of jobs lost" instead of tens of thousands, and it's doubtful that anybody but the reporter who'd written the article in 1992 would notice the plagiarism.)

At every stop in the various gymnasiums and community centers where Clinton would be speaking, local bands blared "Don't stop thinking about tomorrow." We enthusiastically greeted reticent residents, handed out reams of campaign materials and served as the governor's own personal cheering section. Unfortunately, most of the prospective voters who were filing into the centers had probably endured so much over the past couple of years that the last thing they wanted to do was think about what tomorrow would bring. Then Clinton would begin speaking, offering them not just hope but his plan for "putting people first." For many, fears turned to cheers for the man from Hope, Arkansas.

"Clinton and Bush Swamp Opponents in Sweeps of the Southern Primaries."

But it was my third and final trip to New Hampshire with a busload of more mature Arkansas Travelers that stands out in my mind all these years later. Some of the Travelers were long-time, personal friends of Bill (FOBs) and all of us were political FOBs.

It was the weekend before the primary, and Clinton had dropped 17 points in the polls following the attacks on his character, charges that now included draft dodging. He'd countered that charge by releasing a letter he'd written as a college student to a high-ranking official in the Arkansas National Guard thanking him for having helped ensure that he was allowed to enlist in the Guard, but painfully explaining that no matter how much he opposed the war, he felt compelled to serve if he was called and therefore would not be following through on serving in the Guard after all; instead, he'd be putting his name back into the lottery for the draft. That letter was dated December, 1969, twenty-two years prior to his running for president.

God knows, I understood his ambivalence. My stepbrother had come home from Korea in a body bag. My brother-in-law had served three tours in Vietnam, been shot when the Viet Cong had overrun his outpost during the Tet Offensive, been nearly deafened by the shelling at Khe Sahn, had finally come home, his hair as white as snow, and died at 48 of a brain hemorrhage.

Apparently, a lot of other people didn't condemn Clinton for following the dictates of his conscience either. They included James Carville, Clinton's tough-as-nails political strategist and former marine who'd served during the Vietnam years but had, in his own words, been fortunate enough not to have been sent to Vietnam. He'd advised him to just release the letter and let people decide for themselves how they felt about it. Apparently that was good advice. Polls reflected that 64 percent of voters hadn't made up their minds who they would vote for until after he'd released the letter.

At the Merrimack Inn on the night of the primary, we greeted Governor Clinton with the grace and decorum we usually reserved for cheering on Arkansas' Razorback Hogs football and basketball teams (screeching "Whoooooo, Pig, Sooie" to the top of our lungs). It's doubtful that he heard us above the shouts of the swarm of media crowding around him, some for comments on the more titillating issues; others wanting his comments about how he'd fought his way back from certain disaster to a strong second place in a crowded field. He'd garnered more than double the number of votes cast for any of the remaining four candidates. That showing was due in no small part to the huge turnout in which "they voted in masses," in "the biggest crowds in a dozen years at many polling places," making him, in his words and our hearts, the "Comeback Kid."

In one of the more prescient remarks during that wild and crazy evening, one of the Arkansas Travelers, marveling at the media coverage and having given up on trying to get close enough to the governor to congratulate him, turned to his friends and said, rather sadly, "Well, he's not ours anymore. He belongs to the world." That prediction would soon prove to be true, but Clinton would lose in the next three states, making Georgia a must-win for him to remain viable in the race.

With the help of a full-court press by the Travelers, he won with 57 percent of the vote. The effectiveness of the Travelers now well established, Sheila would go on to marshal her forces and lead them into key states from coast to coast, campaigning from door to door from dawn to dusk for Bill Clinton, all the while coordinating their efforts with staff of the national and statewide campaign offices and local supporters in each of the states. The day after Super Tuesday, the *Washington Post* reported (in inch-high headlines above the fold on the front page, "Clinton and Bush Swamp Opponents in Sweeps of the Southern Primaries." The Clinton juggernaut to the nomination and his eventual election had begun.

"Well, he's not ours anymore. He belongs to the world."

I didn't get to make any of those trips. I was too busy working in the campaign's office in Washington.

CHAPTER 38

Washington Operations Office

I must have convinced them that I knew what I was talking about because toward the end of the campaign, I represented the campaign in a couple of meetings with national advocates ... people who were as obsessed with homelessness as I was.

Back in Washington the day after the New Hampshire primary, I went back to "temping." I spent every spare minute after work, and 12 to 15 or 18 hours a day when I wasn't working (including every weekend) in the campaign's cramped office space in a historic building on F Street, just down the street from the National Press Club and around the corner from the White House. I went home late every night, taking time out only for occasional forays to the grocery store to stock up on the cheapest food and household supplies I could find.

Within a few weeks, Gloria Cabe, Clinton's chief of staff until he resigned as governor to work full-time on the campaign (and she resigned to do the same) arrived to take charge of the office. She was smart, tough, politically savvy, and the link we needed to the national campaign staff in Little Rock. Best of all (for me), she brought me on board the campaign full-time, with a stipend of $1,000 a month. It wasn't much because the campaign didn't have much, but it was enough to pay my $650 rent and the phone bill ... and to survive, which was all I was doing by temping anyway. There was no guarantee that I'd work every day in "temping" and, worse, no interest in what I was doing and no progress whatsoever in getting to where I was supposed to go to do whatever I was really supposed to do.

In the meantime, if there was any doubt in my mind about what I was doing, or why I was doing it, it was dispelled every time I walked past all those homeless people bedded down for the night around the escalator at McPherson Square, the covered subway stop nearest the campaign office and the White House.

As the campaign heated up, except for a couple of flying weekend trips home in Old Blue, I poured everything I had into working in the campaign office.

Headquarters

As the primary season expanded from coast to coast and the national campaign office expanded its reach, the Washington office expanded as well, taking over the entire floor of the building and signing up more than 5,000 of what surely must have been the most overqualified part-time volunteers in the history of a political campaign. Unlike the vast majority of campaign offices, there were no signs outside the building that would lead anybody to think that a hotbed of political activity was going on inside.

The largest room was used for volunteer operations (primarily phone banks, mailings, and campaign materials and communications). One large office was occupied by a trio of brilliant young men who worked day and night at their computers doing "opposition research," occasionally taking time to let off steam by playing Nerf basketball on the walls. Opposition research was a new term for me but as best I could tell it was a lot better than the feckless, often fact-less mudslinging of the tabloids.

Gloria, on conference calls every morning with the rest of the senior campaign staff, had her own office and didn't mind at all that her furniture looked as if it had come from a thrift store, which it (and the rest of the furniture and equipment in the office) probably had. That included the furniture that Iowa Senator Tom Harkin had passed along or sold to the campaign when he dropped out of the race for the Democratic nomination. His staff apparently hadn't taken his gracious withdrawal from the campaign as well as he had. When we opened the desk drawers, we found notes (in what I would learn was a time-honored political tradition) telling us where we could go straight to, while others wrote "F--- you!" Gloria just laughed, said it was the first campaign she'd ever worked on where she didn't have to clean the toilets.

I knew that I was finally doing what I was supposed to be doing.

Another office, just big enough for a couple of desks and three or four chairs, was set aside for senior political staff needing a place to work from when they were in DC, which to my delight was often, and, especially for domestic policy staff, for extended periods of time. In the months ahead, that would give me an opportunity to talk to them (every chance I got) about homeless people and homelessness and what we needed to do about it. It also opened the door for me to submit occasional memos with new information about subjects I was basically obsessed with, namely, in addition to homelessness, the core issues of mental health and substance abuse. Yes, that was where I was supposed to be.

I must have convinced the political staff that I knew what I was talking about because toward the end of the campaign, I represented the campaign in a couple of meetings with national advocates. It was in those meetings I knew that I was finally doing what I was supposed to be doing. These people were as obsessed with homelessness as I was. Beneficial to me, on the steep learning curve where I'd found myself, they all were way ahead of me in their understanding of what was happening in homelessness nationally and legislatively. (But, in my defense, they were not necessarily ahead of me in understanding homeless people and the root causes of homelessness. My five years in the mines had served me well.)

Primarily, though, for the first few weeks in the campaign office, I just did whatever needed to be done, which included answering a flood of phone calls, mostly from people wanting to volunteer, but many from people wanting information about Clinton, what he'd accomplished, and what he planned to do as President. I knew a lot about Arkansas and what he'd been able to do there, and because I'd absorbed every word from the plethora of campaign materials I'd helped distribute, I knew enough about his overall plans for improving the economy and education and health care to talk about them. When callers wanted to talk about international or controversial domestic issues, I had sense enough to just listen, take notes and promise to pass along their ideas or concerns to senior campaign staff.

Not all the calls were about the candidate or serious issues. We got a flood of calls complaining about Hillary's comment to the press when they questioned her activism and career choices. She'd responded that she guessed she "could have just stayed home and baked cookies." Never mind that by then she'd already been twice named in the list of "The 100 Most Influential Lawyers in America" by the *National Law Journal*. Not to worry. The calls gave me a chance to tell the callers why she hadn't stayed home and baked cookies.

She didn't care just about her own child. She cared about theirs as well and had been working to make life better for children for decades. Some of the people calling really wanted our mailing address so they could send cookies, but we had to urge the callers not to send them. (We weren't sure what they might put in those cookies.) Later, the campaign sent us a few "Bill Clinton" cookie jars filled with cookies made from Hillary's cookie recipe. (No offense, but her decision to focus on improving the lives of children in America instead of baking cookies was a really good choice.)

With the approval of policy staff in Little Rock after we promised a one-day turn-around, I'd begun editing the campaign's position papers on specific issues that had been produced in-house at the national office and then

... we Arkansans couldn't afford to make any mistakes at all in the information capital of the world where a misspelled word, even if it's a typo, can earn one a withering glance.

sent to us to copy and distribute on the Hill and in the Washington area. It wasn't as though there were a lot of typos or grammatical errors. There weren't, but my 24 days of experience on the Hill had taught me that we Arkansans couldn't afford to make any mistakes at all in the information capital of the world where a misspelled word, even if it's a typo, can earn one a withering glance, and a misplaced comma can change the meaning of a bill and lead to endless debate on its meaning.

I'd already begun editing the copies of Clinton's stump speeches (transcribed verbatim, complete with "cough" or "unintelligible—sound of sirens in background" that somebody at the national campaign had begun sending to us for copying and distribution on the Hill. In addition, Gloria had also begun asking me to "craft" letters that needed an especially thoughtful touch, and soon put me in charge of responding to the correspondence that came to the Washington office. Reviewing, drafting, editing, and managing correspondence soon consumed most of my time.

Nights and Weekends

Since I was the only one of the campaign staff in our office with no social life whatsoever, I was in charge of operations at night and on weekends, overseeing volunteer operations and working with advance teams to make sure that enough volunteers were on hand at campaign events to help with crowd control or, conversely, crowd building. If phone banks or major mailings were being done, the folks in charge during weekdays came in and ran the show and I just pitched in.

Being in charge at night meant that I was also responsible for making sure that the next morning's edition of the Washington Post was picked up as soon as it was available, rarely before midnight. If there were male volunteers in the office, which was rare on Friday, Saturday, and Sunday nights, I'd send them. If not, I walked the few blocks myself regardless of the weather and waited outside the building with a handful of other people who, for whatever reason, wanted or needed the *Washington Post* "hot off the press."

I didn't mind doing it; walking past the White House and cutting through Lafayette Park where homeless people were sleeping was a powerful motivator. As soon as the paper got to the office, no matter who'd picked it up, I'd scan it for any articles that the campaign's vaunted high-tech "rapid-response" team might need to respond to the next morning, cut the articles out, scotch-tape them to sheets of copy paper, then copy and fax them to the designated contact in Little Rock before I went home.

If the campaign strategists expected bad press from some of the other major newspapers, we sent someone to the airport to pick up the earliest editions and on more than one occasion, when the campaign expected something more damning than the usual stories published by the *Washington Times* (the ultra-right newspaper founded and owned by arch-conservative Reverend Sun Myung Moon of the Unification Church) I basically risked my safety and maybe my life by driving Old Blue out to a deserted warehouse area at midnight to pick up a copy. Only later did I realize I was part of the campaign's rapid response to the press.

We caught a welcome break from the office one day in early April when we literally followed our leader, running down the middle of Pennsylvania Avenue from Capitol Hill to Lafayette Park wearing t-shirts that read "I'm Bill's Running Mate" and while it garnered some priceless publicity in the *Washington Post,* the Washington establishment had yet to be convinced, even though by then, he'd racked up wins in 17 states. He would follow that up with a couple more in April and another 15 in May. Then Ross Perot, a short Texan with a great big hat, a whole lot of cattle, and a homespun way with words entered the political arena as an Independent candidate and by June was leading Clinton and Bush in national polls, casting a cloud over both campaigns.

Nevertheless, Clinton had won primaries or caucuses in 39 of the 51 states and the District of Columbia. Now we were headed to the National Democratic Convention in New York, mindful that nothing in politics is sure until the votes are counted and validated.

But once again, politics took a back seat in my thoughts and in my heart when I got a call from the Street Ministry. Mimsy had called to tell me that Herbert, one of our "regulars," had been shot and killed. He was only 26, but because his brain injury, probably from birth, had left him with low impulse control and an incendiary temper, he'd never had a real chance at the normal life he craved. In fact, he'd even been barred from the mental health center because he'd attacked his case manager and terrified the rest of the staff. His premature but entirely predictable death was one more painful, potent reminder of why I'd come to Washington.

Herbert always called me Mom.

CHAPTER 39

Clinton–Gore 1992

"Catch the wave, Al, catch the wave," I said,

with an urgency that surprised me,

and even though I wasn't sure what it meant.

The last thing I'd done on my last day as an intern in Senator Gore's office was sit down with him in his office for a brief interview. We hadn't had a conversation during the time I'd been there and I hadn't expected to since I wasn't on his staff or a personal friend. From time to time that fall, he'd stuck his head in the office where Jacquie, Marla (his press secretary) and I were at our desks and he'd spoken or at least nodded in my direction. I understood how busy he was and I'd told

Jacquie that all I really wanted was fifteen minutes of his time so I could add his perspective on mental health to my research paper. In retrospect, there was clearly something else on my mind.

His office was impressive, spacious and orderly with a couple of comfortable leather chairs facing each other in

"Mental health services for everybody who needs them," I said, mindlessly, ...

front of his desk. I sat down in one and he sat in the other, balancing a cup of something, coffee or tea, from the pot on his credenza. I thanked him for allowing me to intern in his office, told him a little about my research project and that I wanted his perspective, then began asking questions, knowing very well what most of his answers would be. What I really wanted and needed was a direct quote about the state of the mental health system. His response was dead-on target. "Fragmented, full of holes," he'd said. Then I asked the question I hadn't really planned to ask and didn't know the answer to, "Are you going to run for president in '92?"

"I don't know," he said, "why do you ask?"

"Well," I replied, "you may think I'm crazy, but there have been times in my life when there was no way I could have known it, but I just knew that something really bad or really good had happened or was going to happen. Sometimes it's something really specific and sometimes it's not. Maybe it's just heightened intuition, and it's only happened a few times, but when it does happen, I've learned to pay attention to what I'm sensing or seeing in my mind's eye ... and I'm seeing something."

"What are you seeing?" he asked, with just a touch of curiosity.

Searching for the words to describe it, and using my hands to illustrate it, I said, "It's like I'm looking at the ocean and it's relatively calm, but in the distance I can see the ripples of water moving and those ripples begin to turn into bright white sparks of light to form breakers and then there are more and more of them and the breakers get bigger and bigger and then they all come together in one huge wave." By this time, I was using my arms as well as my hands to describe what I was seeing.

"And then what?" he asked (to my relief that he apparently didn't think I was completely nuts).

"Catch the wave, Al, catch the wave." I said, with an urgency that surprised me and even though I wasn't sure what it meant.

I should have stopped right then. What I'd sensed in my gut and seen in my mind's eye was exactly what I'd told him, but then he'd asked, with just a hint of urgency, "What else do you see?" and I went blank. The truth is that I didn't see anything beyond what I'd already told him, and I wasn't sure what it meant myself, but instead of telling him that, I blurted out something I hoped would happen if he caught the wave.

"Mental health services for everybody who needs them," I said, mindlessly, probably leaving him wondering if I needed some of those mental health services myself. A week or so had passed before I realized that the wave I'd envisioned was my intuition; that a wave of change was building across the country. But it wasn't just change, which can be negative as well as positive. What I was sensing was that the wave was much like the wave of progressive policies and politics that had taken Franklin Roosevelt to the White House during the Great Depression, and the wave I was seeing could take Senator Gore to wherever he was supposed to be, just as I felt that wave was taking me to wherever I was supposed to be. It didn't occur to me until years later that if I hadn't caught the wave myself, it could have wiped me and my dreams out.

VP Talk; Pitching Al Gore

A year and a half later, I was sitting on the balcony of a condo in Alexandria, Virginia, overlooking the Potomac River, talking with Jim Blanchard, a former governor of Michigan and one of the insiders that Clinton had invited to help with his selection of a vice presidential running mate. Jim's wife, Janet, a petite, pretty, warm, outgoing, smart and politically savvy woman, was on the staff at the DC campaign office (which had been re-named the Washington Operations Office so we could put it on our resumes for possible employment in the Clinton administration). Janet had invited all of the staff over for dinner. (I now was a really long way from Turrell, Arkansas!)

I'd opened the conversation with Jim by asking how the vice-presidential selection process was going and he'd responded that there were a number of people who were being considered (which I knew). He'd mentioned several of the eleven potential candidates (seven sitting senators including Al Gore, one former senator, two U.S. Representatives, and one governor) confirmed as finalists by Clinton insiders. Some of them would have probably been pretty good choices but I'd responded with comments about why I thought each one wouldn't necessarily be the best choice. Some I thought were too powerful in their own right to be willing to give up that power to serve as vice-president and others I thought wouldn't bring anything to the campaign or administration that Clinton didn't already have.

He hadn't gone through the whole list before I asked, "How about Al Gore? He's very, very smart, he's tough, he served in Vietnam, his personal life is squeaky clean, he 'gets' the need for health care (not to mention mental health care), he's serving on the Armed Services Committee and is strong on defense issues. He could offset Clinton's perceived weakness in defense, Vietnam, and the environment. Gore's a policy wonk and he's passionate about the issues he cares about, especially technology and the environment and global warming. He has a lot of power as a senator but he could do even more to advance those issues as vice president than he can as one of a hundred senators. I'll admit that he's not exactly charismatic but when he gets wound up, he's a good stump speaker, and he's drop-dead good-looking. Plus, his wife is a real asset, smart, caring, pretty, and a 'people' person who'd be a great campaigner."

I didn't even need to add that she had a Masters degree in psychology and was an active and very effective advocate for homeless people and mental health.

"Damn," said Jim, "you know more about this than some of the people I'm working with." Jim was appointed ambassador to Canada and he and I never talked again. I have no illusions that my lobbying for Senator Gore or my encouraging him to "catch the wave" had much, if anything, to do with his becoming vice-president, but it's nice to think that in some infinitesimal way, just as one grain of sand helps to build a beach, it might have helped.

Not long after that conversation, defying the tradition that presidential nominees never picked someone from the same area, much less a bordering state, as his running mate, Clinton announced that he'd picked Gore. Their lives shifted into over-drive for the convention just one week away, and so did mine, albeit on a much lower level.

Some of the staff had volunteered to man a support desk at the hotel where the Clintons were staying. They were to run errands, pick up families and close friends of the Clintons and Gores who'd come to the convention, ferry people back and forth, and basically be helpful. But I had other plans.

Homelessness in New York ... a View

I volunteered to provide support to the political staff who'd be working throughout the convention. They didn't really need me, but Stephanie Solien, Clinton's national political director, put me on her list, giving me the credentials I needed to get into the "Garden" and the freedom to do what I really wanted to do—see for myself what homelessness looked like in New York. This included going to a candlelight rally of homeless people in Chelsea Park instead of going to the glitzy event on Ellis Island that the DC government had invited our staff to attend.

There weren't many people at the rally and the home-less men and women there didn't look any different from the homeless people in Memphis, but the small crowd in-cluded Norm Siegel, already famous for his vigilant advocacy for the rights of homeless people. It also included George McDonald, who'd started helping homeless people in Grand Central Station by giving them sandwiches and asking them what they needed. When the vast majority told him

In the middle of that small crowd of kindred souls, I knew I was getting even closer to where I was supposed to be.

"a job," he invented "Ready, Willing, and Able," a program that gave them one (along with the recovery services they also needed) and soon would gain national attention and funding to expand it.

Nomination and Election

As one of the Arkansas Travelers and as a member of the campaign staff (even a lowly one), I'd ridden up to New York on the "Victory Train" with a mob of campaign people and supporters, but the perks for some of us went further than that. We Arkansas Travelers who'd made it to New York were invited to be with Clinton and his family and close friends as we all awaited his nomination.

That evening we gathered in a meeting room in Macy's basement with a sumptuous spread of shrimp and strawberries and chocolate that, after months of Taco Bell, McDonald's, popcorn and pizza, was like manna from heaven for me. Then Bill, Hillary and Chelsea came into the room and, amid our raucous welcome, walked over to stand in front of a television mounted on a stand high enough that most of us had to look up to watch the voting and the delegate count.

I was standing not much more than three feet away from the Clintons when the delegate count went over the number of votes he needed for the nomination and as he and Hillary and Chelsea hugged, I broke down and cried like a baby. It seemed that everything he'd worked so hard for all his life and so much of what I believed in and had worked for was now possible, and he hadn't forgotten the people who'd worked so hard to help him get there ... And there wasn't a soul in the room who didn't know how hard Hillary had worked and how critical her support had been.

Waving goodbye as the bus pulled out, I felt like I was watching them go off to battle ... probably because they were.

Those of us in the room in Macy's basement then escorted him and his family down an alley to Seventh Avenue and on to the convention center, and, because I had campaign credentials to get onto the floor of the hall, I made it into the bedlam that followed. Standing behind the Arkansas delegation in front of the stage and cheering wildly when he made his acceptance speech, cheering again when Gore was introduced, I was ecstatic, energized and exhausted. The next morning, I sat on a sawhorse outside the International Hotel in a light misting rain, with quarter-size confetti blowing through the air and on my hair, and watched Bill and Hillary and Al and Tipper take the small stage, all of them happy and smiling, then watched them leave on their 1,000 mile bus tour from New York to St. Louis. Waving good-bye as the bus pulled out, I felt like I was watching them go off to battle ... probably because they were.

Back in DC, we boxed up all the Clinton for President campaign materials, made room for the Clinton-Gore campaign materials that would soon arrive, and went back to work. Gloria had already put me in charge of the correspondence that came to the DC office. The amount of mail had increased significantly and we needed more space. In one of the last office spaces, just big enough for me, a good-sized desk and chair, several computer stations, and a few of our vastly over-qualified volunteers, we ramped up our operations. Our lives now revolved around reading the letters that came to the office, highlighting key words and phrases, sorting them and drafting responses, usually incorporating standard language that was being used to respond to the thousands of letters flooding the correspondence office at the national campaign in Little Rock.

I loved it, loved reading about the concerns and hopes and dreams of ordinary Americans and drafting the responses that needed a special touch. We then shipped the letters and the drafts of our responses to Little Rock for final review and signature (the vast majority by autopen). As the campaign progressed and the Little Rock correspondence office became even more overwhelmed, they began shipping some of the mail to us to process as well.

I had no idea that whatever writing, editing and organizational skills I'd developed over the years would take me to the next step on my journey.

The polls taken during the last two or three weeks before the election were looking really good for Clinton-Gore. Gloria had already left for Little Rock and we'd been told to close the office down a couple of days before the election so we could be in Little Rock on election night. As usual, I was one of the last to leave the office and so I was the one who scooped up the fax that came in late that last night. "I hope you people are happy now that you've helped elect that pot-smoking, draft-dodging, skirt-chasing (bleep) president of the United States!" If it wasn't from Mary Matalin at Bush's campaign office, it was from somebody who had a fax sheet with her name on it. I'd never met Mary Matalin but I disliked her every bit as much as she disliked Bill Clinton (and I'd give anything if I'd kept that fax instead of tearing it up in little pieces and flushing it down the toilet.)

On election night, having ridden down to Little Rock with a few of my favorite volunteers who had also become good friends, I was standing in front of the Old State House where the Clintons and Gores were when the newscasters announced that Clinton and Gore had won. Once again, Clinton gave Sheila and the Arkansas Travelers a lot of credit. "Time after time," he said, "when this campaign was about to be counted out, the Arkansas Travelers exploded out of this state, around the country to tell the people the truth about what we had done here together; how we had pulled together, what we believed in, and what we could do as a nation."

A couple of weeks later, the campaign flew us down for the party to end all parties. The president-elect was so exhausted and hoarse that he couldn't speak and could barely shake hands. (It didn't slow the party down at all.)

It was a dream come true, but back in Washington a few days later, most of us were wondering what would come next as we packed up the office—and at least one of us was wondering where her next paycheck would come from—that would be me.

CHAPTER 40

Presidential Transition

However, the U.S. Interagency Council

on the Homeless was totally focused

on homelessness and there were

a few positions open for policy analysts

and program analysts ... I knew I'd found

where I was supposed to be.

We'd almost finished clearing out the campaign office when Mark Gearan stopped by one day. He'd taken Gloria's place when she left toward the end of the campaign to go back to Little Rock. He told me that the presidential transition office would be opening in the next few days in another office building a few blocks away. (Mark didn't mention that he was the deputy transition director and would go from there to work in the Office of the President at the White House. If he knew that after that, he'd be the next director of the Peace Corps, he didn't mention that either.) He just said they were expecting a lot of mail during the transition and needed me to help set up the correspondence office. I didn't even ask what would happen afterward, and I didn't have a plan. It was simple, I'd caught "the wave" and I fully intended to ride it to wherever it was going to take me.

After recruiting a few of our best volunteers, we moved to a high-rise a couple of blocks north of McPherson Square, where what was left of our supplies had been carted and our aged computers had been moved and connected. The suite set aside for the correspondence office was bigger than our entire office had been on F Street, but that wasn't the only difference. Instead of the modest number of letters that we'd been processing every day, the mail was now being delivered in huge mail bags. That is, after they'd all been scanned by the Secret Service to make sure that none of the letters contained anything that could explode or otherwise hurt somebody. We called in more volunteers and went back to work.

A week or so later, David Watkins, one of Clinton's top campaign officials, came by to see me. During our conversation, he told me that the director and a few of the key staff from the correspondence office at the national campaign would be coming to DC when they finished up in Little Rock. The problem? They still had a lot of mail to process and he didn't know for sure when that would be. Until then, he said, I'd be the director of the transition's correspondence office, would be getting a real paycheck instead of a stipend, and we'd work out what would happen after the Little Rock staff arrived.

The (Harmless) "Letters Bomb"

Then he dropped the bomb. "We're expecting about half-a-million letters and cards to the president-elect, plus mail to the other principals. What do you need to get started and make sure we've responded to everything we need to by the end of the transition period?"

After I caught my breath, I started calculating. I knew that the transition period, by law, began the day after the election and ended 30 days after the inauguration. November was half over already, meaning that we had three and a half months, or about 105 days, counting weekends and Christmas, to process all those letters and cards, a mind-boggling average of 4,700 per day. We also knew how much time, on average, it took for us to process a letter that didn't need special attention and how long it took to process the ones that did. Fortunately, the vast majority of the ones we'd reviewed so far hadn't needed special attention. After one last calculation, I told David that we'd need 60 new computers and 120 full-time volunteers, which we'd augment with part-time volunteers in the evenings. He didn't bat an eye; just asked if I thought we'd really be able to do it with all volunteers.

I assured him that we had plenty of over-qualified volunteers who'd be more than happy to work full-time for a stipend of $1,000 a month. They weren't currently employed anyway. The majority were probably hoping for a job in the administration, and we might be able to connect some of them to some of the transition people who then might be able to help them.

Two or three days later the computers were installed. Within a week we'd brought in all of the full-time volunteers we needed, (all of who were happy to get the $1,000 a month in exchange for proximity to the transition personnel, especially those who were working in the personnel office next door to our office) plus another 500 part-time volunteers. As soon as Nancy Hernrich, Clinton's long-time assistant, approved the "boilerplate" responses I'd drafted, we were rolling, and so were the canvas mail carts, some as big as dumpsters, filled with huge bags of mail.

The next couple of months were a blur. With my two awesome administrative assistants, we managed the volunteers, streamlined our processes, put out fires, and worked with the Secret Service to resolve issues with threatening mail. That latter included some that were harbingers of the hate that would be unleashed over the next eight years; others were unbelievably threatening and truly frightening. There were threats to rape or murder Hillary or Chelsea and grisly descriptions of what the writer would do to the president and his family—clear signs of warped minds. Some of the worst ones became less frightening after the Secret Service told us to first check the postmarks to see if the writer was an inmate in a state correctional facility. He then explained why.

I returned the favor to the Secret Service by explaining to them after they came rushing into the office that the letter we'd called them about (per our established protocol) wasn't really dangerous even though the small package had "Caution! Dangerous Materials Inside! Poisonous!" and other caution-ary words written in red, black, and green "magic marker" ink all over it. "It's just somebody's anti-psychotic meds," I said. "Whoever sent this is severely mentally ill, probably has paranoid schizophrenia, and thinks his medications are poisoning him and causing his demons to harass him."

They took the package with them when they left the office, carrying it cautiously even though the bomb-sniffing dog had ignored it. The next day the same two men came back to tell me that I'd been right and one of them asked me, jokingly, "You want a job?"

Threatening the president is a federal offense and the inmates who wrote those God-awful threatening letters to the president were "lifers" who were hoping to be tried and found guilty so they could get transferred to a federal prison where the food and conditions are usually much better!

I did, but I was busy. Along with everything else we were doing, I was still drafting lots of letters that needed more specific (or more carefully worded) responses, including "special messages" to recognize accomplishments or to send messages to groups whose goals Clinton shared and work that he admired. We'd set up a correspondence unit for Hillary's mail, as well, and assigned a few of our best and brightest volunteers to it. A couple of the most overqualified ones would go to the White House with her and not necessarily because they wanted to work on her correspondence. They loved Hillary. Alice Pushkar would not only manage her correspondence at the White House but continue when the First Lady became the junior Senator from New York. Kelly Carnes, a lawyer, would serve as an aide and go on to serve for four years as Assistant Secretary of Commerce for Technology Policy. Both of them loved working for the tough-as-nails First Lady who was also warm, caring, and thoughtful with her staff.

We'd also set up a correspondence unit for Tipper's mail and one for the transition directors. The vice-president-elect preferred to use a couple of his former senate staffers (which was fine). One of the volunteers we'd hired (who spoke at least six languages) had recruited other multi-lingual volunteers and we'd carved out a space for them. There they translated, sorted, and responded to a flood of letters, some written in languages I'd never heard of. (The letters from heads of state and other VIPs around the world were promptly sent over to the State Department.)

We'd hired 160 of our best volunteers and had a small army of volunteers reading the letters, highlighting key words and phrases and sorting them into piles for processing, and sixty computer operators going full-blast drafting responses. We also had lots of proofreaders to be sure there were no typos and that we weren't responding to concerns about international affairs when the people who'd written to the president-elect were concerned about health care. We were rolling. We just couldn't get anything out the door.

In mid-January, Sandy Hudnall, the director of the campaign's correspondence office (who had also managed Clinton's correspondence department when he was governor) arrived, bringing with her the autopen and the authority to use it for letters not requiring Clinton's actual signature. Also with her was a wonderful young woman who went up and down the rows of tables with a plastic laundry basket, picking up drafts of letters and carrying them to the proofreaders who had also arrived from Little Rock. They were phenomenal and I was ecstatic. The mail was moving. Years later, I'd learn that thousands upon thousands of the half million letters we'd been expecting in Washington during the transition had been mailed to Little Rock and processed there.)

On our last day at the transition office, I walked out the door as another Arkansan who'd also worked on the campaign and transition turned out the lights. She was going to drive a truck loaded with materials from the transition to Little Rock to be sorted and filed away for the presidential library that would be established when Clinton left office. I walked the two blocks over to the Old Executive Office Building (OEOB), carrying the cardboard box filled with the last of the letters, not at all sure of what lay ahead for me.

Everybody else had moved on, including my phenomenal administrative assistants. Lynda Rathbone would be working for Mack McLarty, Clinton's old friend and chief of staff, at the White House. Allen McReynolds would go to the Department of the Interior as a Special Assistant to the Secretary for Lands. Brian Thompson, who'd quickly moved from the transition's correspondence department to personnel, would go to the Office of Presidential Personnel as a deputy director, then on to the National Archives where he would serve as White House Liaison and work on the initial planning for the Clinton Presidential Library. I didn't know where I was going.

David Watkins had come by to see me as we were winding down our operations to tell me that an old friend of Clinton's from California would be named director of White House correspondence but that he'd be glad to make sure there was a place for me in the department. I was halfway tempted to tell him that I'd like to write "presidential messages," which I'd been doing for months and enjoyed, especially after I learned that was a full-time position at the White House, or, more correctly, at the adjacent OEOB, but I didn't say it even though I knew it would be an adventure.

I did have sense enough to thank him and tell him that I might take him up on his offer. Writing presidential messages from the Office of Presidential Correspondence next door to the White House wasn't a bad "Plan B." It just wasn't what I'd come to Washington to do.

The Plum Book

At the OEOB, I went to the office of presidential personnel to keep an appointment I'd made with Michael Whouley, Clinton's field director who knew as much or more about who'd done what, when, where, how, how well, and for how long on the campaign than anybody else. After explaining to him that we'd just closed down the transition office and these were the only letters we hadn't had time to respond to, I asked him to see that the director of correspondence got them, then told him what I'd done on the campaign and the transition. I finished by telling him that I needed a job, that I'd come to Washington to work on homelessness issues, and that if he could help me I'd appreciate it, adding that until I found a job somewhere, I'd be glad to help as a volunteer if he needed me.

When I finally stopped talking, he leaned across the desk, looked me in the eye and said, softly, "Pat, I think it's time we helped you." And they did.

Within the "Plum Book" was an opportunity for me to work on a system for better meeting the needs of home-less people.

Before I left his office, Michael handed me a copy of the "Plum Book," a plum colored, letter-size, paperback book listing all of the "plum" jobs in the U.S. Government that the incoming president could appoint and the names of the people who were currently in those jobs. "Take this," he said, "and see if there's anything in there that you think you'd like to do—within reason of course—and let me know what it is. We'll assign a White House Liaison to help you through the process."

That night I pored over the "Plum Book," aka the *United States Government Policy and Supporting Positions,* marveling at all the jobs the President can fill—Secretaries of the various departments, Assistant Secretaries and Deputy Assistant Secretaries to manage the various units within the departments, and Directors and Administrators of agencies such as the Federal Emergency Management Administration (FEMA), and the Peace Corps. The approximately 1,800 lower-level, "Schedule C" positions were also appointed by the president but didn't require Senate confirmation. However, "because of the confidential or policy-determining nature of the position duties," they were required to have the expertise needed for the jobs they would be doing.

I didn't have a clue that the Council consisted of the Secretaries and Administrators of 18 Federal Departments and Administrations with programs to help homeless and other disadvantaged people (basically the President's domestic cabinet) or that the Council would soon become a working group of the White House Domestic Policy Council. Nor did I know that while the Council had the responsibility for organizing the federal government's programs for homeless people, HUD's huge Office of Community Planning and Development would soon have the leader, the money, the ideas, and the tenacity to develop and implement what I was looking for—a system for better meeting the needs of homeless people.

The vast majority of the "Schedule Cs" served as special assistants to the higher ranking appointees in the various governmental departments and agencies but there were very few that specifically dealt with homelessness. Since I wasn't a mental health professional, I knew I wasn't qualified for some of them, and since I wanted to work on more issues than housing, I didn't really want to work at the U.S. Department of Housing and Urban Development (HUD).

However, the U.S. Interagency Council on the Homeless was totally focused on homelessness and there were a few positions open for policy analysts and program analysts. Feeling the chill running down the back of my neck, I knew once again I'd found where I was supposed to be.

CHAPTER 41

Lead, Follow, or Get Out of the Way

"You're hired," said Andrew.

"Resumes don't always tell us

everything we need to know.

When can you come to work?"

"This is Andrew Cuomo," said the unmistakable New York voice on the other end of the phone, "I understand you want to work at the Interagency Council on the Homeless."

"That's right," replied the unmistakably southern voice at my end.

"Well, I guess we need to talk," he said. "When can you come by?"

"How about now?" I asked, adding, "I'm across the street at the Department of Education and I can just walk over."

"I'll call downstairs and tell security to send you up."

I spent a couple of minutes straightening up the stacks of letters I'd been working on, picked up my purse and turned out the lights as I left. All the regular employees who worked in the office had already left at a normal quitting time, something I hadn't done in more than a year and wouldn't do again for at least six years.

HUD and Andrew Cuomo

The U.S. Department of Housing and Urban Development (HUD) occupies a huge, ten-story building, shaped in a semi-circle and built of precast concrete. Hailed as a model of modern architecture when it had been completed a couple of decades earlier, Jack Kemp, the most recent Secretary of HUD, had described it as "ten floors of basement." The halls did look like long, narrow basements with lots of doors painted in different, bold colors in various sections for a reason that nobody seemed to remember, but I knew a little about what to expect because I'd been there before.

Like a complete idiot, I'd sat in the spacious, well-decorated reception area in the HUD Secretary's office with Henry Wing, Henry Cisneros' chief of staff, and told him clearly (a couple of times) that I didn't want to work at HUD, I wanted to work at the U.S. Interagency Council on the Homeless, which I assumed would be chaired by Cisneros.

To make it worse, this was after one of the senior transition officials had called me aside one day toward the end of the transition period. "I don't do this very often," she said, "but you've done a lot for us and I want to help you get a position in the administration." After I'd thanked her and told her I wanted to work on homelessness, she'd added, "Good, I'll call Henry."

I'd then skipped taking the elevator and just floated back upstairs since I knew that President Clinton had nominated Henry Cisneros, former mayor of San Antonio, to be Secretary of HUD. The *Washington Post* had reported that when he'd arrived in Washington, he'd been so appalled at the number of homeless people on the streets, including an eight-months-pregnant woman he'd found sleeping on the lawn of the Justice Department, that he'd gone out and spent a couple of nights on the grates with them. This was a man with a heart for homeless people.

I already had a letter of recommendation for a position in the administration from Tipper Gore, one of the four "principals," a prerequisite for ensuring that my resume wouldn't get lost in the thousands that had poured in. The president-elect, Hillary and the vice-president-elect had more important things to think about. Tipper did too but she was more accessible and glad to recommend me as an expert on homelessness.

A phone call to "Henry" from someone else in power wouldn't hurt if I wanted to work at HUD, but then I'd gone through the Plum Book and found the Interagency Council listed and though Cisneros would likely be the chair, he also had HUD's entire portfolio of housing programs to deal with. I'd come to Washington to work on homelessness and I wanted to work where the focus would be on homelessness and homeless people and the multitude of issues that were part and parcel of homelessness— not just housing.

A couple of days after I'd met with Cisneros' chief of staff, the White House liaison who was working with me called to see if there was a problem with my potential placement. There was. Nobody had told me that while the President of the United States was appointing me as a program analyst at the Council, I'd be wearing two hats. I'd also be a Special Assistant at HUD, while also assigned to the Council which was staffed and housed at HUD. (I hadn't noticed that their addresses were the same.)

Luckily, Cisneros had approved my employment anyway, and though I didn't know what Cuomo's role in the Council would be, I didn't intend to screw up again. The press had been pretty tough on us Clintonites from Arkansas and I was hoping he wouldn't write me off as a southern redneck or a political hack who didn't know enough about federal programs for homeless people to do the job. The truth is that I didn't know much about "homeless" programs funded by the government, but I knew it wouldn't take long for me to learn about them and how they worked—or not.

"You're hired," said Cuomo. "Resumes don't always tell us everything we need to know. When can you come to work?"

The hall on the seventh floor where the Assistant Secretary for Community Planning and Development's (CPD) office was located had the same basement ambiance as the one on the Secretary's floor, but his three-room office suite, though much smaller and not at all elaborate, was much nicer than the lower-level, utilitarian government offices where I'd worked as a temp. Nobody was in the outer office when I got there, but the Assistant Secretary and his senior advisor, Mark Gordon, were kicked back in Cuomo's office in a couple of easy chairs next to a low, circular coffee table. One of them had his feet on the table that also held a few bags of chips and a couple of half-empty soft drink bottles. "Want to have dinner with us?" Cuomo asked.

"Sure," I said, sitting down on the sofa and shaking a few chips out of one of the bags.

"So you've been working with homeless people," he said.

"Yeah, I ran a drop-in center for street people for five years as a volunteer. They're all drunk," I said, off-handedly, in what was surely not my most accurate or politically correct utterance of the day. (I was really tired, too tired I guess to add that many of them were mentally ill and most were self-medicating with alcohol or other drugs.)

"You're hired," he said. "Resumes don't always tell us everything we need to know. When can you come to work?"

"The sooner the better," I said, "I'll be finished with the project I'm working on at Education in a few days." Diane Rossi, one of the key staff people at our campaign office, had been appointed chief of staff to the Secretary of Education, and knowing that I hadn't landed anywhere a week or so after the transition, had called and asked if I'd come in and process all the letters that needed to go out to the people who'd applied for positions but hadn't been appointed or hired. I was sick of correspondence by then but I'd said I would because I needed the money.

A week or so after I'd met with Andrew, (I soon learned that all the political appointees and most of HUD"s senior staff called him Andrew) I walked the four blocks from my apartment to HUD, signed in at the front desk in the lobby and went straight to the suite of offices set aside for the Council. There I met the three career people who were "holding the fort" until the Clinton appointees arrived. All of them would remain on the Council staff and one in particular, George Ferguson, would be enormously helpful—the epitome of what a civil servant should aspire to be—professional, knowledgeable and unfailingly helpful and kind to anybody and everybody who needed help or information.

I took time out one morning to meet with the Secret Service for my background check. It didn't take long since I'd already been "vetted" when I took the job at the Peace Corps and passed with flying colors. In fact, the agent who'd checked my background stopped by my desk as he left after giving the report to Dan, looked me in the eye, shook my hand, and said, "It's an honor to have met you." I also took time to be sworn in and get my HUD ID and attend a training session for political appointees. Other than that, I pretty much buried myself in a mountain of minutia. It didn't take long at all to learn about the Council, who served on it and what it had been created to do. Its mandate: coordinating the McKinney Act-authorized programs for homeless people at the various federal departments and agencies. But I still had a lot to learn about how it all worked—or not.

Inter-Agency Conflict ... a Show Stopper?

One of the staff members, a professional woman who'd apparently been close to the departing director but was unfailingly kind and helpful to me, made it clear that we were the staff for the Council and that we didn't have anything to do with "those people across the hall." Those people across the hall were the staff in CPD's Office of Special Needs Assistance Programs (SNAPS) that administered the department's McKinney Act "homeless" programs. It was not an auspicious introduction to collaboration.

The Council had a staff person out-stationed in each of HUD's ten regional offices who was paid by HUD, and whose job it was to coordinate McKinney Act and other federal programs for homeless people that were being administered by different departments and agencies. If we couldn't coordinate with HUD staff across the hall, how effective could we be?

The people who knew me best were really surprised that I was able to adapt to working in the federal government. I'd never been much of a follower, frankly because it stands to reason, at least to me, that if I'm going to follow somebody, whoever it is has to be ahead of me and going in the same direction that I want to go since that's the only way I'm going to go. Following Bill Clinton and working my butt off to help him get elected had been a no-brainer. He would always be light years ahead of me (and everybody else I would ever know) in more ways than I can even conceive, but what mattered to me even more is that he genuinely cared about people, especially poor people.

When Secretary Cisneros had outlined for the president what he planned to do for homeless people, which no doubt included or was based on what Andrew planned to do, and asked Clinton what he thought about it, he'd replied "Do I like it? This is what I ran for office to do."

"Do I like it? This is what I ran for office to do."

The president had the entire federal government, not to mention international affairs to deal with. He couldn't lead the charge on homelessness himself but he'd picked people I could follow as well—Cisneros as Secretary, Cuomo as Assistant Secretary, and Jacquie Lawing as Deputy Assistant Secretary. All three of them were deeply committed to making a difference in the lives of homeless and other disadvantaged people.

Andrew, a lawyer and the son of New York Governor Mario Cuomo, had founded Housing Enterprise for the Less Privileged (HELP) in New York. Within a year, his organization had constructed its first transitional housing program for homeless families, HELP I, which would be recognized by the U.S. Congress as a national model. He'd also served as chairman of the 18-member New York City Homeless Commission, which was charged with developing policies to address homelessness in the city and developing more housing options. His plan, which was adopted by the commission, set the stage for major improvements in the homelessness "system" in New York City, and would become the template for cities all across America.

Despite her relatively young age, Jacquie's passion for helping people in poverty, plus her experience and expertise in working on homelessness and housing legislation in Gore's senate office had made her a natural choice as a deputy to Andrew. Her work ethic made serious workaholics look lazy. Most of the work that I'd do for Andrew would flow through her.

When President Clinton signed an Executive Order (that had probably been drafted by Cuomo and company) for the Interagency Council to develop a national plan to "Break the Cycle of Existing Homelessness and Prevent Future Homelessness," we had our mandate. My only contribution to the Executive Order was "suggesting" that we shouldn't promise something we knew we couldn't deliver. What we could do was break the cycle of homelessness and prevent future homelessness for millions of people. We'd end homelessness if and when we ended the social ills that create and perpetuate homelessness and that would be when we fixed the social service system and created an adequate stock of housing affordable for the poorest of the poor.

Given that HUD had made homelessness the department's top priority and Andrew was responsible for administering its "homeless" programs, he would have primary responsibility for coordinating development of the plan. He'd have lots of help from Jacquie in working with the 18 federal agencies that would have to sign off on the plan, and Dr. Marsha Martin, who'd left her job as the director of the Mayor's Office on Homelessness and SRO Housing in New York City to be the new director of the Council. Marsha would serve as director long enough to play a major role in development of the federal plan and implementation of the pilot programs called for in the plan.

To get input for the plan, a series of 18 "interactive forums" were held in cities across the country. My role was to work with representatives from other Federal departments and agencies to design the format for the workshops to be conducted in these forums. To solicit the input we needed for the federal plan, all of the workshops concentrated on the big picture rather than having separate workshops specifically for providers of services, advocates, and other stakeholders for the various sub-groups of the homeless population. To ensure that we had knowledgeable input from each of the cities, we invited people known to be knowledgeable about homelessness in those cities as "resource" participants, many of whom facilitated, or helped to facilitate, the workshops.

I then compiled a report of the questions we'd asked and the responses we'd received, which then served as the template for the next step, a national survey of stakeholders. Fred Karnas, former executive director of the Council, HUD's Deputy Assistant Secretary for Special Needs Programs, described the outcome of the forums in testifying before a Senate committee in 2000:

> By the time the last of these forums was held ... HUD had heard from thousands of not-for-profit providers of services and housing, advocates, economic and community development leaders, state and local government officials, and homeless and formerly homeless persons. To supplement the input from the forums, HUD sent a questionnaire to more than 12,000 organizations and individuals asking for recommendations. HUD then completed an analysis of the problem and, in cooperation with its federal partners, crafted a plan of action, entitled *Priority: Home! The Federal Plan to Break the Cycle of Homelessness.*

Forum participants and survey respondents had reported that there was little or no comprehensive planning at the local level, that their efforts to address homelessness remained fragmented, and invariably their focus was on short-term emergency assistance. HUD, which administers more than 80 percent of the targeted homeless funds, proposed a two-fold response. First, implement the Continuum of Care as a new, seamless system for providing both housing and services to help homeless people—with a special emphasis on achieving independence and self-sufficiency. Second, increase federal funding to adequately address the problem of homelessness. This two-track proposal was adopted as the centerpiece of the Federal Plan.

The most obvious outcome of the forums was the clear directive that what was needed was a way to bring the providers together in their communities. That fit perfectly with Cuomo's plan to ask congress to double HUD's existing allocation of "homeless" funds. Doing so enabled HUD to use some of the additional funds as a "carrot" to encourage communities to come together to assess numbers, identify needs and gaps in services and housing, coordinate existing resources, and develop additional programs to fill those gaps. The additional funds would also be used to help fill those gaps.

The Plan

Priority! Home, the Federal Plan to Break the Cycle of Homelessness was great. It covered all the bases—described the history of homelessness and used research data to explain the wide disparity in the numbers that advocates and providers and the government had been arguing about for years. The report also outlined the reasons for homelessness. Those reasons included "structural" issues that included low-wage jobs and a dearth of affordable housing. They also included the inability of the social service system to provide an adequate level of education, job training, and health care, along with mental health and substance abuse treatment for homeless and other disadvantaged people. Combined with "individual risk factors" that, not surprisingly, include low educational levels, illiteracy, physical and developmental disabilities, mental illness and substance abuse, homelessness was (and still is) a predictable outcome.

What I especially liked about the plan was that it would strongly encourage (and ultimately require) communities to work together to develop a system comprised of well-coordinated elements of outreach, emergency shelter, and transitional housing for up to two years for those who needed more services than were ordinarily available in emergency shelters. After the plan was released, with the full support of the president, Andrew even had the chutzpah, given that HUD at the time was seen by many as the poster child for dysfunctional government, to ask congress to double the funding for HUD's programs for homeless people, which they did!

This gave the Department the funding needed to use as a "carrot" to further encourage communities to work together, beginning with pilot programs. A particularly important pilot program, the DC Initiative, was established in Washington,

DC where lawmakers could see for themselves whether or not the plan had a chance of working.

Best of all, the plan strongly encouraged development of permanent housing options with supportive services for homeless people with long-term disabling conditions—the Alepeachies of America. The only part of the plan that concerned me was my fear that calling the system a "Continuum of Care" would be castigated by conservatives who would attack it as "cradle to grave" government. I even had the audacity to tell Andrew that I thought he should consider giving it another name.

He didn't, and I am very happy to have been dead-dog wrong. In fact, the concept and term were incorporated across the federal government, and decades later, the term was codified in the Homeless Emergency Assistance and Rapid Transition to Housing Act of 2012.

On the outside chance that any of us had gotten so caught up in the politics of homelessness that we'd lost sight of why we were working so hard to end it, we were brought back to stomach-churning reality before the plan was even completed. A homeless woman died "of natural causes" on the bus bench directly across the street from HUD—another casualty of the concrete killing fields.

The "Continuum of Care" proved to be enormously successful in helping thousands and thousands of individuals and families break the cycle of homelessness and go on with their lives, but it hadn't reduced the number of homeless people.

For the next six years, I was in love with my job. I threw myself headlong into work, much of which would bore anybody and everybody on the planet except the most committed or committable policy wonk, political junkie, or advocate. I loved it—loved learning about all the Federal programs for homeless and other disadvantaged people and the programs across the country that were, or soon would be, funded by some of those programs. I even loved, as painful as it sometimes was, reviewing and summarizing studies and reports about homelessness and the myriad of issues that go hand-in-hand with poverty, homelessness and other social ills. I loved working with the competent, caring HUD staff across the hall, all over headquarters and across the country, along with policy and program staff from other federal departments, national advocates, and providers of services to homeless people from coast to coast.

At every step along the way, I brought to the table everything I'd learned about homelessness, homeless people, mental health, mental illness, alcohol and other drug abuse and addiction, suicide, domestic violence, child abuse, illiteracy, learning disabilities, food stamps, welfare, disability benefits, veterans, jobs programs, housing, service providers, and the under-funded, fragmented, full-of-holes social service system that was never designed or funded to meet the needs of the Alepeachies of America. And every time I got a chance, which was often, I told Alepeachie's story. And if I could work it in, I told Akaretha and Anthony's story too.

During most of those years, I'd known that I was where I was supposed to be, doing what I was supposed to be doing. The "Continuum of Care" had proved to be enormously successful in helping thousands and thousands of individuals and families break the cycle of homelessness and go on with their lives, but it hadn't reduced the number of homeless people. Health care legislation had gone down in flames. Democrats had lost control of the Congress, and continued budget cuts to mainstream treatment programs for mental health and substance abuse and other social service programs resulted in "dumping" the most vulnerable people into the "homeless" system.

God only knows how many lives were saved or how many people's lives were transformed because HUD was willing to use their funding to help ensure that mental health and substance abuse services and treatment were available for homeless people.

But things were changing. After Clinton's re-election, Cisneros, beloved by most HUD employees, had resigned under pressure for not being totally truthful about a marital affair to the FBI agents who'd "vetted" him. Andrew (who was not exactly beloved by many HUD employees, mainly because he was a tough taskmaster) had been appointed Secretary and was well on his way to making HUD the most improved federal department in the government, and the staff in the Office of Special Needs Assistance Programs (SNAPS) was doing an excellent job of administering the Continuum of Care program.

Time to Move On

In my mind, I'd done what I was meant to do in Washington. I hadn't been at all shy about having input into national policies, programs and the politics of homelessness. I'd traveled to major cities all over the country to help with conferences. I'd assessed the effectiveness of programs for homeless people and identified "best practices." I'd reviewed hundreds of applications for funding as part of SNAPS "expert" panel and provided technical assistance to countless people from public and non-profit agencies and organizations from coast to coast.

On the broader level, I'd represented HUD on the U.S. Interagency Task Force on Child Abuse and Neglect, worked with the various HUD program offices at headquarters and the staff of the White House's Domestic Policy Council on developing the administration's plan for implementing the Children's Health Insurance Program. On a literary note, I'd represented HUD in working with the U.S. Department of Health and Human Services in developing a guidebook and resource manual to "strengthen homeless families," a euphemism for preventing child abuse and neglect.

After eight years, I didn't know even one homeless person in the city.

After Andrew had been appointed Secretary, I'd moved up to direct the Office of Executive Secretariat, managing all the correspondence to the Secretary and the Freedom of Information office. I had a huge office and more money but I wasn't working on homelessness anymore. I wanted to go home.

First and foremost, I missed my three sons. Milton and Mitch, my oldest and youngest sons, were now married and Milton had two sons. Mike, my middle son, had a wonderful apartment overlooking the Mississippi River and with every visit home, it had become harder and harder to return to Washington. My trips home had become much more frequent, sometimes flying, sometimes driving the entire 880 miles in a 16-hour day, spending a couple of days with the people I loved the most, and driving all the way back in another long, long day.

But there was another reason why I wanted to leave Washington. After eight years, I didn't know even one homeless person in the city. My first few attempts at outreach had been a complete bust since I didn't know where any of the shelters or services were located or what their policies were. By the time I'd found out where they were and what they did, my gut was telling me not to get involved with any program because I'd lose my focus on what I'd come to Washington to do.

After I went to work at HUD and the Interagency Council, connecting with homeless people on the street became impossible. All I did was work. And even if I'd had any spare time (which I didn't), it would have been a conflict of interest for me to volunteer in the programs because I was reviewing their applications to HUD for funding. I missed the interaction with homeless people, missed being in the trenches, and missed the warm fuzzies. I knew a lot about a lot of things—but what I didn't know was that I was clueless about some of my personal issues. Issues that I needed to work through. I didn't know it, but going home would eventually help me find the peace that had eluded me for most of my life.

CHAPTER 42

Memoirs of a Turrell Girl

But 1999 brought a reprieve for the president

(and me). In February the Senate voted

to acquit the president of perjury

and obstruction of justice charges

and I felt free to come home.

The moving van had come at the crack of dawn the day before. I'd left later that afternoon, spent the night in some cheap motel somewhere in Virginia, had been driving all day and had just passed the exit that meant I was almost home when Neil Diamond began singing "Hello, my friends, hello. It's good to be back home." I cried the rest of the way into town, my nose as red as Rudolph's when I got to Mike's apartment, only to find that in the time-honored tradition of middle kids, he'd been especially helpful. In addition to meeting the moving van at my apartment, he'd had the movers place my furniture where he thought I'd want it and seen to it that my utilities and phone were connected. Tears flowed as I looked around and marveled over his thoughtfulness, mixed with relief that I was finally back home. The next morning I'd make a beeline to see my other sons, their wives and my grandsons.

I couldn't have been happier. By my calculation, I was about three years overdue. In what I'd thought was one of my more practical moments, I'd given myself two years to work, worm and/or elbow my way into a spot in Washington where I might have some influence or input on policies, plans or programs to help homeless people. If I bombed out, a very real possibility, I'd hang it up and go back home, but if I managed to pull it off, I'd given myself another three years to do whatever I could do—a total of five years. The first part of that plan made sense. The second part of my "plan" was either nuts, a classic example of the Christian concept of "stepping out on faith," or my heart telling me that I didn't want to be so far away from my family any longer than five years. (It was definitely my heart.)

By my own measure of success, I felt that I'd done what I'd set out to do.

I'd had no idea that would include helping to elect a president and vice-president who not only cared about homeless people but were willing to make helping homeless people a priority, but that had been the key that opened the door for me to work in a policy arena I hadn't even known existed.

I didn't know that so much hate and animosity could be concentrated in one place or on one person.

If I hadn't gotten involved in the election, I'd probably have been home in two years. But as thrilled as I'd been at the first meeting of the Council when most of the president's cabinet members filed into the room and took their seats, and as much as I valued having played a small part in the national effort to break the cycle of homelessness, I was just as grateful for everything that I'd learned and would put to good use when I got back to Memphis.

On the other hand, when my five-year, self-imposed deadline had rolled around, it was an election year and I was still enough of a political junkie to want to wait until after the election and inauguration and things died down a bit. They never did, and the man from Arkansas who'd inspired me to do more than I'd ever dreamed I could do and given me the opportunity to do it was in trouble. I didn't know that so much hate and animosity could be concentrated in one place or on one person.

The vast majority of the letters to the president-elect as he prepared to take office for the first time had been positive, but a disturbing number had been full of hate. But that wasn't all. The atmosphere in Washington, frigid when the Clintons and the Clintonites arrived, had simply been a frosty cover for the antipathy and antagonism that never went away. Most new administrations get a "honeymoon" period of 100 days before the jackals attack. Not this one.

Dark Days

"Travelgate" had been the first major brouhaha, with the opposition enraged that the president had chosen to exert his prerogative to appoint people he trusted to be in charge of travel for White House Staff and reporters instead of allowing political appointees from prior administrations to remain in appointed positions. The administration was also concerned with what was, at best, sloppy record-keeping in the travel office. With the opposition's charges of influence peddling by sources close to the President, the Independent Counsel appointed to investigate the charges found that the employees, as political appointees, "served at the pleasure of the President" and that he had the right to dismiss them.

He certainly didn't have to find places for them in other governmental offices but he did, for all of them except the one charged (but acquitted) of embezzlement. Nevertheless, that nightmare went on for three years.

Another "scandal" that didn't consume Washington for nearly as long, also concerned political appointees, but these were in the Office of White House Correspondence who had either been asked to resign or fired, or probably both, by the president. When the administration changes hands after elections, political appointees are expected to submit their resignations. Many do so gracefully and just as many do so grudgingly; but all of us are expected to go without having to be fired. I felt a little sorry for the director of children's mail who wouldn't get to be there any longer to tell American University students where she got to ride in the limousine when she traveled with the president, but consoled myself that at least she wouldn't have to be bothered with those "loonies" in Lafayette Park anymore.

And then there was Whitewater, which dragged on for years with two Independent Counsels, including Kenneth Starr, reporting that there was no evidence that the Clintons had done anything wrong with the speculative land deal in Arkansas except lose their own money.

It hadn't helped that the Democrats had lost control of the House and the Senate in the 1994 election, but when the 1995 budget battle had reached the point of no return and the government had shut down, a pretty, sweet, innocent, 22-year-old White House intern had shown her thong (while she was wearing it) to the President of the United States. I have no idea what precipitated that ill-considered, ill-fated action, but the president had then made what was without a doubt the worst personal, political, and painful mistake of his life by getting involved in an utterly inappropriate relationship with her that he would deeply regret as would most of the country.

He'd easily won re-election in 1996, more than a year before the affair became public knowledge, but then compounded his mistake by denying it. (Is there a man on the planet who, if he'd been in his position, would have admitted it if he hadn't been forced to?) By then there'd been so much smoke from "bimbo eruptions" that even I had to admit to myself that there must have been a fire or two in the past, but in my worst nightmare I never dreamed there'd be one in the White House.

The months following were a test and a testament to resilience. What kept me going was that I'd long ago come to believe that there's a little bit of bad in the best of us and a little bit of good in the worst of us. I just added up the good and the bad about the Bill Clinton I knew and the good far outweighed the bad. Shortly afterward, I called the president's office and asked his personal secretary to tell him that I still believed in him and what he was trying to do for our country and that he still had my support. A couple of weeks later, I was really glad I'd called.

There was no way I was going to abandon ship, especially with his impending impeachment by the House of Representatives.

At a pre-planned reception for Democrats from all over the country at the White House, and with Bruce Lindsey, his long-time, ever-present friend and assistant at his side, the president walked into the reception in the East Room. Other than at funerals or grave-side services, I have never seen a human being in so much pain. The desolation I'd seen in his face when he'd lost the governorship so many years before didn't begin to compare with what I was seeing. There was no way I was going to abandon ship, especially with his impending impeachment by the House of Representatives.

But 1999 brought a reprieve for the president (and me). In February the Senate voted to acquit the president of perjury and obstruction of justice charges (all related to the relationship with the intern) and I felt free to come home. And just as I'd taken a lot of good memories along with painful memories to Washington, I'd brought a lot of good memories home with me too, memories of meeting people and going places and attending events I couldn't have imagined when I'd left Memphis. My frame of reference had been far too narrow.

The Good Memories Were Everywhere

There had been times of elation, tromping through the snow in the New Hampshire primary, the Democratic National Convention in New York when Clinton was nominated for his first term, partying in the "war room" on election night, the staff party in Little Rock a couple of weeks later, the inauguration, election night when he'd won his second term and the second inauguration. Other than bragging rights because I had invitations to the most prized Inaugural Balls (the Arkansas Balls), the one I attended was every bit as over-hyped as Washington insiders had told me it would be due to thousands of ball-goers, a couple of people to check coats and a very few more selling tickets for drinks and box lunches, and long, long lines everywhere.

There'd been the magic of sitting in the President's Box at the Kennedy Center (when the president wasn't there, of course). It was the feeling of being transported to another time and place by the Washington Symphony Orchestra and Broadway musicals, including my favorite, Phantom of the Opera, all preceded by sipping champagne in the small sitting room that opened onto the box.

Still, one of my favorite memories was the night when, standing in the front row of the cheapest balcony seats at the center, I'd cheered so long and so loudly that Willie Nelson had looked up from the stage, flashed a brilliant smile, and dipped his guitar to me. (I know he dipped it to me because the only other people around me were a bunch of tipsy fraternity guys.) At another event, I'd been sitting in the cheap seats behind the performers in a huge arena when Luciano Pavarotti threw his arm out in a grand gesture and his perspiration flew all over me, leaving me a bit smelly but still thrilled. At Constitution Hall I'd listened once again to Helen Reddy singing (but this time in person) my theme song, "I am woman, hear me roar."

The picnic on the South Lawn of the White House for Arkansans was extra special and the annual Christmas tours of the White House for political appointees and our guests (in the evenings after work, of course) were always a treat. But the most powerful and meaningful memories, though political in some ways, were entirely personal.

CHAPTER 43

In Memoriam

But once again,

there was something else I needed to do,

so, 44 years after my mother died,

I found and visited her grave.

The National Law Enforcement Officers' Memorial has quiet walkways and gentle waters, guarded by sculptured, sleeping lions. It is a place of infinite peace, not at all what you would expect in what is essentially a memorial to murdered police officers. The almost 19,000 men and women whose names are engraved on that memorial were all law enforcement officers, killed in the performance of duty. I was there to honor my father the day the memorial was dedicated.

On a beautiful October morning in 1991, from our gathering place on the west lawn of the Capitol, I walked with other surviving family members, right down the middle of blocked-off Pennsylvania Avenue, past the silent spectators on the sidewalks, and on to the memorial nestled in the heart of the judiciary complex a few blocks away. Sitting with the other survivors, we listened to Memphis' men in blue, the "Peacemakers," sing of courage and faith, and then heard President Bush honor our dead in a speech that reflected his respect for them and his understanding of what we were feeling.

My dad would have been so proud to be so honored—so proud to be in that honored company—so proud that his life and dedication meant so much to his country—so proud to have risen above his fourth grade education and the pain and deprivation of his childhood and youth to make a difference in the world. As much as it hurt, I was so proud to be there to honor him and all the other fallen officers.

Oftentimes, when I needed to find peace in the midst of the madness of Washington, I'd go to "Daddy's Monument," and the magic of that place would work magic in my soul.

When the memorial to the 34,000 service men and women who'd died in the "Korean Conflict" and the 1.5 million Americans who'd served in Korea was dedicated in 1995, 42 years after the war ended, I was there, too. In July heat so unbearable that 500 people were treated for heat exhaustion, I picked my way through the crowd of tens of thousands of people to get to the memorial. It was far different from standing on the South Lawn of the White House with other invited guests watching the arrival ceremony for the President of the Republic of South Korea, but far more meaningful.

The memorial is directly across from the Vietnam Memorial, divided only by grass and the reflecting pool of the Lincoln memorial. Many in the crowd were veterans, some in wheelchairs, others with canes or crutches, most of them accompanied by their families or friends. Already touched by the tears in the eyes of some of the veterans and the mood of the crowd, I'd stood as President Clinton and the President of the Republic of South Korea dedicated the memorial, then failed miserably at holding back my own tears when the memorial was unveiled.

There on the mall were 19 slightly larger than life-sized soldiers on patrol, helmets on, wrapped in ponchos to ward off the weather, rifles ready, sculptured so flawlessly that one could see and sense the wariness written on their faces and in their posture. Standing there, one feels the need to be very, very quiet so as not to alert the enemy to their presence. But that's not all; on a wall half the length of a football field, the memorial also offers a tribute to those who served in support positions, with 2,500 fuzzy images of medical personnel, chaplains, cooks, supply clerks—and truck drivers like my stepbrother, who'd served with the vaunted 82nd Airborne and survived the war only to die in a frigid Korean quonset hut trying to help keep the peace.

The inscription on the memorial was perfect. "Our nation honors her sons and daughters who answered the call to defend a country they never knew and a people they never met." Billy Joe would have been so proud to be so honored and I'd been so blessed to have been there to see it.

Now, as happy as I was to be back home with my family and friends, and as busy as I would soon be in my new job as director of Partners for the Homeless, a non-profit where I'd be able to utilize everything I'd learned about homeless people and everything I'd learned about programs and policies and funding to help them (and do some one-on-one work with them) I knew once again that I was where I was supposed to be, doing what I was supposed to do. But once again, there was something else I needed to do, so, 44 years after my mother died, I found and visited her grave.

Visiting Mother

I'd flown down to Naples, Florida, to visit my brother, Carlton (AKA Sonny) for a long weekend. We'd driven up to Sarasota, thinking that since our grandmother had been living there when our mother died, she would probably have been living there too. She hadn't, but on the microfilm at the Sarasota library we found a copy of the brief newspaper article in which her death in Pensacola had been listed along with other statewide traffic deaths from that Fourth of July weekend.

Then I just totally lost it. Everything I'd stuffed for years, the longing, the huge sense of loss, the hurt and the guilt all came pouring out in a torrent of grief.

A week or so later, Sonny called to let me know that he'd gotten a copy of the certificate of her death, which included the name of the funeral home in Pensacola where her body had been sent. A call to the funeral home revealed that my mother's grave was located on the grounds of the cemetery where she'd been buried. The death certificate also confirmed my dad's belief that it hadn't been an accident. Several witnesses had stated that they saw her jump.

The next summer, I drove down to Naples to see Sonny, taking the long route along the Florida Panhandle so I could find her grave. It was getting late and misting rain when I got to Pensacola and stopped at a service station overlooking Pensacola Bay. Not really expecting anybody to answer the phone, my hands still shook as I dialed the funeral home from the pay phone outside the station.

There must be a special place in heaven for people who work at funeral homes and cemeteries. The woman who answered the phone listened quietly as I haltingly explained that I needed the lot and section number for my mother's grave and directions to the cemetery. It took a few minutes for her to search their records before telling me gently, "We have her." All I needed to do was turn left as I drove away from the service station and follow the highway along the bay for a couple of miles.

I couldn't do it, and not because I didn't think I'd have enough time that evening. There was a motel nearby and I could have visited her grave the next morning, but the truth is that just knowing that I was within two miles of my mother after a lifetime of longing was all I could handle. Instead, I crossed over the Bay Bridge and drove for another hundred miles before stopping at a motel.

By the time I got back to Pensacola a few days later, my nerves had settled and I'd braced myself for whatever lay ahead. Stopping at the funeral home first, the woman at the desk offered to take me to my mother's grave, which she said was nearby, but I declined.

Instead, I asked for directions to the nearest florist where I bought four long-stemmed red roses, one for each of the children she'd left behind, then drove back to the cemetery, found her grave and gently laid the flowers across her head-stone. Then I just totally lost it. Everything I'd stuffed for years, the longing, the huge sense of loss, the hurt and the guilt all came pouring out in a torrent of grief.

Friends who knew me best asked me later if I'd found closure and to some degree, I had. But the closure I'd felt was simply the closure of searching for her. I'd found my mother, but I couldn't get any closer to her than six feet and on the way back home, I still felt like a motherless child.

A couple of years after my mother's death, Marguerite, her younger sister and, as far as I knew then, her only sibling, had come to see me on her way back home to Indiana. She'd been to Pensacola to visit her mother, my grandmother. Sitting beside me on the sofa in our tiny living room in West Memphis that sweltering summer day, she shivered several times. "I'm sorry," she said, "but you look so much like your mother it gives me the willies." After she'd told me about my mother's "accident" and her funeral service and I'd told her about my dad's death, I'd asked "What was she like," but I guess I had something stuck in my throat because I had to ask her again.

"It would depend," she said slowly, "on whether she was Mildred or Skippy. When she was Skippy, she was happy-go-lucky and funny and sweet; when she was Mildred, she could be hell on wheels."

I didn't have guts enough to ask if she and my mother had been sexually abused by their father as my stepmother had said and I was too afraid of the answers to ask any more questions about my mother. I basically answered my aunt's for the next hour or so, and listened while she told me about my grandmother's diabetes, which was causing her to lose her sight and would soon prevent her from writing.

Neither of us mentioned calling, probably afraid of the truth that might slip out in an unguarded moment. She wrote to me once after that and I responded but I never heard from her or my grandmother again. I guess none of us knew how to cope with suicide and long -buried family secrets.

CHAPTER 44

The Suicide Club

There is an art to getting someone

who is really, really drunk out of one's office,

not to mention one's face,

especially if the drunken one

has a dagger in his shirt pocket.

There's a dagger in my dresser drawer. I've felt it often, usually when sifting through the soft tangle of well-worn lingerie—fingers gently running along the bottom of the drawer in a last-run-before-laundry-day effort to find something that still fits. You'd think I'd have figured out what to do with the dagger since it's been there for more than twenty years now but I still haven't.

It doesn't fit in with the rest of my keepsakes from my Street Ministry days—treasures like the get well card so many of the street people signed when my back had rendered me immobile with pain worse than I'd ever experienced, or the drawing of my head that "Dancing Jimmy," had penciled on a sheet of plain white paper and then hung around for hours outside the building so he could give it to me when I left work.

Everybody knew Dancing Jimmy and lots of people, including me, had tried to help him get off the streets, but nothing had ever worked for very long, and never past St. Patrick's Day when the local pub crawlers would paint him green and let (or persuade) him to lead the crawl from bar to bar. He was run over by a car and killed while I was in DC, but at least it wasn't on St. Patrick's Day; that let a lot of people off the hook.

Then there's the Christmas card from Sam, one of our Vietnam veterans, and the sweet note from Wesley, a young man from Texas wearing coke-bottle-thick glasses held together with adhesive tape; they didn't begin to hide the black eye he'd gotten when he was mugged just hours after he'd gotten off the bus in Memphis. "Dear Pat," he'd written, "thanks a lot, and please don't get mad but I think I love you." All I'd done was make some phone calls and arrange for him to get back home where he had family and friends and tell him about Job Corps where he could get the training he needed to get a decent job. And it was well worth the cost of a bus ticket and money for food to get Wesley out of the streets before the streets got into Wesley. No, a dagger just wouldn't fit with those keepsakes.

Chief and the "Shank"

Some people, especially the ones who've served time in prison, call my homemade, hand-operated sheath of sharpened steel shaped like a flattened dagger, a "shank." Ten inches long, with a six inch blade that measures an inch at its widest, it won't carve a roast or a pumpkin; it won't peel potatoes or slice bread. It has no other purpose than to kill, or at a minimum, maim. I put it in my dresser drawer because I didn't know where else to put it after I stole it from Chief, our only bona fide "regular" of Native American descent. He, on the other hand, probably knew exactly where he meant for it to go when he put it in his shirt pocket and then staggered into the Street Ministry that long-ago day with the tip of the blade inches away from his jugular vein.

I'd expected him to be hurt when his wife left him to live with a relative in another state and angry with us because we'd been trying for more than a year to get her to do just that. But he didn't mention her and didn't seem to be mad at us, just said he needed a couple of bus vouchers. Since he was obviously drunk, I told him I couldn't give them to him. I didn't think the bus driver or the passengers on the bus would appreciate having him aboard. We certainly hadn't appreciated it when people sent us somebody who was falling down drunk (unless the person who was drunk was ready to go into detox or treatment—and then we were very happy). Needless to say, Chief, whose real name was Charlie, wasn't ready to do either one. He was trying to talk me into changing my mind about the vouchers when I noticed the metal point protruding from his shirt pocket, half hidden by his jacket.

"What's that?" I asked.

"Iss mii knife," he snarled.

"You're gonna kill yourself with that; as drunk as you are, Charlie, the first time you fall down it'll go straight through your jugular vein and you'll bleed to death," I warned.

"I 'ont care," he growled.

"Well, I do," I replied, "Why don't you let me keep it for you 'till you sober up?"

"Uh uh," he grunted; a clear no.

"Tell you what," I said, "I'll swap you the bus vouchers for it. When you sober up, I'll give it back to you."

It took him a minute or two to think about that since he was swaying in an ever-expanding arc by then and most of his attention was rightly centered on remaining upright.

"Nope," he said, still reeling.

If he hadn't been dog drunk, I probably couldn't have gotten the dagger away from him; on the other hand, if he hadn't been dog drunk, he wouldn't have shown up with a shank in his shirt pocket. He'd have had it well hidden in his boot or his bundle or his backpack like just about everybody else who wants to survive on the streets.

There is an art to getting someone who is really, really drunk out of one's office, not to mention one's face, especially if the drunken one has a dagger in his shirt pocket.

It helps to be sure-footed since the art can require walking backward (very slowly) toward an exit from the building, preferably one that can be instantly secured. It also helps to be a good liar since truth becomes expendable in direct proportion to the size and mood of the one who is drunk. I grabbed a book of bus vouchers and got ready to deal.

"Let's go outside," I whispered conspiratorially, "so nobody can see me giving you the vouchers," and the dance began. Without losing eye contact, and holding the vouchers in front of me, I coaxed him out of the office. I could walk backwards sober better than he could walk forward drunk so as we talked about how many vouchers he wanted and how many I'd give him, I'd step back a couple of steps, wait for him to take a couple, then take a couple more steps backward until we'd tangoed all the way down the hall to the door that opened onto the parking lot.

"Come on out," I said, holding open, with my left arm, one of the double glass doors, "and I'll give you the vouchers. I can't give them to you as long as we're in the church." As soon as he was outside the door, I snatched the dagger by its point from his pocket, yanked the door closed, and slammed the heavy metal bar across the double door that now separated him from me and his dagger.

His response was a guttural roar, his face contorted with rage only exceeded by the agony in his eyes and a furious attack on the heavy glass section of the door with his fists. By the time he'd staggered out into the parking lot, somebody had locked the front door to the church and called the police and somebody else had ushered out the people who were still in the waiting room and who knew enough about Chief to understand why they needed to get as far away as they could as fast as they could. That door was quickly locked as well. I was glad they'd called the police even though I knew they'd be taking Chief to jail, which also served as the biggest and worst detox center in town. But, I thought, it beat dying with a dagger in his throat.

Nobody really understood why I refused to give up on Chief but part of the reason was his Native American ancestry. In his defense, it didn't take much alcohol for him to get knee-walking drunk. Whereas lots of alcoholics can drink lots of alcohol before they appear to be drunk, one drink seemed

I had personally done nothing at all to Native Americans, but I had done nothing at all for Native Americans either.

to send him staggering. At least part of the reason why he had zero tolerance for alcohol was because Native Americans as a people had zero history of alcoholism (or alcohol use) until our Anglo-Saxon forebears introduced firewater to the New World. Without at least a few thousand years of alcohol use and alcohol abuse under their belts to inoculate them against the disease, Native Americans found themselves especially vulnerable to alcoholism.

And that, I admit, was part of the reason I'd fought to keep from barring Chief from the Street Ministry for anything but the most outrageous or dangerous conduct. I know I don't need to feel guilty about Chief's alcoholism. I didn't introduce alcohol to the New World and I didn't buy Manhattan Island for a string of beads and I didn't kill all the buffalo or send the Cherokees down the trail of tears. I had personally done nothing at all to Native Americans, but I had done nothing at all for Native Americans either.

But that wasn't the only reason I didn't want to give up on him. I'd known Chief for several years by then, and though he was no doubt the toughest and most fearless of our "regulars," I'd never forgotten the first time I'd met him. I'd gone into the waiting room to be sure everybody had left before we locked up for the day. He'd put his head down on the table where we kept the sign-in sheet and gone to sleep, his tear-streaked face resting on arms as big as hams. He raised his head slightly when I touched his shoulder. "It's time to go," I said, as softly as I could.

"I got no place to go," he mumbled. His daddy had died, he said, (which turned out to be a lie) and he (Chief) said he'd been sleeping on a roof somewhere. We talked for a little while or rather he talked and I listened. It wasn't the first time he'd been homeless; the cycle was already painfully familiar. He'd been in jail lots of times but "I fight," he explained, "I don't steal." Short, dark, and powerfully built, he said his daddy was a "big Indian, real dark, maybe a chief."

I asked him about the possibility of staying with other family members. "Noooo," he wailed, "they call me Boogie Man, but I not want to be Boogie Man. I want to be gooooood." It didn't take long to figure out that he might be having difficulty in being good. With one lightning swift movement, before he'd even finished saying "gooooood," he stuck his fist into an empty ashtray on the table, sprung his short, stubby fingers open and in one smooth swoop brought the heavy glass ashtray within an inch of my nose.

I didn't have sense enough to be scared, but Sedden, one of our newest volunteers, said later he'd been scared enough for both of us. He'd walked into the room just in time to see Chief sweep the ashtray off the table and bring it so close to my nose that it made my eyes cross. But Sedden wasn't just scared; he was smart. While I was sitting there with my eyes crossed, he bought the ashtray off of Chief for a dollar. Chief had been a regular ever since, sometimes sober and subdued by street life, usually drinking or drunk.

Chief was barred for two weeks for bringing a weapon into the Street Ministry but a few days later one of his friends came in and told one of the volunteers he didn't want any help, that Chief was outside and he'd just come in to give me something that Chief wanted me to have. It was a paperback copy of Robert Louis Stevenson's *The Suicide Club and Other Stories*. On the cover of that book is a drawing of a dagger stabbing into the heart of an Ace of Spades. The shadow cast by that dagger looks exactly like my dagger—and the book had been in my dresser drawer, next to my dagger, for at least twenty years before I finally summoned up enough courage to read it.

CHAPTER 45

The Last Lesson

My father used to say, jokingly I thought,

that "ignorance is bliss."

The more I learned about suicide

the less I believed he was joking.

I now knew more than I'd ever wanted

to know about suicide.

Just because it took me so long to psyche myself up enough to read *The Suicide Club and Other Stories* doesn't mean that I wasn't interested in the subject of suicide. I was. I'd just become a master at avoiding any conscious thought of what my mother must have been thinking and feeling when she put her hand on the door handle on the passenger side of the truck and hurled herself out into oblivion. But studying suicide from an academic perspective wasn't the same as living with the results of somebody else's suicide, so I'd taken several courses in psychology when I went back to college. That would be safe, I'd figured, and even if it wasn't, I would have some knowledge of the subject.

If I expected to have a credible voice when talking to mental health professionals about homeless people with mental illness, I needed to understand the basics and have a working knowledge of the terminology of mental health and mental illness, which would surely include suicide. I could handle it. After all, I'd already "walked the walk" when it came to having lost somebody I loved to suicide; I just needed to learn how to "talk the talk."

It had taken three semesters for me to work my way up from Psychology 101 to Abnormal Psychology, a class taught by Dr. Allen Battle. Even then he was a legend in his own time for his encyclopedic knowledge of the normal and abnormal human mind. His legend included a thorough understanding of why people commit, or attempt to commit, suicide, and how to help prevent it. What I learned in his class validated my initial perception that Chief hadn't been dead set on killing himself that day. If he had been, he probably would have.

Statistically, women are more likely to attempt suicide than men, but men are more likely to succeed at it, most often choosing guns, knives, or jumping from high places as the means. As far as I know, he didn't have a gun, but if he'd been fully intent on dying that day, he could have gotten one. Downtown streets were, and still are, full of them, and there are plenty of tall buildings in the event he decided to jump from one. On the other hand, he'd checked out a book about suicide from the library and gone to the trouble to make his own dagger. It's pretty clear that he either hoped he'd kill himself accidentally or he hadn't much cared if he lived or died that day when he'd put the shank in his shirt pocket and staggered into the Street Ministry.

God knows he had enough reasons. He'd surely been struggling with many of the issues that drive people to take their lives, or attempt to do so. Like every homeless man and woman I've ever known, he was under enormous stress. To say that he had financial problems would be a gross understatement. He had no finances, no tangible assets, nothing that he could call his own. Not only was he unemployed, he was, for all practical purposes, unemployable.

Like 90 percent of people who try, or succeed in killing themselves, Chief was surely depressed, but we'd never even tried to get him assessed for clinical depression. That would have made him eligible for a disability check. We hadn't, however, probably because we knew he'd have drunk it up the way so many of our homeless friends did. We understood that drinking a depressant would make one more depressed, but we had yet to learn how often the clinical depression was present even before it was masked by alcohol and drugs.

By almost any measure except his will and ability to endure homelessness and his willingness to fight at the slightest provocation and win the fight, he was a failure. Elizabeth, his wife, who'd met him in the waiting room and married him in Squirrel Park a few days later, had just left him and he was hurt and angry at her and at us for not only encouraging her to leave him, but helping her get away from his abuse. Had he died that day, making sure that we knew he was contemplating suicide could well have been, as Professor Battle pointed out in class, "the ultimate revenge."

Hope, the Saving Grace

On the other hand, it is entirely possible that Chief didn't die that day because he didn't have what some researchers state is the single most prominent indicator of suicide—a pervasive sense of hopelessness. Despite the hell that he and Elizabeth had experienced together as they huddled in an abandoned building dubbed "Hotel Siberia" by the inhabitants of the homeless community, and the hell that Elizabeth had endured from his abuse, he knew she loved him and still had hope that she'd come back. (He had good reason to hope; she was back a week later!) He hadn't entirely given up hope for himself either. He'd even agreed to go into a residential treatment center for his alcoholism and was only four days away from graduating from the program when he got in a fight and it took six staff members to throw him out.

It helped me to be able to think, and finally believe, that Alepeachie's death from a heart attack instead of suicide meant that he too hadn't totally lost hope that things would ever get better for him. One can only wonder, though, how much loneliness and hurt a human heart can endure before it simply implodes. But whatever comfort I gained in thinking that apparently Chief and Alepeachie hadn't totally lost hope, that comfort was obliterated by the reality that in one thought-less, irreversible moment I had killed whatever hope my mother had that her children would welcome her back. I was sure she had forgiven me but I hadn't forgiven myself.

> *I found a measure of relief in learning that the vast majority of people who make a suicide attempt aren't intent on dying.*

Since a suicide attempt is often a cry for help, for a day or so I reasoned that maybe my mother hadn't really meant to kill herself. Perhaps she died because the man she was riding with hadn't been able to grab her in time to keep her from jumping, something my dad had been able to do when they were married.

Then I read that people often grasp at any possibility that the death was really an accident and not suicide, which took me back to square one. Making an attempt to jump out of a moving vehicle in the subconscious hope that somebody will prevent you from doing so could well be a cry for help, but it isn't an accident and it wasn't enough to convince me that she hadn't meant to die. There had to be more.

Predictors

The Federal government's National Institute on Mental Health (NIMH) lists eight predictors of suicide. I am very sure that my mother had at least three of them. She'd experienced family violence in the form of sexual abuse by her father, and though I don't recall any blows ever being struck or even any pushing or shoving, she'd been so terrified of my father on the one night I remember, that she'd been hysterical and had a pistol hidden underneath a pillow. In addition, she was no doubt depressed and likely had been for much of her life, although, to be honest, she appeared very happy and carefree in one of the photos my grandmother sent to me. In that photo, she and a nice-looking, well-dressed, older man are sitting at a table, having cocktails at some club somewhere. I don't know who he was or whether he was the man she'd left us for. I do know that the photo didn't tell the whole story. My mother's agonized letters to my dad and the first of the few letters my grandmother wrote to me after my mother's death and before her own eyesight failed told a much different story. My mother had "never been happy—always grieving over her children," my grandmother had written.

My father used to say, jokingly I thought, that "ignorance is bliss." The more I learned about suicide the less I believed he was joking. I now knew more than I'd ever wanted to know about suicide.

And then I finally got around to reading The Suicide Club. The book, written in the florid literary style of the late 1800s, consists of three separate stories. The first, The Suicide Club, is about a Bohemian prince and a young military officer who serves his master as confidant and companion in the prince's nighttime "rambles," undertaken whenever the prince is bored and seeking excitement. Visiting in London, bored with his life and basically looking for trouble, by the end of the evening the prince and his companion find themselves visiting a club where all the members (except the president of the club) want to die.

Yes, they want to die but they are either afraid to kill themselves or don't want to embarrass or hurt their families, (or lose their property and money to the government) by taking their own lives. For what, to the prince, is a modest sum, he joins the club where, on a designated night, the president of the club shuffles and deals a deck of cards. The man dealt the Ace of Spades is to be the next to lose his life, and the man dealt the Ace of Clubs is to be the one to take it.

Stevenson's description of how the prince feels when he sees the president deal the cards to the next victim and the next murderer and sees their reaction is masterful.

The prince was conscious of a deadly chill and a contraction about his heart; he swallowed with difficulty, and looked from side to side like a man in a maze.

Death is no longer an abstract concept or possibility, and the club has one less member by the next meeting. The next time the cards are dealt, there are only two cards left to be dealt and one of them is the Ace of Spades. The prince's response is even more pronounced.

When he saw his fate upon the table in front of him, his heart stood still. He was a brave man, but the sweat poured off his face.

Then he turned over the card he'd been dealt; the Ace of Spades.

A loud roaring filled his brain, and the table swam before his eyes. He heard the player on his right break into a fit of laughter that sounded between mirth and disappointment; he saw the company rapidly dispersing, but his mind was full of other thoughts. He recognized how foolish, how criminal, had been his conduct. "God," he cried, "God forgive me!" And with that, the confusion of his senses passed away and he regained his self-possession in a minute.

That his more realistic companion rescues the prince from his potential murderer, and that the prince and his companion kill the president of the club, who they believe to be a mass murderer, was almost irrelevant to me. It was the prince's response when he realized he would actually be killed that took my breath away.

As she was falling to her death, had my mother had a split-second of clarity and realized that she hadn't really wanted to die?

CHAPTER 46

The Road to Healing

On my knees at the altar,

I experienced my own personal epiphany—

the realization that the spiritual reunion and

healing I'd sought at Dorothy Lee's grave

didn't happen because that cemetery was too

painful a place for my mother and father.

The little potted plant with the tiny, delicate, white blooms was just right for a toddler's grave, or so I'd thought before my brain and gut kicked in to remind me forcefully that nothing can be right about a toddler's grave. Nevertheless, the tiny flowering plant nestled in between the much larger, blood-red poinsettias on their way with similar purpose to similar spots, had seemed like the best choice under the circumstances. And it sat there with its own single-minded purpose in the passenger seat as I drove out to the cemetery on what I felt sure would be the last stop on my road to healing.

In late September, after carrying around a card with the section and lot number on it for twenty years or so, I'd finally made time to call around to the cemeteries in Memphis to find my sister's grave. Procrastination isn't enough to explain it. Denial and avoidance of pain are far more likely explanations, but when the woman who answered the phone at Forest Hill said, ever so kindly after she'd taken a few minutes to check their records, "Oh, yes, we have her," instead of feeling pain, my heart skipped a beat. I'd known there was something I needed to do and this was it.

A few days later I drove out to the cemetery. At the office, the woman who'd answered the phone when I called gave me a map pinpointing the section where my sister, Dorothy Lee Phillips, age 18 months, had been buried in 1937, about two years before I was born. Possibly because I have a tendency to pay far too little attention to directions and maps, but more likely due to another subconscious delaying tactic on my part, I drove around the cemetery for at least half an hour before I found the section.

For the next hour or so, I walked slowly back and forth among the rows of markers and headstones, reading the names and ages of the infants and children buried in and around the "Babyland" section, trying without success to avoid absorbing even part of the pain that permeates the area. When I'd thoroughly searched the section without finding Dorothy Lee's grave, I called the office, confirmed that the cemetery hadn't required that markers or headstones be placed on the graves, and asked them to have their groundskeepers locate the exact place where my sister was buried. Then I drove back home, sure that I had finally found something I could do for my long-deceased mother and father. I needed to do something to make amends to my mother and I wanted to do something for my father simply because he'd done so much for me.

I'd known since I was a child that I'd had a sister who'd died when she was only 18 months old. I'd thought about her from time to time as I was growing up, even written about her my freshman year in college, describing her as the teenaged girl I'd often wished I was, not the one I really was with the skinny legs that stuck out from under my cheerleader's skirt like a couple of toothpicks.

My dad had told me as much as I guess he could bear to tell me—her name, how old she'd been, and, with a long, deep sigh that told me as much or more than his words, that he'd been holding her in his arms when she died of pneumonia. I'd asked him once where she was buried and he'd told me the name of the cemetery, which I'd forgotten, remembering only that it was in Memphis. I didn't have the heart to ask him anything else. The unutterably sad look on his face the few times he mentioned her invariably faded to a wistful, faraway look that I understood took him back to that time. After I had children of my own, I couldn't, in my worst nightmare, imagine what it would have been like to lose one of them. Leaving the cemetery, I could, however, imagine how it must have haunted them to have been too poor to buy a headstone for her grave.

The Headstone

A few days after I'd been out to see where the groundskeepers had marked with a little white flag the exact spot where Dorothy Lee's grave was, I walked out of Memphis Memorial Studio with the receipt for the headstone I'd just ordered and paid for. It was to be engraved with a tiny girl with angel wings cuddling a lamb, her name, the year of her birth and the year of her death (because I didn't know the months or days of her birth or death).

Back in my car, even before I'd had time to put the key in the ignition, I felt my mother's presence. She was back again, filling my mind, my heart and my car with her invisible presence, but this time my tears were tears of joy. I had absolutely no doubt that she knew what I'd just done and she was happy. And so was I. As small and belated a gesture as it was, it was the first time in my adult life that I'd been able to think about my mother without feeling guilty.

But there was still something I needed to do.

Now it was the day before Christmas Eve, and I was on my way to do it. I was armed with a little blooming plant that I could easily hold in the palm of my hand, envisioning as I drove along the expressway on my way to the cemetery some sort of spiritual reunion with my mother and my dad at my sister's grave. When I got there, I placed the little blooming plant tenderly on Dorothy Lee's marker, thought about the tiny child buried there, the dozens of other children buried nearby, and waited for the heavens to open and the spiritual reunion to begin.

It didn't happen. Back in my car, chilled to the bone and deeply disappointed, for a minute I just sat there.

Then, from somewhere deep inside me came that same guttural voice, but instead of crying, "I'm sorry, I'm sorry, I'm sorry," through a flood of tears I heard myself screaming, "I didn't mean it! I didn't mean it! I didn't mean it!"

And I hadn't meant it when I'd told my mother over the phone that "I'm sorry. My mother is sitting at the dining room table." I knew perfectly well who my real mother was, loved her unconditionally, had longed to see her again ever since she'd left, and would have been thrilled beyond measure to have her back in my life. At the only opportunity I'd ever had or would have, I hadn't told her. Now I was telling her, but she wasn't there.

Now, upset that my plan for closure hadn't worked, I sucked it up again, drove to the cemetery in Arkansas where my father, stepmother and stepbrother were buried and placed flowers on their graves. Then made a commitment to myself to do it more often and drove away, feeling empty and alone.

An Epiphany

The next day, Christmas Eve, I spent most of the afternoon and evening with my family before I went to midnight mass at Calvary. On my knees at the altar, I experienced my own personal epiphany—the realization that the spiritual reunion and healing I'd sought at Dorothy Lee's grave didn't happen because that cemetery was too painful a place for my mother and father. They were with their baby daughter; they'd moved on from the pain of the past and it was time for me to do it too.

I'd spent the better part of a quarter of a century trying to help homeless people and telling their stories in the hope that it would bring healing and hope to them, only to find that it would happen to me when I told some of their stories—and mine.

But there was still one more thing—I knew what it was.

CHAPTER 47

Finding Alepeachie

There was no changing the subject

as I stood at Alepeachie's grave

more than two decades after his death

and promised to continue telling his story.

But he didn't hear me.

His spirit had moved on too.

Driving out to the cemetery in one of the decidedly less affluent sections of Memphis, a scant seven miles from downtown and my little cracker box house a five minute walk from the mighty Mississippi River, I don't know what I expected to find. To get there, I'd taken the interstate, then doubled back a few blocks and crossed over a four-lane overpass with a freight train rumbling and wailing below. It was literally a stone's throw from the spot where the directions reflected that the entrance to the cemetery would be located.

I couldn't enter the street where it was located from the turn lane at the bottom of the overpass either. It didn't match the way the exit and entry from the street were marked. In short, though it was probably great for the companies that owned the railroad and the manufacturing and chemical plants nearby and for the jobs they produce for the mostly blue-collar folks who live in the area, building an overpass and railroad track practically at the entrance to the cemetery didn't show much respect for the dead.

Insensitive was the first word that entered my mind. I thought the overpass placement was especially insensitive since the cemetery had clearly been there first (since 1865) and all of the people buried there are veterans or their immediate family members, mostly wives, many of them buried in their husband's graves. Still, if I hadn't been forced to get to the entrance to the cemetery through a few side streets, my first full look at the cemetery wouldn't have been as powerful.

The commercial area bordering the cemetery was a hodge-podge of used-car lots and auto repair shops spilling over with older model cars and trucks. All along the side streets I took on my short, circuitous route were small "cookie cutter" houses like those that had sprouted in subdivisions all over America in the decade following World War II. A few were well kept, more were showing years of neglect, and even more were dilapidated. On one dead-end street all of the houses were dilapidated, or worse, dilapidated and abandoned. Somebody had posted a home-made sign that warned "DON'T DUMP HERE!" which had clearly been ignored. Whatever I'd expected to find, I now expected to be worse.

I was dead-dog wrong. The cemetery was a jewel.

Despite the overpass and its graffiti-covered concrete columns and the railroad tracks, partially walled off by a fence no more than twenty yards away from the front of the entrance and the cemetery's small office complex, the cemetery was amazing. It was beautifully kept, with row after row of upright, snow-white marble tombstones—thousands of them—a smaller version of the hauntingly lovely Arlington National Cemetery. Interred there are veterans from the Civil War, the Spanish American War, World Wars I and II, the Vietnam War, and wars that killed thousands of Americans but were never officially declared wars, including the Korean "Conflict." Veterans of more recent wars and military actions, such as the Persian Gulf War and Operation Iraqi Freedom are also buried there.

Interspersed among the headstones in several areas of the cemetery were rows and rows of small (and smaller) upright marble posts, more than 8,000 of them marking the graves of unknown soldiers. Most of those died in the Civil War, or, as the inscription under the State of Minnesota's giant-sized Union soldier with the flowing bronze cape called it, "The War for the Preservation of the Union."

The cemetery was a jewel. The cemetery's other major monument, a sarcophagus with a uniformed, bronze soldier lying in state on a granite bier, stands as a powerful, poignant monument to Illinois' dead. It struck me that both of the memorials were to men who'd fought and died so that people like Alepeachie could be free from the bondage and horror of slavery. And though I know it was pure coincidence, I found the sign on the narrow lane leading to Alepeachie's grave even more comforting. It probably won't make much sense to anybody but me, but in finding his grave on a lane called Morgan Road I knew once again that I was where I was supposed to be, doing what I was supposed to be doing.

At His Grave

"Ale Peachie Broadnax, Pvt, U.S. Army, Vietnam," his marker read, followed by his date of birth, February 12, 1956, and date of death, September 3, 1989. A small cross is engraved at the top of his headstone and on the headstones of most of those buried in the section. It is there that I was finally able to find a measure of peace with his loss.

I hadn't been there when Alepeachie was buried. His funeral service had been held at eight on a Sunday evening, a week after his death, probably delayed to give the medical examiner time to complete the autopsy and for the funeral home to prepare his remains for "viewing." The latter is an archaic practice that, at least in the south, forces us to get past the denial stage of grief and, if we're lucky, feel that the deceased didn't suffer before his death.

On the printed program from Alepeachie's funeral, I'd written that he looked as if he were sleeping. Only the silk-lined casket and the ill-fitting suit he had on made it painfully clear that he was surely dead. I remember that I would have tried to comfort his family but I was, on the surface, in worse shape than any of them, so much so that if anybody at the funeral told those of us who were there when or where his burial would take place, I didn't hear it. I know it wasn't in the program because I still have it more than two decades later and there's no mention of his burial.

I could and should have asked where and when he'd be buried. Deep down, however, I was afraid that the answer would be Shelby County's "potters' field." That was the "paupers" cemetery where men, women, far too many children, and far, far too many babies are still being buried when their families or friends are unable or unwilling to pay for a plot. I didn't ask because I didn't have the money for a burial plot for him and I couldn't bear any more guilt than I was already feeling about having failed him.

Reading the program at his funeral, I'd been surprised to find that he'd spent four years in the U.S. Army. Once I'd finally found his grave and asked for the minimal amount of information the cemetery could disclose to a non-family member, I wasn't at all surprised to find that he'd only been in the Army for about three weeks and that the Vietnam engraved on his marker meant only that he'd been in the Army during the Vietnam War era, not that he'd actually served in Vietnam. In fact, he'd entered service on September 30, 1974, the month he should have begun his senior year at Tennessee Preparatory School, and been released on October 21, three weeks later.

I don't know if he was drafted or whether he enlisted or why he was released so quickly. It's entirely possible that they found the heart condition that eventually killed him and discharged him for medical reasons, but it's just as possible that the symptoms of severe mental illness that often begin to become evident when a youth is 17 or 18 had been the reason for his discharge.

What I am very sure of is that it could only have added to his sense that "nobody wants me; nobody likes me; everybody hates me." No wonder he felt that nobody wanted him. The U.S. Army that had drafted thousands and thousands of men for the Vietnam War didn't even want him. The last American troops had left Vietnam the year before.

And, in one more instance of his isolation, nobody but his case workers seemed to know how to spell his name. We'd spelled it Alapeachie, but I'd begun spelling it Alepeachie when Mike and Willie (who were working with his SSI (disability income) and Medicaid records) began spelling it that way. His funeral program had spelled it Aleepeachie. The school had spelled it Alpeachie during all the years he'd been there. The marker on his grave had Ale Peachie.

Near Alepeachie's grave was a towering, aged oak tree and even nearer was what I thought at first was a chinaberry tree. It was leafy green, even in the winter, with the clumps of green berries that I remembered from the tree that grew next to our porch. It was there that I'd spent so many days watching and longing for my mother. The Books of Knowledge that I'd read, sitting in the crooks of that tree, had given me a sense of destiny; that there was a wider world than the one I was living in, and that there might be a place for me in it. I wondered if going into the army had given Alepeachie that feeling, only to have it dashed after only three weeks.

One day I'd asked him what he would do if he could do anything in the world he wanted to do. His usually inscrutable face softened into a faraway dreaminess before he replied "I'd drive a truck all the way across the country."

Since it would be a couple of decades before recovery from mental illness became the mantra, the hope, and a real possibility for many people with severe mental illness—and since I didn't think there was a chance he'd ever be able to do it—and I didn't want to lie to him or build up his hopes, I changed the subject ... I actually changed the subject a lot.

There was no changing the subject now as I stood at Alepeachie's grave more than two decades after his death and promised to continue telling his story. But he didn't hear me. His spirit had moved on too. And then I went home to write, adding to his story how profoundly his all-too-short life had affected mine.

Afterword

This year marks the 50th anniversary of the assassination of President John Kennedy and the legislation that he championed, commonly called the Community Mental Health Centers Act. At the time, there were 600,000 people in mental institutions; now there are approximately 70,000. In his remarks to Congress, the president said (and no doubt believed) that "When carried out, reliance on the cold mercy of custodial isolation will be supplanted by the open warmth of community concern and capability." He must be rolling over in his grave.

On a single night in January 2012, a total of 111,993 men and women with severe mental illness were reported to be homeless in America. Of those, 46,550 were sleeping unsheltered—on the streets, in parks and abandoned buildings, under overpasses and bridges, in tents, sheds, barns—and other places "not meant for human habitation."

"Norman," wasn't among them. He was in a group home for homeless individuals with severe mental illness, or at least most of him was. After sitting in an alcove of the old, boarded-up police station in Memphis for years, refusing shelter, housing, and services—even blankets—during bitter cold, his feet had been amputated to save his life.

Tens of thousands of others weren't counted either. They were in jail or prison.

Dr. E. Fuller Torrey is the executive director of the Stanley Medical Research Institute and a prolific, noted author of books about homeless, mentally ill people. He is also a board member of the Treatment Advocacy Center, which released a report in May, 2010, that validates his militant advocacy for assisted outpatient treatment. That report, *More Mentally Ill Persons Are in Jails and Prisons than Hospitals: A Survey of the States,* reported that "there are now more than three times more seriously mentally ill persons in jails and prisons than in hospitals." The report went on to state that "America's jails and prisons have become our new mental hospitals" and that "40 percent of individuals with serious mental illnesses have been in jail or prison at some time in their lives." At its heart is the reality, expressed by Dr. Torrey in October, 2013, that "It is almost impossible to get someone committed."

Nobody gets the bottom line of the issue better than the National Association of Mental Health Directors who reported in 2012, that "We are spending money in all the wrong places —prisons, emergency departments, and homeless shelters—when the illnesses become more serious." Nobody gets the need for changes in the system better than the families of those who are heartsick at what is happening to their loved ones—or worse, what may happen to them or others if he or she becomes one of the small minority of those who are too dangerous to themselves or others to remain in the community without effective mental health treatment.

Lest we forget, also among the total of 633,782 homeless people located in the "point-in-time" count were an additional 274,611 individuals unaccompanied by children, and 84,030 families with children. Shamefully, 19,428 of those families were also sleeping unsheltered (many of them in the dead of winter in some of our coldest and most rural states). The total number reported to have been homeless—at some point in time for some period of time—during 2012 was 1, 502, 196. For most of these families, safe, decent, affordable housing could end their *houselessness*, but rebuilding their lives to help ensure that their children will not become homeless adults will take much more—including health and mental health care to deal with the trauma of homelessness.

As this is written, the federal government has just re-opened after having been shut down for 16 days, at a cost of billions of dollars, and immeasurable cost in confidence in government. The shutdown was due to the relentless efforts by a vocal, divisive minority to repeal the Patient Protection and Affordable Health Care Act (AKA Obamacare). Their opposition is apparently oblivious to its own claim that the recent rash of mass shootings, which killed 70 people, including the soul-sickening slaughter of 20 children at Newtown, were solely the result of untreated mental illness and the failure of the mental health system. (Never mind that those who were killed and the 90 that were wounded were shot with guns meant only to kill or wound multiple numbers of people.)

If and when fully implemented, Obamacare is expected to provide health insurance for 60 million Americans, including those who are homeless and currently lack health insurance. The insurance would also cover mental health and substance abuse treatment (except for those who are too sick to sign up for insurance or accept the care they so desperately need). I remain hopeful that Americans of good will can and will find a way to ensure that none of our most vulnerable men, women, youth and children, further traumatized by homelessness, are left behind. My basis for that confidence?

President Kennedy's words, spoken at his inauguration, are inscribed in stone at his gravesite in Arlington National Cemetery, one of the first memorials I visited when I moved to Washington. "With a good conscience our only sure reward, with history the final judge of our deeds, let us go forth to lead the land we love, asking His blessing and His help, but knowing that here on earth God's work must truly be our own."

About the Author

Pat Morgan is a self-confessed political junkie and "Arkansas Traveler" veteran of the Clinton for President, and Clinton-Gore campaigns. She is also a mostly unsuccessful political candidate (won 1, lost 2), a former elected official in county government, an unabashed policy wonk, and relentless (ask anybody who knows her) advocate for effective services, especially mental health care, and housing for homeless people.

Pat is also an expert on the subject, having received numerous awards, including the U.S. Interagency Council on Homelessness' 2006 Innovation Award (in a Republican administration) for her contributions to ending chronic homelessness. Learning enough to be an expert on homelessness, she says, might have been deadly dull if she hadn't learned her most important lessons from listening to hundreds of "street people" with "staggering levels of disabilities" and battling to secure the services and housing that would help them break the cycle of streets, shelters, hospitals and jails.

A real estate broker and former banker (occupations not necessarily noted for altruism), Pat answered the call from the concrete killing fields of homelessness—found her calling—and lived out her dreams.

It's been a "wildly improbable ride," she says, one that has taken her from the cotton fields and dusty streets of a tiny town in Arkansas to the Street Ministry in the heart of the concrete killing fields of Memphis, Tennessee to the highest level of federal policy making in the nation's capital.

Totally frustrated with the lack of resources for homeless people, and deeply concerned at the rising body count from the concrete killing fields, Pat resigned as the unpaid director of The Street Ministry and enrolled in Rhodes College "mostly to get the credentials to go with what I'd already learned so I'd have a more credible voice in developing policies." She already had a degree from the "school of hard knocks," having graduated magna cum laude in "street smarts." Luckily, her three grown, independent sons were supportive (after she promised not to go out for cheerleader), especially after she was selected (at age 50) by *TIME Magazine* as a "Rising Star," one of "20 Outstanding College Juniors in America. Being featured in *TIME* led to a Washington Semester in American Politics at American University, and an internship in the office of then-Senator Al Gore, for whom she'd campaigned when he'd sought the Democratic nomination for president in 1988.

But it was her long-standing, rock-solid support of then-Arkansas Governor Bill Clinton that would result in a presidential appointment to the U.S. Interagency Council on Homelessness, then a working group of the White House Domestic Policy Council. That would come after she'd tromped through the snowy streets of New Hampshire, worked days, nights and weekends at the Washington Operations Office, and then organized and directed the Office of Presidential Correspondence at the Office of Presidential Transitions. Throughout it all, she was driven by the memories of the "street people" she'd loved and lost to the concrete killing fields and those still most at-risk.

An engaging, experienced public speaker with a refreshing sense of humor to balance the seriousness of her work, Pat is available for speaking engagements, short-term consulting, and even shorter advice by email.

Reach her at:
PatMorgan1@comcast.net • (901) 525-8498
www.PatMorganAuthor.com • www.Homelessness101.com
Twitter followers, become one of Pat's Peeps at: @PatMorgan110
Facebook: www.facebook.com/pat.morgan.9081